Practical and Inspirational Guidelines for *Winning*

Practical and Inspirational Guidelines for *Winning*

J. David Irwin

RESOURCE *Publications* • Eugene, Oregon

PRACTICAL AND INSPIRATIONAL GUIDELINES FOR *WINNING*

Copyright © 2021 J. David Irwin. All rights reserved. Except for brief quotations in critical publications or reviews, no part of this book may be reproduced in any manner without prior written permission from the publisher. Write: Permissions, Wipf and Stock Publishers, 199 W. 8th Ave., Suite 3, Eugene, OR 97401.

Resource Publications
An Imprint of Wipf and Stock Publishers
199 W. 8th Ave., Suite 3
Eugene, OR 97401

www.wipfandstock.com

PAPERBACK ISBN: 978-1-6667-0472-3
HARDCOVER ISBN: 978-1-6667-0473-0
EBOOK ISBN: 978-1-6667-0474-7

05/26/21

Carretto, Carlo, *Letters from the Desert*, Orbis Books, 1972

"Living without Calculating Costs," by Rev. Sebastian White, O. P. Used with permission © Magnificat, July 2020. www.magnificat.com

Scripture texts in this work are taken from the *New American Bible, revised edition* © 2010, 1991, 1986, 1970 Confraternity of Christian Doctrine, Washington, D.C. and are used by permission of the copyright owner. All Rights Reserved. No part of the New American Bible may be reproduced in any form without permission in writing from the copyright owner.

To my loving wife, Edie

Contents

Preface | ix
Acknowledgement | xi
Introduction | xiii

Part I: Fundamental Considerations | 1
   1. Putting Our Act Together | 3
   2. Personal Development | 12
   3. Understanding the Basic Parameters | 21

Part II: Strategies for Success | 43
   4. Successful Team Players | 45
   5. The Successful Manager/Entrepreneur | 57

Part III: Putting it All Together | 95
   6. Looking out for Numero Uno | 97
   7. Winning as a Way of Life | 132
   8. The Ultimate Strategy | 162

Appendix: Book Club Discussion Questions | 195

Preface

THIS BOOK CONTAINS A compilation of lessons I have learned over a lifetime of study in the school of hard knocks through a wide spectrum of activities that range from family interactions on the one hand to complex business/professional involvements on the other. As a result, numerous personal examples are provided that serve to illustrate the ideas and concepts that have been applied to achieve a winning outcome in these environments. It is important to indicate at the outset that I am not a trained psychologist, and yet I believe much can be learned from an examination of the lifestyles of those individuals who have achieved success in essentially any endeavor. The wisdom displayed by these outstanding people, within the context of their environment, is coupled with God-provided inspirational material that underpins the philosophy proposed. Within the context of this book, winning refers to the attainment of a successful outcome, regardless of the context, and although the concepts are generally applicable, they are primarily directed at Christian-oriented individuals who aspire to lead in some capacity in situations where interpersonal interactions play a significant role.

As we strive for success in any endeavor, we are secure in knowing that all of our activities are in the hands of Almighty God, since he is the architect who has designed the plans for our lives. Although the road ahead is unknown to us, our omnipotent and loving God can see clearly the path ahead. His guidance is always available, and we tap into it when we link our minds and hearts with those of our Divine Savior in prayer. Because he made us, no one knows us better. Therefore, he alone is in the best position to direct our steps in order to ensure that we achieve success, which may include material gain, but will definitely include eternal joy and peace. When we ask for and obtain his guidance, we can be absolutely confident that while our journey may contain pain and heartache, it will end in indescribable joy.

Although many of the concepts and ideas discussed will be confined primarily to the interpersonal relationships among individuals and presented in the framework of a business or family environment, they are also applicable when dealing with members of a civic organization, a church group, a professional organization, or any other group where people interact or work together for some common goal.

JDI

Acknowledgement

I AM DELIGHTED TO acknowledge with great respect and deep appreciation the help of two outstanding individuals who read the manuscript and made numerous suggestions for improving it. They are Dr. W. Harold Grant, a counseling psychologist, deceased, and Karl E. Martersteck Jr., Vice President of AT&T Bell Laboratories, retired. However, the individual who has made the most significant impact on this manuscript is Mary Ann Rygiel, retired English and math teacher, who has a PhD in American literature. Her critical review and strategic suggestions have vastly improved the presentation. I am most grateful to her for the time and effort she invested to support this activity.

JDI

Introduction

THIS BOOK WAS WRITTEN for one purpose: to present some winning strategies for personal development that I am convinced are widely applicable in a variety of circumstances. Specifically, I will provide some ideas and support them via various means, which will help us deal more effectively with our coworkers and live a happier and more productive life as we progress through the rungs of our ladders of success, whether our ladder is horizontal or vertical—i.e., our goal is to be happier and more productive in our current situation or our goal is to be happy through greater success as we move vertically within our organization, and of course success in the former often leads quickly to success in the latter.

There are a number of excellent books that rival this one and address some aspect of the issue presented here. Many of them fall under the banner of self-improvement and their focus is such things as (a) advice for dealing with the internal negative thoughts and feelings that keep a person from failing to achieve all they are capable of being; (b) guidelines for self-care that have their foundation in self-empowerment and self-knowledge; (c) prescriptions for finding balance across a spectrum that includes career, family and friends; (d) how one's "self", which is endowed by God, can achieve mental and emotional health while simultaneously dealing with life's inevitable problems; and (e) A step-by-step strategy for becoming the best you can be.

While all of these books, as well as others with similar themes, provide good advice, their focus is limited to a small subset of the topics addressed here. As the remainder of this book will illustrate, the material presented will expand upon some of the ideas and concepts that these books present through a wide spectrum of ideas for successful personal interactions, supported by real-life examples, and implemented in a

Christian lifestyle in order to achieve success and happiness in a wide spectrum of life's endeavors.

My own history in approaching this subject matter began in Minneapolis, Minnesota where I was born, and soon thereafter moved to Montgomery, Alabama where I grew up. I entered Auburn University, then called Alabama Polytechnic Institute, to study electrical engineering. In the summer between my freshman and sophomore years, a group of my high school friends arranged to have as many young adults as possible attend a Sunday morning Mass, and then get together afterwards for a social gathering to renew friendships and catch up on everyone's activities. I arrived late for Mass, but from the back of the church I could see where all my friends were sitting as a group. So, I climbed into a pew and sat next to a young girl with a huge circular hat. I could not get a good look at her face during Mass, but I knew the girls in my graduating class, and I was sure this young lady sitting next to me was not one of them. I met her at the social event after Mass, and learned that she too was attending Auburn. Edie and I dated for the balance of our undergraduate studies, she graduated in June, I graduated in August on a Thursday night, and we were married in a nuptial Mass approximately thirty-six hours later. We left for Knoxville, where I attended graduate school at the University of Tennessee, and left about five years later with three children and two degrees. I went to work at Bell Telephone Laboratories, which was the research and development arm of what was at that time the Bell System. I was promoted to a supervisor in about eighteen months, a process which typically took five years, but left to pursue my life's calling as a professor about a year later. I joined the Auburn faculty as an entry-level assistant professor and three years later was promoted to head of the department, a position I held for thirty-six years. I continued to teach sporadically along with my administrative responsibilities, which included not just managing the department, but chasing money, equipment, new faculty, outstanding students, and working with our alumni. There is an old cliché that states that managing faculty is like herding cats, because the good faculty are entrepreneurs and have a mind of their own. Therefore, my approach to management was to provide as much support for the faculty as possible, and then get out of their way. I am a workaholic by nature, and during the time I was department head, I believe I encountered essentially every conceivable problem that could possibly occur in that environment. At the same time, I spent what seems like my entire professional career building an international reputation for our department. As

Introduction

the department head, I felt it was my responsibility to lead the way. So, I became an editor-in-chief of an international technical journal and the president of technical societies; I wrote books and technical papers, and ran international conferences. Our outstanding faculty, who prior to my appointment as head had little or no involvement in national or international professional activities, followed suit and became internationally recognized professionals in their field as a result of their involvement in a host of worldwide professional activities.

Edie and I have now been married for fifty-nine years. Like every other married couple we have had to deal with numerous problems, the most serious of which was Edie's fall a couple of years ago. While exercise walking in the house on a rainy day, she tripped and her head went straight into the edge of the sofa, crushing discs three through seven in her neck. She laid on the floor completely paralyzed from 9 AM until about 5 PM when I got home from school. She went through almost seven hours of surgery, six days in ICU, five weeks in a rehab hospital, about eighteen months of outpatient rehab, and she has enough titanium in her neck to build a model airplane. She has worked very hard with great courage on an exercise program, and as a result has managed to achieve limited mobility at the present time.

While this incident has drastically changed our lives, there are a number of important lessons we have drawn from it. First of all, there is only one spot in her exercise path where a fall would encounter furniture. At that particular spot the floor is smooth, no transitions to carpet or rugs, so there was absolutely no reason to trip. So, we are convinced that this accident was not an accident, but an event planned by God. In addition, although Edie could not move an inch, and therefore could not call for help, she was never afraid or in any pain. In fact, she will tell you that she felt that God was there holding her hand through it all. So, although we would never have chosen this path, we are at peace in the faith that God knows best.

Our family has had to make a number of adjustments to deal with Edie's condition. However, our children have gone overboard to help. One of our kids is in town and the other two with their spouses have come from their homes in Atlanta at a prodigious pace, and all worked in cooperation to provide us with every conceivable form of support. They have been so attentive that we lack for nothing, and every problem that occurs in the house is addressed and fixed immediately. Edie and I are so blessed and believe that her fall has provided the opportunity for us to experience our children's love and support in a most phenomenal way. The incident and the aftermath have also given us an opportunity to show others that they too can experience God's miracle-working power in some of the more difficult trials of life.

Throughout our married life, I have gained experience through all levels of jobs (ranging from summer jobs to high-level academic jobs) from family, and personal interactions with people in a variety of professional, religious and civic organizations. All of this has provided me with a unique perspective from which to approach this material. I did not always do everything right, but I tried very hard to learn from my mistakes and not make the same one twice.

At the outset it is important that we clearly understand the context in which the word "winning" is used. Although this word is often used to refer to the attainment of some victory, it also means success, and by extension, one who succeeds. There are literally a myriad of things that each of us encounters at which we would like to succeed, and in general they range from simple tasks, such as cleaning a room, to those that require monumental effort, such as rising to become CEO of some company.

It is critically important to remember that although God has created us in his image and likeness, each of us is unique. There has never been, and there will never be, another person on this earth exactly like us. Because we are unique, it is absolutely impossible to fairly compare ourselves to anyone else. Such a comparison would be like comparing blueberries to watermelons! Even children who have grown up in the same household, are the same sex, have the same teachers, play the same sports, etc., often bear little resemblance to one another. Therefore, in our desire to win at anything, the competition is really internal, and the only realistic comparison is between ourselves at present and that which we strive to become. For example, if you are a golfer, have you progressed from regularly shooting in the nineties to a routine score in the seventies? Have you gone from being late for work every day to regularly being on time? These are fair comparisons, and they are a good indication of our success.

With the notable exception of Almighty God, change is the only constant in our lives, and the winners of tomorrow will be those individuals who can adapt to change and profit from it, or at the very least survive it. This is especially true in families and businesses. The transitions taking place in families today are enormous. The family unit itself has taken on multiple configurations. Both parents, if the household even has two parents, often find it difficult to make ends meet and must of necessity work multiple jobs. This situation is exacerbated when there is only a single parent. As a result, children are left more and more to their own devices. Because of the tremendous advances in information processing and telecommunications technology, unsupervised children are easily bombarded with audio and video content that is at the very least inappropriate and in too many cases absolutely dangerous. If we look at the vast array of content that is immediately available to them, it would not be unreasonable to assume that they could easily believe that anything they wanted to do could be considered normal behavior. This is an alarming situation for parents who want their children to grow up in a Christian environment to be good, honest, and productive citizens. In view of these and similar type issues, our ability to cope—what's more, to prosper and develop a healthy and happy lifestyle—is often a desperate struggle requiring special skills in working effectively and smoothly with one another. Of course, it is also in this environment that our faith plays a critical role in providing a foundation upon which to build Christian relationships that maintain our families on the straight and narrow while under constant attack from the dark forces that try to lead us astray.

It is no exaggeration to say that this world in which we all live is in a constant state of flux. We need only consider the machinations in politics that are projected instantly throughout the world to see that inherent instability clearly exists. Within this dynamic and ever-changing environment, businesses are continually being forced into uncharted waters. In essence, the world has shrunk with the enormous amount of global interaction, and interpersonal relationships have taken on a new meaning when our colleagues have an entirely different culture which we may not appreciate or understand. Cooperation rather than confrontation must be the hallmark of our business relationships, and this philosophy is especially important in industry, and especially those industries that operate in an environment of global competition. The world-class products produced by world-class businesses will have to be made by world-class people who are participative, cooperative and believe beyond any doubt that it is in their own best interest, as well as that of the business, to not only adapt to the forces that drive their industry, but excel in this changing environment. We need look no farther than our cellphones to see a product that, while literally revolutionizing communications with billions of devices worldwide, is designed and manufactured in locations throughout the world by individuals of different cultures.

While adapting to the changing tide is a constant struggle, it is very much a matter of attitude. After all, it is our attitude that stimulates and motivates us to make necessary changes. It is this same attitude which ultimately sets the pace and influences our colleagues to pick up the banner and run with it. Winners do not sit around waiting for others to act, they either do it themselves or they set in motion all the forces required to accomplish the task at hand.

There are always times in our lives when we are suddenly placed in positions which call for us to exhibit our very best in interpersonal relationships. If we can be effective in these situations, we emerge winners. If we do a poor job in a critical situation the result may be catastrophic in the short term, a disaster in the long term, or both. As a general rule, in interpersonal relationships, we truly win only when the other person doesn't lose. For example, it is reported that at a party attended by Winston Churchill and Lady Astor, Mr. Churchill became somewhat inebriated. Lady Astor told Mr. Churchill, "You are drunk," to which Mr. Churchill replied, "My dear, you are ugly, but tomorrow I shall be sober and you will still be ugly." Was Mr. Churchill a winner in this situation? I doubt it. Instead, I suspect that after they exchanged unpleasantries, Mr. Churchill was promptly and summarily dropped from Lady Astor's social network.

While throughout our lives we may pursue a large number and wide variety of goals, it is through the Christian lifestyle that we can achieve the two goals that supersede all others. These goals are (1) an enduring and sustaining relationship with our God and (2) the achievement of happiness, and the former will ensure the latter.

I am convinced that if we understand the ideas that are presented below and put them into practice in our daily life, we will become a very positive force in any environment in which we play or work. We will be better prepared to optimize our own strengths and minimize our weaknesses; and as we see more clearly our relationships with others, we will be in an excellent position to correctly interpret their actions. A thorough understanding of what motivates the people with whom we work provides us with the best vantage point from which to effectively interact with them in any given situation. In the remainder of this book, I will strive not only to achieve that vantage point but to attain a better understanding of how we can most effectively apply our own talents in any given situation.

Part I

Fundamental Considerations

1

Putting Our Act Together

The Basic Inventory

AS WE BEGIN TO examine some of the techniques that will help us develop a winning behavior, it is important for us to first take a realistic inventory of ourselves. For example, Benjamin Disraeli, the former Prime Minister of the UK, once said, "The secret of success in life is for a man to be ready for his opportunity when it comes."[1] Through an objective analysis, we can determine the type of individual that we are, and correctly assess and understand our inherent strengths and weaknesses.

Each of us was born with certain traits. We have acquired others as we have grown older and learned from the people and circumstances which we have encountered. These elements of our repertoire determine the type of individuals we are and the type of work we are best suited to perform. We are all uniquely qualified to perform certain jobs well. The happy and successful individual is that person who has achieved a match between their interests and talents and some specific job. There is an old cliché that states the following: "I may not be much, but I am all I've got." However, what we've got is not only sufficient, but very effective when it is properly applied in the right position.

In the 1950s, the cardiologists Meyer Friedman and Ray Rosenman began studying personality types and their relationship to health, specifically their anticipated incidence for heart disease.[2] Out of this study came the phrase "Type A Personality" which became so common that it was

---

1. Disraeli, "Benjamin Disraeli Quotes."
2. See Scott, "What It Means."

simply referred to as Type A. As a result, people were classified as Type A or Type B. The dichotomy between Type A and Type B, as it relates to health, is also germane to our discussion, and therefore because of its simplicity, we will employ it also.

Perhaps the one word that best describes a Type A individual is competitive. These people are typically impatient, have short fuses, and their focus is on accomplishment. These workaholics live their lives in the fast lane, streaking along at a breakneck pace. They are fast burners who engage in a minute-by-minute race with the clock to accomplish their tasks with an attitude that basically states—get out of my way or you will be trampled. They exhibit a killer instinct that essentially means they are willing to make extraordinary sacrifices to get things done.

In contrast to Type A's, Type B's are more relaxed, and do not view life as a race to accomplish as many things as possible. They are not compelled to manage everything. Neither do they measure their success in terms of the number of tasks completed, but rather they are more quality conscious. They do not forget to smell the flowers along the way, as opposed to Type A's who may not even see the flowers. They enjoy leisure rather than being scared to death that they will be caught in a moment of it.

Regardless of whether we are Type A or Type B, we all possess certain assets and liabilities. From a very simplistic point of view, our personality type, together with our strengths and weaknesses, determine our basic modus operandi. By weighing our personal assets and liabilities against the task at hand, we would know whether we should play a lead role, a support role, or perhaps not even participate; because we are not a good match and there are others more suitable to this task that could engage to complete it. For example, a couple that operates a home decorating business may divide the responsibilities as follows. If the wife has a flair for color schemes, matching furniture, and selecting flooring, and the husband is a well-organized administrator, then the business can be congenially and efficiently operated if she makes the decisions, and he implements them.

These concepts, although very simple, can have a profound effect not only on our careers, but our daily state of mind as well. If we have carefully done our homework so that we completely understand the reality of any situation and our potential role in it, we are then prepared to make an educated decision as to whether we should participate, and if so, how. For example, in applying for a job, we should ask ourselves do we have the background, education, experience, personality and the interest in a particular position. It is often helpful if we also seek advice from others who are interested in our welfare in order to help us be more aware of all the issues involved because they will view the situation from an entirely different perspective. If, however, we haven't done our homework carefully and are not excited about what we would be doing, then even if we somehow obtained the position, it may turn out to be an unsuccessful endeavor. Of course, there may be situations in which we need a job and we are willing to do what is necessary even though we are not fully qualified and the job requirements do not match our talents and interests. While this latter case may be a necessary, but suboptimal solution to a job search, to the extent possible, we should try to do the things we enjoy doing and are suited for, since in the final analysis our job is *our* job, and therefore our own judgement must prevail.

Quite often in business, problems are attacked by teams of people and sometimes even multiple teams depending upon the magnitude of the problem. Each person or group plays a key role, and one individual has to ensure that everyone works in concert to finish the job on time within the performance and economic constraints. While an individual may be a kingpin in one area, that person may be called upon to act in an advisory or support capacity for another. Although he may not be the lead individual, he can play a significant role and may actually be the person who, because of his unique expertise, makes the entire project a success. For example, suppose this individual works for a company that manufactures toys and games, and he is in charge of all electronic games. He may have an entire line of his own game products but, in addition, is capable of having a significant impact on toy sales by enhancing their capability with electronics that permits the toys to walk and talk. Therefore, he actually plays a dual role. He is the lead individual for one or more product lines, but plays a support role for others. As a result, the success of the company may be critically dependent upon him. Because of this critical dependence, it is extremely important that he not only possess the technical know-how, but is also optimistic, enthusiastic, reliable, imaginative, cooperative, stable, flexible, compassionate, and responsible. In fact, it is very unlikely that he would even be in such an important position if he did not exhibit most of these traits.

Isn't it interesting that when we first meet someone, we form an opinion of that individual within a matter of seconds, or minutes, at the outset? This first impression, while not always correct, will typically last until something is done to change it, and is essentially an overall assessment of that person. Our colleagues who work with us have an opportunity to view us for long periods of time under of variety of circumstances. From their vantage point they are able to obtain a fairly accurate picture of what motivates us, because they have acquired a large quantity of data on us via regular observations. This concept is very important in numerous areas of our lives. For example, consider a couple contemplating marriage. In addition to the love they have for one another, which should be paramount since love can overcome many problem issues, doesn't it make sense for two people who are thinking about spending the rest of their lives together to invest the time prior to marriage to be sure they thoroughly know and understand the other individual? "Do they both want children?" "Do they have the same attitudes towards money?" "Do they have the same values?" The answers to these questions provide data that support an intelligent and realistic decision, and may save a lot of grief and heartache if it is later learned that answers to such questions is "no" when we believed they would be "yes."

In a business environment, if we are astute judges of character and are able to recognize the type of personality and the strengths and weaknesses of others, we can devise a viable strategy for working with them in almost any capacity. This is especially important if we are in a position of authority. An intimate knowledge of those who report to us allows us to effectively work with them to generate tasks and responsibilities that match their interests and talents, thereby supporting their professional development in an atmosphere of cooperation. The ability to achieve this situation with employees is one mark of a good manager.

Of course, our inventory could not be complete without faith: faith in God and faith in ourselves. Our faith in God provides the foundation for everything we do. God is in charge of our lives. Therefore, our lives are not some random set of events, but rather a sequence of steps within a carefully designed plan. He created us, and therefore no one knows us better or can predict what we will do under any set of circumstances. When we cooperate with him and seek his help, he provides constant directions on a regular basis to lead us to our highest good.

God has given each of us a free will, and thus we are free to choose the manner in which our lives will unfold. Our choices are based upon faith in ourselves, but this faith is based upon our faith in God. The realization that our every action, whether large or small, has been carefully designed a priori by the creator of the universe should provide us with all the confidence necessary to move forward with trust and assurance. Although the path ahead is unknown and may contain roadblocks and pitfalls, when we cooperate with God's guidance, we can feel as surefooted as a mountain goat in steep and dangerous terrain.

Regardless of our station in life, we all desire to be happy and appreciated for what we do. We want our efforts to count for something, and we want to be a part of the solution, not a part of the problem. A careful and realistic inventory of ourselves provides us with the first phase of the roadmap we need to set the course to achieve our goals. Let us now examine the next step, which is the establishment of these goals.

Goals

If I decide to simply leave town but do not have a particular destination in mind, then any road that exits the city will do because on such a road I can *leave* town. However, if I have some specific destination in mind, there may be a very limited number of roads that will take me there, and there is probably one road that is better than all the others. In addition, if my destination is far away, it would be ideal if I were enthusiastic about the trip and had all the means necessary to get there. A moment's reflection indicates that achieving our goals is somewhat related to making such a trip. As Oliver Wendell Holmes, a famous American physician and poet has said, "The greater thing in this world is not so much where we stand, as in which direction we are going."[3]

Our goals may range from soup to nuts, and may be concerned with any aspect of our lives. For example, our goal may be to run a mile in five minutes, lose ten pounds in three months, purchase a 2020 grey Mercedes 500 SL automobile within a one-year time frame, or become a millionaire by the age of forty.

In general, a goal is a broad statement that defines the achievement of some desired result, and objectives are intermediate results that lead to the accomplishment of the goal. For example, if the goal is to become a licensed real estate agent, the objectives would include successfully filing the application, passing the licensing exam, and paying the necessary fees.

Objectives and the goals they support must have certain qualities. They should be (1) relevant—directly related to what is to be achieved; (2) specific—spell out in no uncertain terms what is to be accomplished; (3) achievable—they can actually be accomplished given the specific circumstances; and (4) measurable—it will be well-known whether or not

3. Holmes, "Oliver Wendell Holmes Quotes."

they have been achieved. The importance of these factors becomes clear when contrasted with some nebulous goal such as—I want to be a better person tomorrow than I am today. Wow! What does that mean? How will I know if I have achieved it?

Performing a realistic assessment, up front, of what is actually involved in reaching a goal is extremely important. If for example I find that my goal cannot be achieved by any means, then I am doomed to failure before I even start, and the pursuit of the goal is a total waste of time and energy. Whenever I think of the naivete with which some people approach goals, I am reminded of a conversation with Astronaut Hank Hartsfield in which he commented that an individual with whom he was talking could not understand why going to the moon was such a big deal—after all, he could see it all the way!

A clear understanding of my own personality characteristics is extremely helpful in the establishment and achievement of goals. Once I understand the underlying characteristics of my own personality, I am better prepared to determine how to use them in goal setting. If I am not sure what type of temperament I have, the well-known Myers-Briggs test is a good starting point.

It is important that we understand the type of personality we possess, because if there is a disconnect between our personality and the goals we have set for ourselves, then there is a high probability that trouble and heartache are waiting for us around the corner.

Winners typically have an entire series of goals. They methodically proceed from achievement to achievement, never experiencing the paralysis associated with the feeling they have "arrived." They set a clear, well-defined goal they are eager to achieve and then all their psychological and physical energy are sharply focused toward the objective. With a positive but tenacious attitude they visualize the achievement of the goal and through a steadfast belief in themselves, they work tirelessly to accomplish it.

Planning is a key winning factor in both setting and attaining goals. In fact, planning is an absolutely necessary precursor for accomplishing almost anything. That is why, for example, contractors have completion targets, factories have production schedules and salespeople have quotas. From a career point of view, where we have been or where we are now only sets the initial conditions. The achievement of any worthwhile goal normally takes time, and hence we must develop a plan and execute it in order to be successful. It is unlikely that Almighty God will somehow anoint us to our desired position; we are going to have to work to achieve our goals, and we will not know what tack to take if we don't have a plan. Having a crystal-clear image of exactly what we want to accomplish and a well-defined plan for achieving it is equivalent to firing a heat-seeking missile at a "hot" target. Our internal guidance system will automatically provide in-flight corrections all along the way. This homing device continuously repositions us for an optimum path to the goal, even in the event of sudden setbacks or diversions which are encountered along the way. It is impossible to overemphasize the importance of having a clear "fix" on our goal, for without it we simply drift aimlessly and the probability that we will somehow stumble into it is probably in the sixth decimal place.

Our goals usually involve an accomplishment of some task subject to certain constraints or the minimization of such things as time, money, energy, wear and tear, and the like. As an example, suppose I have several errands to run on a Saturday morning. I have to get a list of items at the grocery store, drop off a suit at the cleaners and fill up the car's gas tank at the filling station. In addition, since I have other things that I would like to do in the morning, and I am not a member of Warren Buffet's family, I want to minimize the time and fuel required to accomplish these tasks. Therefore, simply stated, my goal is to run these errands in the minimum time by driving the shortest distance. Although much of the planning may be done subconsciously, nevertheless, I must decide the sequence of stops to minimize the distance traveled, provided that it is not necessary that the first stop be the gas station. My planning also includes making sure that when I leave home, I have the list of groceries to be bought, the money with which to buy them, and the suit I want cleaned. Thank God it is impossible to leave the gas tank at home. Although this planning may sound simple, apparently it is not. I know people who routinely leave home without at least one of these items. In such a case, clearly an additional sixty seconds of planning would, no doubt, have been time well spent.

An old Chinese proverb states that "A journey of a thousand miles begins with a single step." Some of our goals are like that journey. Therefore, if possible, I recommend breaking up the path to a goal into as many small segments as possible and then attacking them one by one. Some goals, although reasonable, appear at first blush to be colossal in magnitude. However, by splitting the goal into a number of objectives or sub-goals and approaching them in a sequential manner, I can solve a number of small problems instead of one humongous one. For example, several decades ago I decided to write a textbook on electric circuit analysis that would be suitable for courses taken by sophomore students in engineering at the university. From my own experience at the time in co-authoring other books together with conversations with publishers, I determined that the book would have the following approximate characteristics: three hundred thousand words, two thousand mathematical equations, one thousand technical illustrations, and would consume about eight to nine hundred pages of printed text. Given these estimated parameters, deciding how to attack something of this magnitude is non-trivial. Where would I begin? However, I divided the book into seventeen chapters and three appendices, and then further subdivided these items into approximately 180 sections, each of which would average only several pages in length. Now a section several pages in length is something I believe I can handle. In the final analysis, I wrote one section several pages in length, then another and another until I finished the book. Although my goal was to write a book that would be about eight hundred pages in length, I was never working on more than a few pages at a time. The twelfth edition of this book is currently in production, and it has been used both nationally and internationally for more than thirty-five years. This same concept could have been applied if I were cleaning a house, building a barn, designing a skyscraper, or trying to achieve any other goal. In fact, this process essentially mimics the use of PERT charts that are widely employed in industry for project management. PERT, which stands for Program Evaluation Review Technique, is a graphical display of the manner in which to complete a complicated project. It specifies the series of events that must occur along a timeline for project completion, and provides management with the ability to visualize the resources needed and the progress achieved. The execution of our goals is typically performed in a similar manner.

If my goal is realistic and therefore achievable, all I need is TIDE—not the washing detergent, but Talent, Interest, Dedication, and Enthusiasm. In other words, I have to have some aptitude and be totally committed and excited about achieving the goal. The commitment is absolutely critical. History recounts numerous examples of situations in which people have achieved success in battle against almost insurmountable odds by first cutting off every method of escape. They were left with no choice—they had to win.

Although we may not be locked in a life and death struggle, commitment to the things that we are trying to do is just as important today as it has been down through the ages. To be really committed to a task is not a trivial concept or one to be taken lightly. It is sometimes explained by comparing the roles of the chicken and the pig in the preparation of a breakfast consisting of bacon and eggs. The chicken is involved, but the pig is committed!

A happy and successful marriage is for many of us a very important goal. However, why do so many marriages today end in divorce? The answer to this extremely important question would likely appear to be commitment. The partners take each other for better or worse as long as it is for the better. In fact, some couples even agree up front that if things don't work out they will just uncouple. We could all get filthy rich betting on the breakup of marriages that begin with such a prenuptial agreement, since the escape mechanism is already locked and loaded. Marital therapists indicate that maintaining a viable marriage is much too complicated to oversimplify it by stating that commitment is the key. And I would not presume to know or understand all that is involved in counseling couples contemplating divorce. However, on a macro level, it would at least appear that if the love is truly present, an honest commitment will go a long way toward saving the union.

While each of us will typically have a number of goals throughout our lives, and some will be achieved and some will not, there is one goal that, for Christians, is paramount and inherently consistent. That goal is, of course, the ultimate goal; the achievement of eternal happiness with our Lord in heaven. If we have managed to achieve every other goal we have set for ourselves and failed to achieve this one, we are not winners. The series of goals we achieve in the material realm should simply be a part of the mosaic of our lives that leads us to our final goal. When we cooperate with God's guidance these intermediate goals throughout our lives provide the stepping stones along the trail that ends in eternal glory, and those individuals who achieve this goal are the real winners.

In general, those individuals who are winners at any endeavor are the ones who have the following prerequisites: they have carefully and succinctly defined their goal, they have a highly workable match between the goal and their capabilities to achieve it, they are excited about making a success of what they are doing, they have developed a well-conceived plan, and finally they are totally committed. If all of these factors are present, a word of caution is in order—choose goals very carefully, because their achievement is almost certain.

2

Personal Development

Health

TO THE DEGREE THAT we are able we should try to lead a healthy life. Our internists tell us that to a large extent that means eating, sleeping, exercising, and relaxing correctly. In addition, clearly the benefits that accrue as a result of doing these four things in a methodical manner apply to any type of personality.

We are what we eat! Therefore, nutritional foods should be a regular part of our diet. We should have a balanced diet high in fiber and low in fat. We should be willing to maintain our health so that we do not have to pay to recapture it after it is lost. The former is normally much cheaper than the latter. Nutritionists, who are experts in the design of a healthy diet, and the manner in which to consume it, should be our guide in ensuring that we not only eat the proper foods, but do so correctly.

Many people need eight hours of sleep just to function properly the next day. Other people can get by on four or five hours of sleep. It is important to get whatever is needed. Without the proper sleep we cannot do our best, and if we make a habit of losing sleep, it will have a detrimental effect on our physical, mental, and social well-being.

An important part of a healthy lifestyle is exercise. Exercise can be done inside or outside. It can be done before work, after work, or during the lunch hour. We can walk, run, or do a large variety of exercises designed to support the development of any portion of the body. In fact, the Internet abounds with articles documenting the general effects that exercise has on the body, but in particular it is good for the brain, bone density, blood pressure, cholesterol, heart rate, muscles, the respiratory system, and the list goes on.

Although exercise physiologists can design a program suited to each person's specific needs, anecdotal data indicates that by investing only two hours per week in thirty-minute intervals spread throughout the week, we can achieve some rather dramatic results.

As important as exercise is to our health and well-being, it is even more important to approach it in a safe and careful way. If I have had health problems in the past and/or have not been involved in a regular exercise program, then the first step in the development of my program should be a counseling session with my physician. Once a program has been established, moderation should be its hallmark.

Personal trainers typically recommend a program in which in each exercise session is bracketed by a period of ramping up the intensity of the workout on the front end and ramping it down on the back end. In addition, the regularity with which exercise is approached is key. Many years ago, I was a member of a club that contained a variety of exercise equipment. One evening a gentleman came in to exercise. I had never seen him before and learned later that he was a very successful businessman but he rarely showed up at the gym. I assumed that he could not find time in his schedule to exercise on any type of routine basis and when he did come, he tried to make up for a lot of loss time in a big hurry. On this particular night he collapsed in the gym and later died at the hospital. This very tragic event is an example of what can happen when we put sudden and irregular stress on the body.

The fluid intake both during and after exercise is very important. If our exercise causes us to perspire a lot, that fluid in the body should be replenished. However, the type of fluid used is extremely important. This issue reminds me of what happened to a friend of my parents. He was a man in his mid-fifties. One day in the hot summer months, he went into his house after cutting the grass. He was hot and tired; so he sat down in the kitchen where it was cool and asked his wife for a cup of coffee. Within five minutes, he collapsed and died. When the sequence of events leading up to his death were explained to their physician, the doctor's explanation was quick and simple. Because of the vigorous exercise involved in cutting their grass, his heart was beating at a rapid rate. Coffee is a stimulant, and therefore after drinking the coffee, his heart tried to beat even faster. It could not, and bingo.

Since I am over fifty, I have a medical checkup every year. For younger people with no record of medical problems, it may not be necessary. However, my internist believes that it is important to keep an eye on the critical parameters, if for no other reason than to identify trends. In fact, he has told me that if an emergency arises, he would probably treat things different in the absence of data, than he would if he has a history of my critical parameters over a long period of time.

Finally, from a health standpoint, it is important to relax, even if we have to force ourselves to do it. Behavioral specialists indicate that any kind of hobby, sports, or similar activity is an excellent outlet which not only diverts our attention away from work, but makes us a more well-rounded individual. Like too many other things in my life, I had to learn this the hard way. My undergraduate years at the university preceded the personal computer and programmable calculator, and so the complicated engineering problems were solved with a slide rule or what we called a slip-stick. I recall working one Saturday all afternoon trying to solve a complicated engineering problem that required a large number of mathematical calculations. I worked the problem over and over trying to get the right answer. Each solution took me approximately one hour. I kept making the same type of mistake over and over each time I worked the problem. I became exasperated as I searched for the mistake. Finally, late that afternoon, some of my buddies came over to get me, and we all went out to eat and to a movie. After church the next morning, I sat down to attack the problem I had unsuccessfully worked several times the day before. Within minutes I found the error! It just seemed to jump off the page at me. If it was so obvious on Sunday morning, why couldn't I see it on Saturday afternoon? I think the answer is that I was in tunnel vision and could not look at the problem with the proper perspective. I completed the problem in record time on Sunday, and the solution was correct. However, never again would I keep banging my head against the wall trying to solve problems in a marathon mode. I take breaks, even small ones, that give my mind a time to clear and ensure that whatever the problem is, I want to be able to see it from as many different perspectives as possible.

Health is certainly not a prerequisite for winning; however, it helps. If you have achieved some goal, regardless of how important it is, and failed to maintain your health in the process, did you really win?

Education

Education is extremely important because as the American author Napoleon Hill has stated, "Whatever the mind of man can conceive and believe, it can achieve."[1] In order to be competitive in a world that is constantly changing, we must be capable of adapting to those changes. We must educate ourselves to get a job and, in our rapidly moving environment, we must continue to learn new things in order to keep one. In a mode of continuing education, we are constantly preparing ourselves to do our jobs better and more efficiently. Hopefully, this education also leads to more job satisfaction and enjoyment. If we wish to change jobs, there is a high probability that we may require some additional education. Failure to remain in a viable position can have some serious consequences.

For Christians, continuing education should be an ongoing exercise. As a general rule, it may take a lifetime of study to really comprehend all that God is trying tell us. Even rereading passages in the Bible often provides new insights that were never discovered earlier. It is through this study that God speaks to us to help us address the issues that we face at the time. Therefore, it is critically important that our religious education be a continuing and integral part of our lives so the guidance we need is readily available.

I will never forget several years ago I went shopping for a new lawnmower. I visited several stores to compare prices and machines. At one of the stores I asked the salesman about one of the mowers that I thought would meet my needs. I first asked if the mower was a two-cycle or four-cycle machine. The salesman said he did not know. I asked about the warranty. The salesman replied that he did not know. I had a list of about a dozen questions, and as I quickly went through them, his answer to each was the same—I don't know. Finally, in desperation, he said, "Look fellow, I don't know anything about these machines, I just sell them!" I just smiled and walked away as the little computer in my head was trying to figure out if the manager of the store had any clue what this guy was doing. He was totally unprepared for the job, and as a result he was trying to sell me an unknown device, and I had no intention of buying one of those.

Planning for change not only applies to us as individuals, but also collectively in the form of a corporation. Do you remember the handheld calculator that was called the Bomar Brain? The guts of the calculator were an electronic chip that was manufactured exclusively by Texas

---

1. Hill, "Whatever the Mind of Man..."

Instruments. Bomar had no viable alternative for these chips. So, when Texas Instruments decided to enter the calculator business, they cut off the supply of chips to Bomar, and the Bomar Brain went the way of the Dodo Bird.

As another example, consider the McDonalds restaurant chain. They have always been considered an outstanding fast-food restaurant, right? You bet! But why have they remained so successful over so many years? There are, of course, lots of reasons. However, at least one of them is their adaptability to the changing environment. They went from the Big Mac to the Egg McMuffin to the quarter pounder to chicken McNuggets, etc. And you can bet that whatever they have when you read this book will change soon as they adapt to the market needs. Why? Because their competition is not going to roll over and play dead. In order to remain competitive and at least hold, and preferably gain, market share they have to be innovative and learn to anticipate people's needs and desires. In other words, they have to keep educating themselves about the market and its controlling parameters.

Our education can take anyone of a number of different forms and may deal with many different aspects of our lives. Consider for example our work. First of all, we should be interested and excited about what we are doing. If this is not the case, we are probably in the wrong job. Assuming however that we have achieved a good match between our talents and interests and some position, we should strive constantly to be in the learning mode. If we know our own job extremely well, then we can learn as much as possible about others in the company. The more we know, the more valuable we are as an employee. In fact, if we understand a large number of jobs and their interactions, we may be able to suggest ways to improve the company by streamlining the operation or cutting operational costs. If we can do this, we will not only be an extremely valuable employee, but one of the first to be promoted, the last to go if a problem develops, and one of the first to get reestablished if the company for some reason goes belly up.

The workplace is a very dynamic and competitive environment, and for most companies change is a way of life. Those individuals with a willingness to continue to educate themselves in whatever manner they can are the least affected by the inevitable changes in the work environment. The technology that is having, and will continue to have, a large impact on companies and their current workforce is artificial intelligence, or AI. This technology is rapidly replacing low-level jobs at a prodigious pace, and it is forcing people in these positions to seek alternative employment. However, those individuals who prepare themselves for change with a mindset for embracing a different environment can move to other jobs where their skills are not only useful, but needed. Three specific companies that have experienced explosive growth by employing people to work at their own schedule, on a part-time basis, are Angie's List, HomeAdvisor, and taKL. For those people who are less aggressive in their approach to adapt to the changing times, Uber and Lyft are possibilities.

Because we are a product of our history and our environment, change is one of the only constants in our lives, and we must not only accept it, but prepare ourselves to thrive in it. As Thomas Carlyle, a British historian, philosopher, mathematician, and teacher has said, "Today is not yesterday. We ourselves change. How then, can our works and thoughts, if they are always to be the fittest, continue the same? Change indeed is painful; yet, ever needful."[2]

I have had some type of job since I was old enough to have one, and I believe we can all learn something from each job we have. For example, between my freshman and sophomore years at the university, I worked all summer in a plywood factory in north Montgomery, Alabama. I worked from 7:00 AM to 4:00 PM. The plant was hot as the proverbial hinges and reeked of the formaldehyde that was used to make the glue. Every day I would sweat like a stuck pig, and in spite of taking a bath every night, by noon I was not fun to be around. However, I learned something that summer that was very simple, and yet for me profound. What I learned was "come hell or high water, I was going to get an education, because I was not going to spend the rest of my life in that job or one like it!"

Social Welfare

If we want to be happy and successful, our fundamental mode of operation should be a Christian lifestyle, which means a strict adherence to the Commandments. If we "love our neighbors as ourselves," all of our social interactions will provide a happy and healthy environment for us and all with whom we come in contact. From a pragmatic standpoint, we should take pride in ourselves, and in so doing we can literally package and market ourselves for success. Since first impressions are very important, we should make a good one. These impressions, which others have

---

2. Carlyle, "Today Is Not Today..."

of us, tend to influence their actions. For example, if we look good, we are treated with respect. Others just naturally assume that if we are neat, clean, and look sharp, that our appearance is important to us. If we look important, we feel important, and this feeling also builds our confidence. On the other hand, if we look like an unmade bed, people will assume that we ourselves feel unimportant and, as such, we will be ignored or at the very least given only casual attention.

If Edie is going shopping in a store that sells high-quality merchandize, she always dresses up. She says that the salespeople will tend to ignore her if she is not appropriately dressed. Our son, John, who recently retired as a Senior Vice President at AT&T, wore dark suits, matching ties, starched white shirts and well-shined shoes, and all of his colleagues did, too. Therefore, he would not be caught dead in any other uniform. I even remember as a child commenting to the local beer distributor, who was a friend of my dad, that he had one of the most expensive automobiles in town. He explained to me that he was required to do so in order to clearly demonstrate that not only was he very successful, but more importantly, that his product was a real favorite with the beer-drinking public.

Do you realize that millions of dollars are spent each year on industrial design for the products we buy? For example, such things as pictures of the product, color schemes, and the size and shape of the package, are typical variables. Regardless of the type of job we have, we are also normally selling ourselves and our ideas on a regular basis. Therefore, we should take care to package ourselves so that we too look our best. We all believe what we perceive, and our perception is influenced by nonverbal, as well as verbal inputs. That is why, for example, a simple smile is so important. Just as we make snap decisions in a grocery store on which product to buy, our perception of another individual is also typically lightning quick.

I have known a number of students at the University who, during their years in school, walked around looking like they lived on the street. When I look at them, I am not really sure whether they are men or beasts. However, when they are about to graduate and start interviewing for a job, a metamorphosis occurs, and they start looking like they just stepped out of a fashion magazine. Sanity has prevailed. It had better, if they want a job. Business takes a dim view of interviewing people who look like tramps.

Clothes are a critical part of our image investment portfolio. Therefore, our dress should be appropriate, comfortable, and look good. Looking good is important in one's business and, as a general rule, a suit is normally a sign of authority. Admittedly, the West Coast often marches to a different drum. In California, it is not uncommon to find the male officers of the company working in jeans and golf shirts, and the female officers in an equivalent attire. In fact, today this philosophy has spread across the country and it is more prevalent in many industries. Nevertheless, if we see someone who is very well dressed, we can be confident we are looking at a successful individual.

We need to dress so our clothes don't do the talking for us. An individual I know was a member of a singing group. One evening the group was to perform at a nursing home. My friend was going to a costume party immediately following the performance, so she wore a tiger costume, complete with a four-foot tail, to the nursing home. The music was very good, but some of those old people, many of whom could not even see well, were so confused they didn't know whether they were being entertained by a choir or a circus.

Sometimes the problems with appropriate dress can be very subtle. For example, right after we were married, Edie and I went to the wedding of two of our classmates. The wedding was in the afternoon, and the sun shone brightly in the church windows. We were sitting in the pew, waiting for the wedding to start when I looked up and saw a kind of aurora borealis, dancing all over the walls and ceiling of the church. It was so bright that many of the people in the church noticed it. I knew if it continued during the wedding, it would detract from the ceremony. I started looking around trying to figure out what was causing it. I was having a difficult time determining the source, when I noticed that every time Edie moved, the constellations on the wall and ceiling moved too. I finally figured out that Edie's cut glass earrings were refracting the sunlight and causing the problem. When Edie took off the earrings, everything returned to normal.

As a general rule, dress is important and in some places failure to adhere to the dress code can produce a speed bump in your career. Therefore, we should dress for success if we want our head above the crowd.

Having the proper social graces, however, involves more than simply dressing properly. It also means such things as knowing how to select an appropriate present, having the proper table manners, and knowing how to converse with a wide variety of people at various occasions. For example, as W. Somerset Maugham, an English playwright, novelist, and short-story writer, has said, "At a dinner party one should eat wisely but not too well, and talk well but not too wisely."[3] It is important for us to remember that the people with whom we socialize can have a profound effect upon our careers. If these people are good Christians, they will play a vital role in our personal development. Therefore, we should try to confine our personal interactions to solid, positive, forward-looking people who will encourage us and be happy for our every success. Negative thinkers or gossip junkies, on the other hand, poison our minds and tend to pull us down with them. Some of these people believe that by tearing down another individual they will make themselves look better. This approach is, of course, ridiculous. If I painted my neighbor's house chartreuse and pink, it would not make my house look better; instead it would appear that I lived in a wacko neighborhood and my own sanity would come into question.

Variety is indeed the spice of life and other people can add complete new dimensions to our lives. By mixing with many different types of people, we can significantly enhance the scope of our social orbit. When these people are religious individuals, they can have a significant effect on our lives. In general, people are fascinating and each one knows things we don't know and can do things that we can't do.

Regardless of our situation, winners should try to operate in a social mode that is honest, congenial, pleasant, and does not embarrass us. In addition, winners should strive to enjoy our interactions with others so that they add zest and pleasure to our lives. When winners are not completely satisfied with their social progress, they should take steps to correct it now for after all, as someone pragmatically stated, "Today is the very first day of the rest of our lives."

---

3. Maugham, "At a Dinner Party..."

3

Understanding the Basic Parameters

WINNERS SEEM TO INHERENTLY understand that the soup of success will always contain at least three critical ingredients: time, information, and power. Although they may be present in varying degrees depending upon the circumstances of the situation, they are typically present in any successful endeavor.

Time

Simply stated, success takes time. While this statement is not very profound, it is true. I have never known a really successful person who did not work long and hard at what they do. They have paid the price and earned the right to be successful. This time commitment is also a fundamental characteristic of the Christian way of life. How can we possibly become close to Our Lord if we don't invest the time to know him and communicate with him. He will not force us and we are free to do as we please, but the consequences of ignoring him can be quite serious. We need his guidance, and we receive it through our prayer time spent with him. After all, he knows the way ahead and through our communication with him, he reveals the optimum path to us. Winning in any aspect of life is easier when God is controlling the traffic signals in our lives.

Time is a commitment. It is an investment in an individual's success in this life, and hopefully in achieving it in the next. It is also a requirement in the process of acquiring or applying knowledge or skills. We may acquire knowledge or skills through education whether formal or informal and/or on-the-job training, such as an apprenticeship. Either way, we have to invest a great deal of time in learning the things that will help us to be successful. Consider, for example, the following simple cases.

Suppose we wish to become a successful real estate salesperson. In order to be licensed to sell real estate we must first pass a state exam. Preparation for the exam will take at least a couple of months of study either independently or via some course offered by an individual who is a practicing professional. As soon as we have passed the exam, we are ready to go out and start selling millions of dollars of real estate—right? No! First of all, you have to work for a real estate broker, and so you need to find one who will hire you. Passing the real estate exam simply illustrates we know the fundamentals involved. In general, we have little or no detailed knowledge of contracts, closings, techniques for obtaining listings, what to say and what not to say when selling an individual, the idiosyncrasies involved in selling rural, residential, or commercial property, and so on ad infinitum. The real estate market is also dynamic. There may not be the same kind of demand for commercial real estate in the near future, if the market for malls and big box stores changes, as a result of the growing acceptance of Internet purchasing. It will normally take considerable time and hard work to "put it all together" and become a very successful real estate salesperson.

There are quite a number of people who believe that they have a flair for investing in the stock market. Perhaps they are familiar with some aspect of the business world and as a result they feel comfortable investing in stocks that are aligned with their interest and expertise. In addition, some people read the *Wall Street Journal* religiously to stay abreast of changing trends. If these individuals have invested the time and energy necessary to know their sectors of the market well, they may be successful. However, it is unlikely that someone who treats this activity as a sideline will make a lot of money in the market. Today, large investment institutions comprise a huge portion of the market. These institutions have portfolio managers who eat, drink, and sleep with the cadence of the Big Board. They watch the market like a hawk and have tremendous impact on moves within the market because they control huge blocks of stock. These managers are backed up by a large research staff that provides advice while keeping track of the complete status of various corporations and correlating their business with local, national, and international events. In fact, in some cases, their firm's computers are programmed to watch the breaking news very carefully, and if a headline appears that would have a negative impact on the market, the computers react within seconds and as a result, the Dow may fall by a significant amount in a precipitous manner. There are many individual investors who try to operate in essentially the same mode. If they are on top of the market on a minute-by-minute basis, they probably do very well. However, if an individual only spends enough time to dabble in the market, it is very unlikely that they will be successful. In fact, even some of the most sophisticated investors have taken a terrible bath at various times in history, e.g., October 19, 1987 or the winter of 2019–20 when COVID 19 became an all-too-familiar household expression.

If we are a parent trying to keep our children on the straight and narrow, we have to devote a lot of our time to them. We have to have the kind of rapport with them that fosters good, honest communication. We have to know what they think, how they feel, what they want, what is important to them, and what pressures they are under. We need to know where they are, where they are going, what they are doing, and who their friends are. It is hard to influence what you do not know or understand. Learning and digesting what is happening in their lives so we can help them with their problems takes time—and lots of it. Anyone who does not have the communication lines wide open and thinks they will get a straight answer to what is really happening is regrettably in for a very rude awakening.

I would have to be completely naïve, even stupid, to assume that developing and maintaining the kind of rapport with my children that is necessary to have a positive influence on them and guide them in good choices is easy. It is anything but that. It is extremely difficult, and we all do the best we can. Today, in order to make ends meet, there are often two breadwinners in the family. As a result, and by necessity, children are left for what may be long periods of time without adult supervision. This can be a recipe for disaster. I am not a psychologist, but common sense tells me that in today' s world with an Internet where I can access essentially anything—and I do mean anything, easy access to a wide spectrum of harmful drugs as well as instant communication via telephone, text, and email—the ability to get into trouble is greatly enhanced. Raising children in this environment would seem to be an almost impossible task. However, many people go to great lengths to ensure that they have a successful family environment. Some people, if they are able, simply decide that the extra money is not worth risking their children's future and trade that money for time. Winners find a way to navigate these treacherous waters by focusing on what is truly important to the success of all their family members. While this process is anything but trivial, winners recognize that their family is of ultimate importance and take steps to secure them first. A person who achieves great success at the expense of their family can hardly be considered a winner. They may have essentially won the battle but lost the war.

There is one particular issue associated with success and family that requires special attention. Many young adults with children are in the process of developing their careers, and as we have noted this process takes time. However, running in parallel with this process is the formative years of their children's development. It is in this period that children learn the lessons that provide the foundation for the rest of their lives. It is imperative that children enter the teenage years having the proper guidance, because once they reach these years, their time is spent with their friends. Mom and Dad will take a backseat position and find it difficult to even spend time with them, let alone influence their behavioral patterns. If children do not enter the teen years with the proper behavioral standards, it is almost impossible to correct the situation, and in many cases disappointment and heartache lie in the path ahead. While it is unfortunate that the process of raising children is never easy under the best of circumstances, it is easier in a Christian household where children have grown up in an environment in which God plays a central role. The discipline provided by an adherence to Christian morals and values is a powerful antidote to many of the problems encountered by children as they seek to establish a sound footing in this world filled with happiness and success.

Of course, it may not be the lack of time spent guiding the children that is the issue. At the other end of the spectrum is a parenting trend that has some very serious consequences. This trend is identified by the terms "helicopter parents" and "lawnmower parents," and the trend involves moving from the former to the latter. These two terms, which are currently in vogue, describe a parenting philosophy in which the parents take on most, if not all, of the responsibility for their children's problems, and thus in essence their successes. In addition, some parents apply this philosophy to their sons and daughters long after they are no longer children.

In the helicopter scenario, the parents hover over their children to ensure that as the children's problems arise, they are ready, willing, and able to handle them. After all, the parents have been around a long time, probably have some experience in areas of concern, and feel that they are in a better position to handle whatever comes along. The lawnmower parents are much more forward-looking, and they anticipate problems that may arise, and then systematically try to eliminate them so the children never even have to address them. In each case, childhood, as the parents would define it, could theoretically continue until death, that of either the parents or the children.

While parenting has always been, and will probably always be, a difficult task because we all ride the maiden voyage, the parents who operate in either helicopter or lawnmower mode typically have only the best of intentions. They love their children and pride themselves in doing more for their children's success than their own parents had done for them. They are investing time, money, and energy to do the best they can to make their children happy and content as they grow up, and they are proud of it. They simply refuse to cut the umbilical cord in an effort to ensure that their children's growth is a problem-free adventure.

While it would appear that attempting to eliminate the myriad problems that will undoubtedly occur as their children try to mature into responsible adults should be applauded, the parent's attempts to keep their children from failing are actually doing the exact opposite. The parent's myopic approach fails to anticipate the results of their actions downstream. When the children do not have to learn to face and solve the simple problems encountered when they are young, how will they ever be prepared to deal with what is almost assuredly the more difficult problems they have to address as adults? For example, if a child cannot deal with failing to make the baseball team, failing to become first chair for flute in the band, failing to get an invitation to a popular party, failing to make an A in mathematics, etc., when will they ever learn to muster the strength to handle problems at the adult level, such as not getting into the "right" college, losing a job, getting a divorce, being stabbed in the back by a close friend, dealing with the death of a sibling or parent, etc.? How can the children become responsible adults, capable of dealing with life's inevitable problems, when they have never been taught to be responsible children? As Ann Landers, the pen name for Esther Pauline Lederer, an American advice columnist and nationwide media celebrity, has said,

> It is not what you do for your children, but what you have taught them to do for themselves that will make them successful human beings.[1]

---

1. Landers, "If I Were Asked..."

Learning to be responsible is one of the key ingredients in successfully moving from childhood to adulthood, and time spent on that activity is absolutely critical. Our job as parents is to make our children as responsible and independent as possible. If we can successfully do this job correctly, the children are well prepared to deal with problems and pursue a successful future whether we are around or not; and of course, we cannot count on being around all their lives.

Learning to handle problems at a young age can make the children very resilient and capable of handling the inevitable adversity that life will typically throw at them. I believe that when the children are young, we have to deal with a whole lot of small problems, but when they are older, the number of problems may be few, but they are normally large at best and devastating at worst. If the children become adults and have not learned to cope with problems, their options are typically professional help, "dropping out," or turning to alcohol and/or drugs as a coping mechanism.

I have a front-row seat for the dropouts in my class every semester. Our students enter the university with high ACT or SAT scores so there is no doubt that the brain power is there. In addition, we provide tutoring for students that costs them nothing. This tutoring is readily available, and I am available to answer questions as they arise. In fact, our College of Engineering has built a large building, well-staffed with people who are solely dedicated to helping our students be successful in school, as well as their subsequent career. Furthermore, I warn my students on the first day of class that in order to be successful in the class, they must study and keep up so they do not fall behind. Clearly, while I can explain the course material to them, I cannot understand it for them. Invariably 20 percent of the class, i.e., one in five, will drop the class after the first exam. There is absolutely no way for the parents to influence their children's performance on my exams. Mama and Daddy have absolutely no impact whatsoever. It is the student's responsibility, no one can do it for them, and some learn much too late they are ill-prepared for what must appear to be a transition from dining on peacock tongue to a steady diet of ramen noodles. Failing key courses that are prerequisites for later courses essentially ensures that the student will have to go an additional semester or two, assuming they actually remain in school, and the cost of those extra semesters is not cheap.

Failing to be able to cope with adversity can also lead to alcohol and drugs. These two coping mechanisms are really dangerous. They may be only disruptive in the short term, but could be devastating in the long term. In addition, the parents may not even know there is a problem in one of these areas until addressing them is way beyond their ability to provide assistance, and the solution requires professional help, if they are smart enough to seek it, and do so in time.

It is unfortunate that some parents believe they have the resources to fix any problem their children will encounter. This mindset is way off track because there are numerous problems their children may encounter that money simply won't fix. In addition, the fix, when possible, provides the child with a false sense of security. The parent's money and their time spent in teaching their children to learn to adjust to problems are not necessarily interchangeable. When time has not been allocated to help their children adjust to life's problems, throwing money at these problems is a poor solution, if one at all, and in the case of alcohol and drugs, the last time I checked, gasoline was not the preferred fluid for putting out a fire.

In 2019, paving the way for children took a nasty turn. Splashed all over the news in living color was the saga of more than thirty very affluent parents, including some movie stars, who were criminally charged for "investing" about twenty-five million dollars in schemes designed to buy their children's admission into some of the country's best universities. The total number of people involved in the process was about fifty, and US Attorney for Massachusetts, Andrew E. Lelling, declared it to be "the largest college admissions scam ever prosecuted by the Department of Justice."[2] Mr. Lelling said that those parents used their wealth to create a separate and unfair admissions process for their children.[3] The vehicles employed in the schemes were fake academic and athletic records, and the investigation resulted in many people being prosecuted while others who were involved lost their jobs. It is difficult to assess the damage done to the children in this drama, but it is unlikely that it added anything to their self-esteem.

Although it is normally very time-consuming and often difficult to force children to grow up by insisting that they deal with their own problems as they arise, the consequences of protecting them from adversity by solving their problems for them are very serious. Our actions have consequences, and it is a tragedy that in our attempts to protect them from failing as children, we may be guaranteeing their failure as adults.

2. Sweet, "Hollywood Stars," para. 2.
3. Medina et al., "Actresses, Business Leaders," paras. 11–12.

Regardless of how we slice it, the bottom line is that there is only so much time. We all have twenty-four hours a day, and Almighty God is not generating any more of it. Therefore, the efficiency with which we use the time we have plays an extremely important role in each and every success we experience.

Information

Information provides the basis for essentially everything we do. Our every action or reaction is a result of the information we have at the time. Some information is of very little value while other information is absolutely critical. Some information, although it may be intriguing, has no impact on us. However, other information could be of enormous importance and perhaps save us a great deal of time, money, or energy, because of the significant impact it has on some critical decision. In order to illustrate the crucial nature of information, consider the following examples.

Let us examine a situation in which I am interested in establishing a new business in town to make masks. Although I am intensely interested in this business and have a real desire to succeed at it, that is far from enough. It is certainly necessary for success, but not sufficient. I need information and plenty of it. For example, can I obtain the initial and long-term financing, and can I do it at some reasonable interest rate? Is the necessary manpower available? Can I purchase or lease all the facilities and equipment I will need? Is there a guaranteed supply of raw materials available at a reasonable price? What is my competition and where are they located? Can I convince the buyers that my product is superior to those currently available? This is just some of the information I need to even begin to pursue my business model. Failure to obtain this information or properly assess its impact on my plans can have some rather serious consequences—like a total loss of my investment!

Let's suppose that I am selling a used car. I have checked the NADA book, and I know the recommended value of this car to the penny. I have been advertising the car for some time with no results. I need the money to pay off a note at the bank, and the interest on the note is continuing to accumulate. Finally, a man and his daughter come to see the car. As they examine the car and ask me questions about it, I try to find out everything I can about them. In talking with them, I find out that this car meets the daughter's needs. They have been looking for the right car for weeks with no luck. They live in the next town and have driven thirty miles just to see my car. Then I overhear the daughter tell her dad that she really wants this car and asks him to please buy it for her. Now I ask you—notwithstanding my own financial difficulties—based upon the information I have just received, will I get my original price for the car? You'd better believe it. However, suppose that when the man and his daughter show up, they don't give me even a single clue to the actual degree of their interest. Now I have no information on them, but I am keenly aware of my own financial situation. If they decide they might be interested in buying the car, will I get my original price? While it is possible, it is unlikely. I have so little information on them that it is difficult to know just how much negotiating room I have.

There are times when it is not the lack of information that is the problem, but the volume of it. We have a plethora of information, and our problem is assimilating it in a fashion that helps support a decision. However, when the amount of information is gigantic, trying to obtain what is needed to make a realistic decision in a reasonable time frame, is often much like taking a sip of water from a fire hose. Suppose, for example, that I am considering changing jobs. I have two good possibilities, Company A and Company B. During my interview with them I have gathered a significant amount of information about each. I have learned that the actual position is better at Company A, but Company B pays more money. My commute to work would be shorter with Company B, but the family as a whole prefers Company A. The medical insurance, because of a dental rider, is better at Company A, but the leisure opportunities are better at Company B. As more and more comparisons are considered, the complexity of the decision increases. Therefore, in an effort to sort out the positive and negative features in each in comparison with the other, I prepare the following list of items:

- Job preference
- Coworkers
- Opportunities for advancement
- Educational opportunities
- Money
- Stock options
- Vacation time

- Medical insurance
- Leisure opportunities
- Climate
- Proximity to suitable housing
- Family preference

Within each of the particular categories there are a number of considerations which determine its relative merit. For example, my daughter may feel that the recreational opportunities afforded her as a result of my accepting the job with Company A are outstanding. However, she also feels that in the summer the bugs are big enough and present in sufficient quantities that they are capable of carrying her to the recreational facilities. In addition, as we examine the list, we note that some items are really much more important than others. Therefore, in order to identify their relative importance some of the items will be weighted by a factor of two. If I now carefully examine the list and assign a relative number between one and ten (where ten represents the highest degree of importance) to each category, I might arrive at a table such as that shown below.

Category	Co.A	Co.B	Weight	Co.A total	Co.B total
Job Preference	9	6	2	18	12
Coworkers	10	5	2	20	10
Opportunities for Advancement	5	9	1	5	9
Educational Opportunities	7	5	2	14	10
Money	6	8	1	6	8
Stock Options	0	3	1	0	3
Vacation Time	10	10	1	10	10
Medical Insurance	10	7	2	20	14

Category	Co.A	Co.B	Weight	Co.A total	Co.B total
Leisure Opportunities	8	10	1	8	10
Climate	8	4	2	16	8
Proximity to Suitable Housing	7	9	2	14	18
Family Preference	8	4	2	16	8
Totals				147	120

In the absence of additional information, the table would indicate that Company A is probably the best overall choice. If the totals were significantly different, it would appear that the choice is obvious. On the other hand, if the totals had been approximately equal, then one choice would no doubt have been as good as the other, and the final decision would probably be based on a gut feeling. Of course, there are times when circumstances seem to dictate the choice, and that can be unfortunate. This situation is often prevalent when dealing with aging parents. There can be so many variables, involving a number of family members, with limited flexibility and resources that the necessary decisions are forced and the final arrangements, which may be suboptimal, are simply the best that can be achieved at the time, and under the current constraints.

The Internet contains a wealth of information concerning the processes involved in decision-making. In general, we should first clearly identify the decision that must be made in a simple and understandable manner, gather the information necessary to identify the viable alternatives, and, given these alternatives, select the one that is best. The example above simply outlines one means by which to accomplish this task. This approach is also applicable when buying a car, a house, or making any kind of decision where it is possible to accumulate large amounts of data. What is typically needed is a process to sort the data in a manner that provides the information needed to make an educated decision.

Before we can effectively use information we have to obtain it, and in general that is not a simple task. We have to do our homework and invest time, money, and energy in the process of gathering data, so that when we come to crunch point we will have at our disposal everything we need. For example, good attorneys spend days, weeks, and sometimes months gathering data for a case. If their counterpart has not been as diligent, they will no doubt lose when they face off in court.

Because of the inherent value of information, we normally dislike and usually distrust people whose primary avocation is snooping into every detail of our personal business. Our real friends use information to help us; however, our adversaries have quite another motive in mind. Therefore, our approach in obtaining information is absolutely critical. If we approach an issue in a demanding or threatening fashion, we will learn very little. People will naturally hide information from us if we appear to have an axe to grind, since they do not know how we will use the information they give us. However, if our approach is "would you please help me with this—I just don't understand," people will tend to tell us even more than we want to know. For example, when someone appears to be confused, I tend to explain things in great detail, and I probably provide them with more information than they actually need.

When my dad graduated from high school, he got a job in a dry-cleaning plant. He was anxious to do well and advance in the organization, and he dedicated himself to learning all the technical aspects of the dry-cleaning process. One night after working late, Dad and one of his coworkers stopped by a coffee shop to unwind. In the course of the conversation, the man mentioned that the owner's oldest son would soon graduate from high school and join the company in a supervisory position. Furthermore, the owner had several other children, all of whom would eventually occupy management positions. As a result, Dad's chances of advancing in the company were approximately zero on a scale of one to ten. Soon thereafter, given this valuable information, Dad left the business for another company where there was real upward mobility.

There are of course times when the valuable information comes too late, and mistakes are made that are difficult, if not impossible, to fix. I will never forget an incident that occurred while I was serving as head of the Electrical and Computer Engineering Department at Auburn University. I was in this position for thirty-six years, and it would seem that every problem that could possibly occur in that environment did during my tenure in the position. During one term a student who was planning to graduate flunked a class, meaning he would not graduate as planned that term. The young man's father called me and wanted to meet with me to discuss this situation. We set up a time, and the father showed up as planned. In the meantime, I had met with the professor, whose class the young man had failed, to make sure I had my facts and evidence assembled and could clearly demonstrate the reason for the failure. When the father arrived, the two of us sat down at my conference table with the professor and the student. I asked the student if we could discuss his record and performance with his father. Of course, I was not concerned that I would get his permission with the father sitting four feet away, but I needed his permission (it is a law that I have to have the student's permission even though the father is paying the bills). Once I had the student's permission to discuss his performance, I completely ignored him and the professor and looked directly at the father. I began laying out the case, point by point, to show the sloppy manner in which his son had performed with a somewhat laissez-faire attitude. I had not gotten very far into my presentation, when the father stopped me. He told me that apparently I did not understand his reason for the meeting. Much to my surprise, he said he was not there to defend his son. Instead he told me that their family owned a big business, and this young man was the eldest son, who would naturally be trained to run the company. So, the father was there to find out if he dared turn the company over to this guy. Wow! I am sure the expression on my face was a dead giveaway. I was so impressed that this father was there to gather information on his son's performance that would support a decision so important to the family's future. He had no intention of turning the company over to this son without understanding if he could trust him with it. I could tell by the expression on the son's face that the father was not the only one who had gathered some information at that meeting. The son had too, but I am afraid it was too late.

There are times when the real information is coded within the data we receive, and all of our senses must be acutely alert in order to extract it. In some cases the real information is not in verbal or written form, but rather in what we call body language.

Body language is a very important subject and there are numerous books, short courses, and websites on the Internet that address its many facets and ramifications. We have all heard the expression "actions speak louder than words," and thus body language is an effective, although often subtle, way in which to communicate. It is a way for me to convey a considerable amount of information without opening my mouth. Body language provides information via such things as posture, eye movement, hand movement, facial expressions, and unusual gestures, just to name a few.

I have seen television news programs in which body language experts are called upon to analyze a politician's performance at some event, such as a political rally. The expert will provide an opinion detailing how the person's body language has impacted his performance, and comment on what is not said as opposed to what is being expressed verbally. It is important to be very cognizant of body language when communicating with someone, especially someone you don't know well, and failure to do so may mean that a key underlying message is completely missed.

As an example, suppose that I am looking for a job. A friend of mine tells me that he knows the president of the XYZ Company and can arrange an interview for me. I report for the interview on time, and I have done my homework. I am very neatly dressed, and I know a lot about the company. I feel that I am prepared to answer any question. The president invites me into his office with the greeting "I've only got a few minutes." At first, we just look at one another and when I realize that he isn't going to say anything, I begin my litany. I am confident and very enthusiastic. As I speak, he begins drumming his fingers on his desk, and I notice that his head is beginning to tilt slightly backwards. His pupils dilate and then start rotating into his eyelids. Just as he is about to lapse into a coma, he catches himself and abruptly stands up while I am still in the middle of a sentence. As I continue to finish my sentence, he starts toward the door. The minute I pause between sentences to breathe, he says "Dave, I enjoyed meeting you. We will be in touch." Did you get any clues as to my chances of getting a job at that company? Being overly optimistic, I would say the probability is in the sixth decimal place.

Many moons ago, I went to a professional meeting which was held at the Intercontinental Hotel on Hilton Head Island. Since all of our children were either working or in college, Edie went with me. While I attended the technical meetings, Edie got out by the pool to get some sun and read a book. One day while she was there a woman whose husband was also attending the meeting started up a conversation with Edie. Before she had learned Edie's name, she launched into an aria about her daughter. Her daughter was adopted and their only child. She told Edie that the daughter went to the very best school in the area, was in the honor's program, could play the piano flawlessly, and was simply outstanding in every possible way. For thirty minutes, Edie heard everything anyone could possibly want to know about this daughter. Finally, she asked Edie if we had any children. Edie replied, "Yes, three." That was apparently the wrong answer, because the lady picked up where she left off as though

Edie had not opened her mouth. She went into overdrive as she told Edie that they lived on a full acre in New Jersey in a big house and that her husband was absolutely wonderful. She continued as she raved on about their automobile. In an effort to at least say something, Edie told her that we had recently had car trouble and she hoped that the lady's car was better than ours. The lady replied, "Oh, it is!" So, in addition to her other wonderful attributes, the lady was obviously clairvoyant, since she has very little information on us, and for all she knew we could have been the Duke and Duchess and simply had trouble replacing the solid gold hood ornament on our Rolls Royce! Nevertheless, with the exception of a couple of very short injections by Edie, the self-advertisement marched on. Edie learned that this lady was trained as a nurse, and although she really did not want to work, her daughter wanted to be with her friends and not her mother (I wonder why?). The lady claimed to be so good, that the local doctors were absolutely pleading with her to come to work. She was so important that she could pick her own schedule, but she would have to be back to work on Friday.

After about an hour of this "conversation," Edie excused herself. In this encounter, the lady had provided a great deal of information, while Edie had provided almost none. While all of the information the lady gave to Edie may be true, the manner in which it was presented made it at least appear to be suspect. In fact, when information is presented in an overbearing braggadocio manner, the underlying information may be quite different from what is actually being presented.

Finally, there are times when the information is in your face, but you cannot seem to see the forest for the trees and are unable to understand its real significance. As an example, I am reminded of the story of two bounty hunters back in the frontier days who were paid for every outlaw they could bring in. One night while the two were camping deep in the woods, one of them was awakened to find that they were completely encircled by about two dozen outlaws armed to the teeth, and so he woke up his partner and said, "Wake up man, we're rich!"

It is often critical to have the right information at the right time and in the right place. The probability of having this information under these circumstances is vastly improved if we are in constant communication with Almighty God. Information from him can be seamlessly transmitted through a hunch or a dream, or the path may be via some circuit through multiple nodes. God alone knows all the circumstances surrounding the information we require, and regardless of the manner in which we receive the information, if the circumstances suggest that it has originated with God, we can trust it completely.

Sometimes, we recognize only in hindsight that God has supplied the key information in the solution of some sticky problem. We may have tried numerous approaches that led nowhere. Then all of a sudden an idea pops into our mind that suggests one additional path that has never occurred to us. After following this new course of action, we realize that it is the path we have been searching for. Why didn't we think of this approach earlier? God has not only supplied us with critical information, but in the process he has also taught us that we can rely on him when we remain close to him.

Power

All too often this word is used in such a way that we associate it with a negative connotation. If someone is trying to abuse, control, force, or manipulate some person or situation, then we refer to this exploitation as an application of power. In this master/slave-type relationship, the individual being controlled is devalued or otherwise hurt in some way. Although there are times when we are dealing with an intelligent adversary and our only viable defense is like that of a forest ranger—to fight fire with fire, winners will take this approach only as a last resort. Real winners will first exhaust every positive tactic in an effort to maintain a situation in which there are no losers. Our approach to power is a very positive one. It is a means to an end, and not an end in itself. It is an important ingredient in our formula for working effectively and successfully with others; for it not only provides a degree of freedom, but the opportunity to be more productive and serve others. In doing so, both parties involved are happier for it.

The library and the Internet are replete with a host of articles on the subject of power. Power is a fascinating subject, and it is interesting that one manner in which to categorize it is to subdivide it into four categories: confirmed, hidden, wasted or unknown.[4] Our power is said to be confirmed when we have it and everyone believes we have it. It is hidden if we actually have it but others don't think we do, wasted if we have it but don't know we have it, and it is unknown when neither we nor others think we have it, even though we may actually have it. Note that the

---

4. See "Power Perception Matrix."

concept that seems to underpin each of these categories is perception. Simply stated, we operate based upon what we perceive to be the situation. So, clearly our perception of power is critical. For example, if I perceive that you will harm me in some way the next time we encounter one another, I will do my best to ensure that we don't encounter one another!

From a scientific standpoint, power is the time rate of change of energy. Therefore, our power is derived from an inherent ability to "make it happen." This power manifests itself in numerous forms, some of which may appear at first to be absolutely powerless. For example, how much power does a five-day-old baby have? If the answer to this question is enormous power, then that response would be correct. When our oldest daughter, Geri, was five days old, Edie and I got up essentially every hour on the hour in the middle of the night just to be sure she was still breathing. Now that's what I call real power, because I would not have gotten up that many times to greet the President of the United States.

Individuals derive power simply by virtue of the fact that they occupy some position of authority. People in such a position can influence behavior in a number of positive ways. For example, by creating a congenial competition or using some kind of carrot, they can produce the desired result in an atmosphere of mutual support. When it is necessary to exercise power, it can be done in a firm but friendly manner.

It is normally never necessary or desirable to wield power in a dictatorial fashion, even using the softer sell defined by the expression "be reasonable, do it this way." Winners in an influential or controlling position can simply take the following approach: "I've heard everything that was said and I certainly appreciate and respect the advice and opinion presented; however, based upon my experience and the data I have, I believe we will need to do it this way." It is not unusual for individuals in authority to possess data that those working for them do not have. There is certainly no need to be nasty; in fact, those who are usually display a part of their character that is best left hidden. As a general rule, we can obtain the results we need and still maintain an esprit de corps that fosters a supportive environment. After all, you may make the decision, but someone else may have to implement it.

There is power in taking calculated risks. In general, we can minimize risk and therefore maximize power through the judicious use of time and information. By understanding every facet of a situation and the impact, if any, that time plays in its execution, we can develop a realistic assessment of the potential gain versus the loss. If we have diligently and accurately assessed the tradeoffs among our choices, and to the extent possible, structured the risk to minimize the downside, we can on an average basis be very successful. We may not win every time; however, in many cases it is not necessary to win every time, just most of the time. There are, of course, exceptions. Suppose the game is Russian roulette with live ammunition. A gain-versus-loss analysis, which quantifies the risk, indicates that the probability of winning is five out of six and the probability of losing is only one out of six (assuming use of a revolver with six bullets). If an individual survives this exercise it is an ego trip, and they become a celebrity with their friends. But if they lose, they are *dead*. Losing, therefore, is unacceptable to anyone in their right mind. If fact, if some narcissistic individual played the game in front of me and won, I would not classify them as a winner, but rather someone in desperate need of professional help.

Experience and expertise are also forms of power. For example, if I need heart surgery, who should I select to do the job—the new young heart surgeon just out of school with almost no experience or the old seasoned veteran who has performed hundreds of these operations?

Knowledge is power. How do we react when the person, who is known as an expert in his area, tells us that we need to replace the compressor in our air conditioner, the cache memory in our laptop or the valves in our car? If we don't know the difference between a valve and a compressor, we are at least at a distinct disadvantage.

Consider the case in which I and my competitor are trying to make a big sale to the chief buyer of some company. My competitor and I have essentially the same product and the costs are basically the same. On the day of the final presentation to the buyer, my competitor shows up with an expert who, because of his intimate knowledge of the product and its numerous applications, can document line and verse why his product is better than mine. Where does this leave me? Given the situation, the question is probably rhetorical, since my position in this deal appears to be out on the end of a limb that is systematically being sawed off behind me.

There is inherent power in an ability to look at things from another person's point of view. This type of insight is essentially invaluable in effectively dealing with others. The ability to see things from another's perspective is, however, obvious only to the psychic. Since we cannot look into an individual's mind, we must develop this insight through observation. By observing someone over long periods of time in a variety of circumstances, we can obtain the individual's performance signature. As we collect additional data, the signature is more accurately identified,

Understanding the Basic Parameters

and we find ourselves in a position of being able to estimate their response to a variety of inputs, and therefore optimize our interaction with them. For example, it would be very helpful to know in advance that every time a colleague is asked to perform a particular task, he appears to become deathly ill. If we are going to ask the question anyway, we can at least do it in the softest possible manner and have the paramedics standing by on full alert.

There is power in being able to predict, with even limited degree of accuracy, the performance of others. We can be much more effective in dealing with people if we can predict their response before we even apply the input. In the absence of some cataclysmic event which could drastically alter our behavior, we typically do the same things over and over again. We develop routines and methodically follow them day in and day out, regardless of how simple or complicated they might be. Although it is in general very difficult to look at something from another person's point of view, if we can and do so from an empathetic standpoint, the rewards that accrue to us when dealing with them are astounding. We can predict with reasonable accuracy what they will do in at least some circumstances. For example, many years ago, I was involved in setting up a national conference on environmental issues which would address the social/technological aspects of air, water, and solid waste pollution. I knew that in order for the conference to be a success, I would have to have a list of very well-known experts in these areas. This was not my area of expertise, and my knowledge of these areas could be described facetiously by my ability to spell "environmental." So, I went to the library to determine who the experts in these areas were. I prepared a list of those people in each area who seemed to be the leaders in their field. When my list was complete, I began calling them. I had no illusions. I knew these experts would not know me from Adam's bird dog, and I had correctly assessed my own position. However, I had a plan, and it was based upon the knowledge of how these experts would react to one another. The first step of the plan was to get in personal contact with at least one expert in each area. I would ask them to participate, and if they could not help, I would ask them, "Who would you recommend to speak at this meeting?" I was absolutely sure that all these big guns would know one another and be impressed that their peers had suggested them for this speaking engagement. This was the big league, and I did not even qualify to be a batboy. However, the plan worked. I would call an individual and tell him that this other bigshot had recommend him. The person I called would almost universally say "Well, if so-and-so suggested me, I will be happy to help." The majority of my refusals to help came from people with hard conflicts. What happened? I was a nobody with a capital *no* and no expertise or visibility in these areas. However, the knowledge of how these bigshots would react under a peer recommendation turned out to be the key to filling the program with recognized experts in the various fields of interest.

We derive enormous power from simply treating others with respect and dignity. If we demonstrate a genuine interest in them and their needs, hopes, and dreams, they will walk through hell for us. In fact, as a general rule, people will tend to reflect our image back to us. Therefore, we should always treat people the way we would like to have them treat us. Sound familiar? If we are feared and disliked because we control through negative power, we may get the job done; however, our environment will always be unhealthy and generally unstable.

Suppose that I am the owner of a small manufacturing plant and that I receive an order for a large quantity of some product I produce. The quantity and time constraints that have been imposed by the buyer will put an enormous strain on my entire manufacturing line. However, if my employees like and respect me, and I explain to them exactly what I am up against, my employees will normally do everything within their power to help me meet the requirements of the order. If, on the other hand, I have little or no rapport and mutual respect with them, it is unlikely that I will meet the schedule. In fact, if I am really disliked, some of the machines in the production line might even break down—on purpose!

As a final example of the many faces of power, let's consider one that may appear to be exactly one hundred and eighty degrees out of phase with the whole concept of power, and yet one that is extremely important when dealing with others in an effective manner. I am referring to situations in which I have made anything from a tiny mistake to a colossal blunder. There is unusual power in being truly sorry, forthrightly admitting the error and being willing to make whatever amends are appropriate. I think this situation is similar to one I observed many times while growing up. There was a huge German Shepherd that lived across the street from us named Prince. Every time another dog would wander into his territory, Prince would rush up to him, flashing those fierce-looking teeth. Whenever this happened the other dog would simply lie down on his back in front of Prince exposing the most vulnerable part of his body. I interpreted this action to be equivalent in dog talk to "Gee whiz, Prince,

I am very sorry that I crossed into your territory without asking permission. It certainly won't happen again. Please forgive me." Prince would sniff around for a minute and then make a royal exit, as if to say, "It's okay, just don't let it happen again."

None of us is perfect. Almighty God is the only one who can lay claim to that position. However, we can essentially disarm a potential bomb from exploding in our face if we quickly admit an error and ask for forgiveness. When we admit an error and criticize ourselves for making it, it is most unbecoming for someone to jump on us while we are in this vulnerable position. For example, I have seen situations in which the individual who made an error starts telling their boss or spouse, "I am so sorry, that was a terrible mistake. This time I really screwed up. I don't know how I could have been so stupid." As long as this is not a regular occurrence, before they get too far into this confession, the other person will invariably step in and interject "Oh, it's not really that bad. We will get around this situation somehow." When we criticize ourselves, people tend to be compassionate and generous, and will act to minimize the damage we incur. For most people, it is a violation of human nature to take advantage of someone who is defenseless, and we make ourselves defenseless through self-condemnation. When this is done in a sincere and honest manner, this approach packs tremendous power. With it, we can not only minimize the flack, but we can often completely reverse another's attitude.

Admittedly, this approach is worthless if we are dealing with the type of individual who, when we expose our vulnerability, takes advantage of the situation and grinds us into the floor. If we have to deal with this type of individual, our options are limited, but it is probably worth considering any tact that will remove us from the environment.

While there are numerous forms of power, and there are a host of ways in which it can be applied, it is of the utmost importance that we are constantly aware of the real source of power in the universe: Almighty God. Thus we need to remember that since all power originates with him, the only responsible application of it is for good. God gives us a free will, and with it we can choose to use the power we have in a positive or negative manner. When it is used to achieve good and serve others, God will bless these activities and perhaps give us even more power while simultaneously expanding our sphere of influence. After all, God is good and the gifts he gives us should be applied to further his kingdom on earth, and as Christians that is one of the most important achievements we can make.

Part I: Fundamental Considerations

Given this analysis of the fundamental components that play a necessary and vital role in winning, let us now examine the strategies for accomplishing success, whether as a member of the team or the one directing it.

Part II

Strategies for Success

4

Successful Team Players

Everyone Contributes

I BELIEVE THAT IT is important at the outset to realize that everyone in an organization is special and has the potential to be a real contributor in some way, shape, or form. Somebody, somewhere thought that each individual was needed and that that individual has a responsibility to fulfill. While we would probably not question for a moment the importance of people at the top of an organization that shoulder the total responsibility, let us consider the other extreme in order to illustrate our point. How important is your garbage collector, or the orderly in the hospital that handles your bedpan, or the janitor who replenishes the toilet paper in the restroom dispensers? They become very important if they fail to do their job for some reason. In fact, there are a whole host of people that play a critical, and perhaps silent, role in our lives. As a case in point, consider the people from all walks of life, who made tremendous contributions to the health and safety of others during the COVID-19 pandemic. This group includes people with special talents, e.g., doctors, nurses, medical technologists, first responders, the police and firemen, but there are a host of others as well, e.g., truckers that delivered the goods everyone needed, grocery store workers, the plant workers that made disinfectant sprays, toilet paper, and the list goes on. These super contributors are owed an enormous debt of gratitude, because they made life more bearable for everyone else.

Working effectively as a team player can be a very rewarding experience. When people work together in a cooperative effort to achieve a common goal, the synergism created produces a whole that is much greater than the sum of its constituent parts. Within the team each individual fills a critical niche, and therefore is very important to the overall success of the group. In order to grasp the enormous impact of a cadre of dedicated team players we need only examine the success of Japan. From an island the size of California they have maintained an enormous role in a vast spectrum of world markets which extend from automobiles to heavy industries. How did they develop this prominence in a short time? The answer appears to be very simple. Every corporation is one big happy team, and every individual, regardless of his position, performs each task to perfection. Hence, the products they produce are of high quality, extremely reliable, and therefore very much in demand. As Andrew Carnegie, industrialist and philanthropist, has said,

> Teamwork is the ability to work together toward a common vision, the ability to direct individual accomplishments toward organizational objectives. It is the fuel that allows common people to attain uncommon results.[1]

Becoming a successful team player can be an end in itself, or a path to a management position. The successful team player may be either Type A or Type B. Each contributes in his own unique way. Many people, regardless of their personality types, have no desire to occupy a position of authority, but can be a tremendous contributor to any effort. On the other hand, those people who have demonstrated a competence at working effectively with others will no doubt soon be tapped for supervisory responsibilities.

While it is always management's responsibility to ensure that everyone in the organization is a solid contributor, each of us, regardless of the position we occupy, can help colleagues be more effective in many ways. If we are truly interested in them and their welfare, we will be happy to do what we can for them. In general, anything we can do to make one of our colleagues more productive will be of benefit to the whole organization. There are many situations in which either everybody wins or no one does. For example, if a proposal is not funded or a product does not sell, everybody loses, not just the one or more people who really deserve, because of their lack of cooperation, to become unemployed.

Genuine interest and encouragement for our colleagues is often the key catalyst in helping someone develop their full potential. After all, none of us was born successful. We all had to start somewhere, and most of us needed help and encouragement along the way. When work is an

---

1. Carnegie, "47 Empowering Carnegie Quotes," 7.

integral part of a Christian approach to life, an interest and support for others simply comes naturally.

There was a young boy who refused to simply follow mundane procedures enforced by his school. As a result of his nonconformist attitude, all of his teachers criticized him and branded him an idiot. However, his mother recognized his potential and she encouraged and supported him in everything that he did. As a result of her very positive influence, generations would benefit from his work. While I doubt that any of us would recognize the names of his teachers, we all have no trouble remembering the young lad's name: Thomas A. Edison.

The Positive Approach

One of the best things we can do as a member of any team is to be a positive influence on everyone with whom we come in contact. Many people in an organization simply go along, whether right or wrong, in order to belong and get along. However, the successful environment must employ the operational mantra, "If you don't have anything to do, don't do it here." Teams that are going to accomplish something don't need people with a mealy mouth attitude. It is precisely this type of individual that no doubt prompted the sign which reads "if you think the dead can't come back to life, you should be here at quitting time."

Successful teams are typically composed of successful people who do not think about, what's more dwell on, the negative. They take a very positive approach to every aspect of their lives. They do their part to create a congenial atmosphere, and within it make the best of any situation with a friendly attitude. Of course, in essentially every organization, there will inevitably be conflicts. In fact, these conflicts, when properly managed, can support diverging opinions that may ultimately lead to a better way of doing things. When the exchange is both healthy and respectful, the ideas discussed may not only lead to such things as increased productivity, but they may help identify the individuals in the organization who are best suited to guide the organization's future.

The manner in which conflicts are dealt with defines the organization's conflict culture. Resolving conflicts is an extremely important function and there are numerous articles, easily accessible on the Internet, that outline the many facets and ramifications of this subject and suggest ways in which to effectively deal with it.[2]

2. See, e.g., "Developing a Positive Conflict Culture."

It is worthwhile to stop for a moment and think about the attitude of our household pets. Day after day our dog rushes up to us with its tail wagging wildly like they are absolutely delighted to see us. The cat rubs against our leg and purrs with a sense of ecstasy just for being near us. However, these animals do not sow or reap. They don't even bring home the food; they just eat it after we have gone to the trouble to fix it.

Management appreciates those individuals who work with a can-do attitude. These are typically the people who move, shake, and change the world for the better. These winners are a part of the solution—not a part of the problem. They make mistakes, sometimes lots of them. However, when they do, they admit it, take steps to correct it, and then keep moving on. There is an old saying that goes something like this: "an individual without a misdeed is not likely to ever succeed." We learn by making mistakes. I have worked with executives who would say that they are looking for people who are right more than 50 percent of the time. The slot machines in places like Las Vegas take our money a little more than 50 percent of the time, and they are real winners!

There are numerous self-help books, e.g., Norman Vincent Peal's book *The Power of Positive Thinking*, that are filled with the stories of people who, supercharged with a positive attitude and a belief in what they were doing, overcame tremendous odds to succeed. These people simply found a way to do things that others would not even attempt.

When I was working at Bell Telephone Laboratories in New Jersey, I asked two of my colleagues, Frank and Harry, a technical question concerning a project in which we were all involved. Frank told me that my question was not important. I asked him to think about it anyway. He said he would, but he probably didn't, and I never discussed it with him again. Harry told me that he did not know the answer, but he immediately went to the small blackboard in his office and started trying to figure it out. After about fifteen minutes of a back-and-forth discussion in which we tried to outline the merits of one approach over another, he figured it out. Harry also turned out to be the biggest contributor among all of us in the overall project. I have not followed Harry's career, but I am absolutely certain that he is well-liked, respected, and an outstanding contributor in every situation.

People want to be associated with and follow individuals with a cheerful, positive approach because these people with a can-do attitude can accomplish so much. Consider for a moment the tale of the stone soup. It was war time and because of the scarcity of food and supplies, the townspeople were hiding and hoarding food. Some soldiers came to town. They were hungry and asked the townspeople for some food. Everyone told the soldiers they had none. Do you know what the soldiers did? They did not roll over and play dead. They went to the center of the town and built a fire. Then they got a huge pot, filled it with water, put a big stone in it and proceeded to cook. The townspeople were intrigued and came to see what was being cooked. The soldiers told them it was stone soup. The people were amazed and wanted to taste it. Soon people began suggesting that the soup could be improved if they added their onion or potato. You can guess the rest.

While history is replete with examples that extol the benefits of a positive approach, it is important to know beyond any doubt that looking on the bright side of any situation at least provides a mechanism for producing fruitful results by stimulating solutions. We always have at our disposal the creator and sustainer of the universe, and if we ask him for help in prayer, and truly believe that he can help, he will answer. His answer may not be what we want or expect. In fact, it may appear to us that he has not answered. However, he knows the road ahead, and we don't. Therefore, the answer may be to sit tight because at this time, and in this place, this is the best solution. As George Frederick Will, an American commentator, has said, "Don't just do something; stand there."[3]

The positive attitude will normally do it every time. We gain absolutely nothing from being down in the mouth. As Mr. Robert H. Henry, a well-known humorist speaker has said "Don't tell people your troubles. Eighty percent of them won't care, and the other twenty percent will be glad you've got them."

Mutual Support

Supporting one another is a fundamental trait in any Christian organization, and one where the team players work in a positive atmosphere of mutual support and respect can be an awesome entity. It is a well-oiled machine in which things can happen quickly and effectively. People adjust to the task at hand and sometimes take on different roles at different times for the benefit of the organization. The same individual may play a leadership role in one task, while participating as a team-player in another. When everyone in the organization focuses their attention

---

3. Will, "Don't Just Do Something."

on a particular task, good ideas come from everywhere, because everyone looks at the problems through their own eyes with their own unique background. Winners seem to instinctively understand the dynamics of this process and constantly work to maintain it.

A cooperative and supportive environment is a very efficient place to work. By helping one another we can expand the bottlenecks and minimize the effect of discontinuities which may exist in a feast or famine flow of work. By covering for one another we ensure that one individual is not drowning in work while a colleague is sitting around filing their fingernails. The congenial and respectful atmosphere supports an efficient work environment, and as a result, the throughput of the organization is optimized.

Our colleagues who are congenial and supportive are an excellent source of advice and ideas. Quite often, because we are totally immersed in a problem, we cannot transform ourselves to a position where we can see clearly the big picture. Our tunnel vision tends to keep our minds focused upon one part of the problem, and it is very difficult for us to extract ourselves to a point where we can obtain an overview of the entire situation. This has happened to me on numerous occasions. I have been so concerned about some particular problem that I could not even imagine some other aspect that completely obviated what I was doing. When I was finally able to see the big picture, I felt like the plumber who was diligently trying to repair a water faucet on the Titanic.

I never cease to be amazed at the creativity displayed by friends and colleagues. They may have absolutely no knowledge of the problem which concerns me; however, if they will discuss it with me in a supportive atmosphere, a number of good ideas may be generated from their free-thinking, unbiased position. In fact, they may be able to look at the problem in such a way that they see some aspect of it that I cannot visualize at all. I have even experienced situations in which, while I was in the process of explaining my problem to someone else, the exact solution I was trying to obtain suddenly popped into my mind. Apparently as I tried to clearly articulate every facet of the problem, my subconscious synthesized the solution.

In a supportive environment, unusual power can be brought to bear when people pull together and recognize every individual as someone special. A family is typically a model example of a group where mutual support reigns king. Our spouse is perhaps our very best supporter. Although she may have an entirely different perspective when examining some problem, she has only our best interest at heart. Therefore, her opinions and recommendations, which may be orthogonal to our own, are always made with our personal welfare uppermost in her mind. In fact, in any supportive environment we must realize that as Herbert Hoover, the thirty-first President of the United States, has said,

> Honest differences of views and honest debate are not disunity.
> They are the vital process of policy-making among free men.[4]

I know from experience that in almost every case in which I did not listen to Edie's advice, I later wished that I had. It is important to note that this reliance on the wisdom of our spouse is not just for those of us who are normal human beings, but individuals whose contributions to this world make our own pale in comparison. For example, Niels Bohr, the Danish physicist who received the Nobel Prize for physics in 1922 for his seminal contributions to our knowledge of atomic structure and quantum theory, was also the benefactor of such advice. One of his sons said of his parents' relationship: "My mother was the natural and indispensable center. Father knew how much mother meant to him and never missed an opportunity to show his gratitude and love. . . . Her opinions were guidelines in daily affairs."[5]

In a family where everyone is encouraged to do the best they can, they often respond by doing more than they are asked to do. People share ideas, and when there is present that genuine interest in helping one another, the ideas sprout like weeds. Everyone is happy and delighted when nice things happen to someone else.

We can even work fewer hours in a supportive environment if we are more productive. By helping one another, if we can make up in smarts what we could spend in time, we have a viable exchange. However, to work less and be paid more without a corresponding increase in productivity is insane. In order to visualize this scenario, we need only extrapolate the concept to the point where we are paid a great deal of money to do essentially no work. Even the US government cannot afford that deal.

There is an obvious benefit for the Type A or Type B individuals who have a genuine interest in supporting their colleagues and also have aspirations of moving up in an organization. If we are ambitious, our colleagues will be delighted to see us promoted. To the extent possible, they will even campaign for us. On the other hand, if we are the antithesis

4. Hoover, "Herbert Hoover Quotes."
5. Pais, *Niels Bohr's Times*, 250.

of congeniality, we will not garner their support because no one wants to work *for* an individual they can't work *with*.

People have survived great tragedies by pulling together and supporting one another. Just think what can happen in an organization when people display the same attitude.

Communications

Successful team players enhance the flow of information within an organization. The more each individual knows about the overall plan, the better prepared he is to contribute to it. Having the proper information often saves time and energy, and prevents us from trying to reinvent the wheel. When I speak of information I am not talking about gossip. We naturally share many of our activities with our friends. However, successful people waste very little time discussing things that may not be true or do not benefit their colleagues or the organization.

When I was a member of the technical staff at Bell Telephone Laboratories, the engineers had a saying: "Communication is our most important problem." The layman may have thought we were talking about the telephone system, but we were really referring to flow of information among ourselves, and this problem was taken seriously. The director of the center in which I worked, three levels of management above me, would wait for the first report generated by a new young engineer. Then he would sit down with his red pen and read it carefully, marking anything and everything that was wrong. If both the content and grammar were not correct, when he was finished reading it, the report would look like he had bled on it. Imagine the impact of having a report come back with a lot of red ink on it. That is a very sobering and sometimes tearful experience. The Director's actions sent a clear signal throughout the organization which in essence said, "There is no need to write it, if I can't read it." The veiled corollary to that statement which also did not escape anyone was, "If you can't clearly tell us what you do, perhaps you should not be here doing it."

Coordination is often absolutely necessary and communication is the means by which it is accomplished. For example, in the past the US government has encountered very serious problems in the production of some weapon systems. These problems occurred because the research and development personnel, who were responsible for the design and development of the prototype units, had little or no contact with the manufacturing organizations that would produce the systems in very large quantities. When it came time to transition the system from research and development to production, the production personnel found that the systems could not be mass produced as designed in a reliable fashion. While each individual part of the system could be fine-tuned by the engineers in the laboratory, such procedures would be impossible in a high-rate production environment. However, if the engineers who were responsible for manufacturing the system in a high-rate production mode had been involved up front in the research and development effort, the system could be designed for production from the outset, and the transition process would have been smooth and efficient.

Consider the following internal memorandum that I sent to Joe Doaks.

> Internal Memorandum To: Joe Doaks
> From: Dave Irwin
> Re: ABC Proposal
>
> At our last meeting on November 12, 2019, the need for a special meeting was expressed so that subject proposal could be finalized. Please inform me when and where the meeting will take place, and the time frame in which I will receive the required proposal documentation so I will be prepared for the meeting.

What I expected to receive from Joe was something like the following.

> Internal Memorandum To: Dave Irwin
> From: Joe Doaks
> Re: ABC Proposal
>
> In response to your memorandum concerning the ABC proposal, let's plan to meet on December 13, 2019 in my office, and I will forward the material requested NLT close of business December 2, 2019.

What I actually received from him was the following.

> Internal Memorandum To: Dave Irwin
> From: Joe Doaks
> Re: ABC Proposal
>
> As you know, subject proposal is an important part of our work. The ramifications of our decisions will have to be judged in view

of retroactive policies that may have deleterious effects on the current status of the operation. Our meeting will of necessity be a discussion with propositions which hopefully will illuminate alternate points of view. The meeting will be held at a time and place which does not interfere with existing commitments, which may unilaterally affect the organization. Specifically, we will definitely plan to meet no later than two weeks after the submission of our current proposals, the submission dates of which are currently unknown. We will, however, ensure that we definitely forward to you the required information during the week in which the current proposals are submitted. I look forward to working with you on subject proposal.

Damn! What did he say? His response was nothing more than convoluted nonsense which is absolutely useless. I just asked for two dates. What I received was—well, I really don't know. Joe could certainly use a short course in communication skills. All he had to do was answer my questions directly, which as indicated could have been done in one sentence.

The Internet is replete with articles and courses that deal effectively with communication in essentially every possible environment and from every conceivable standpoint. It is a tremendous source of information for individuals whose success is dependent upon effective communication.

I have attended meetings in which everyone was told to do exactly the same thing, and then as soon as the meeting was over, everyone took off in a different direction. Amazing as it sounds, it happens all too often. The language problem can be very subtle, as illustrated by the following example.

When I was working in New Jersey, I sent Edie and the three children home to Alabama to visit the grandparents. They were scheduled to fly from Newark to Montgomery. The children were ages two, three, and four. Our son, John, was three. In preparation for the trip, I had emphasized to John that this was going to be a big deal, since he would be able to fly on a plane. John was very active and skipped learning to walk, going straight to running. I wanted John to be excited about the trip and look forward to it, since I knew Edie would have her hands full on the plane with three small children. John had some toy airplanes, and he would wave them around in the air, pretending that he was flying back to see his grandparents.

When it was time to board the plane, the airline let me go on the plane with Edie to help her get the children settled in their seats. The plane was packed and everyone was crawling over one another, trying to get settled. When the time for departure arrived, I kissed everyone and started to exit the plane. At that point, John went absolutely berserk and lay in the aisle kicking his feet in the air. He went into a screaming fit, and I could not calm him down. I kept trying to figure out what was wrong, and he was so upset that he was unable to tell me. Finally, after repeatedly asking him what was wrong with him, he blurted out that he wanted to ride on the plane. I told him he was on the plane and pointed to the wings out the window. Then it hit me—he thought he was going to ride on top of the plane. It was too late. I had blown it. I had to get off the plane, because it was leaving and all I could do at that point was pray for Edie, the stewardesses, and everyone else on the plane as well, since John had excellent lungs.

In preparation for this trip, knowing that the kids would see a black person for the first time, Edie explained to the children that God made some people white, some people black, and some people yellow, etc. While the family was staying at my parent's house, our oldest daughter, Geri, got up early one morning. Before Edie could get up and dressed, Geri went into the den where Maria, the black lady who helped my mother with the ironing, was ironing a shirt. With Edie's comments apparently still firmly in mind, Geri walked up to Maria, and slowly rubbed her arm and said, "God did that to you."

I have always been amazed at how well we can communicate with sign language, and I am not referring to the American Sign Language (ASL). A professional colleague and I were part of a scientific delegation to the Soviet Union in 1976. One afternoon we went to Gorky Park in Moscow. About supper time, we found a little place that looked like a hotdog stand where we could get some food. We could not speak or read the language; so we walked up to this little outdoor restaurant and stood in line. When we reached the front of the line, we stood aside to let others go ahead of us, and we watched what the others ordered. As soon as someone ordered something that looked good to us, we motioned to the proprietor, pointed to the food, and then pointed to ourselves. The proprietor knew immediately what we wanted and dished it up. When he handed us the food, we held out a handful of money, the proprietor took what we owed him, and we sat down to eat.

Because much of our business today is performed on an international scale, the translations between languages, which are not always one-to-one, can present communication problems. For example, at a

1987 Frontiers in Education Conference at Rose-Hulman Institute of Technology, Dr. Sam Hulbert, President of the Institute, told me that PepsiCo wanted to employ the slogan "Come alive with Pepsi" in Taiwan. However, the local translation of this phrase was interpreted as "Pepsi brings your ancestors back from the grave," and some of the potential Pepsi drinkers were not exactly thrilled with that prospect.

In communicating, it is not even necessary to use the proper words in order to get a point across. As an example, during one of the trips that Edie and the kids made to Alabama, my mother and Edie took the children to see *Holiday on Ice* at the coliseum in Montgomery. At one point in the program, a large-breasted female skater in a tiny outfit skated toward the point where the family was sitting. She was on one skate, leaning forward with the other skate outstretched behind her. At this point, John jumped out of his seat and started shouting, "Mama, Mama, look!" At this point, he had the undivided attention of everyone within twenty feet. He turned to his mother and exclaimed, "Mama, look at those big skin balls." He had not used the proper words, but there was no doubt what he was talking about.

5

The Successful Manager/Entrepreneur

Leadership

AMONG THE MANY DESIRABLE qualities of a successful manager or entrepreneur, the one that stands out first and foremost in my mind is leadership. This is a topic that can be easily found on a host of sites on the Internet, where it would appear that every possible facet is identified and discussed. In fact, John C. Maxwell, an internationally recognized leadership expert, has identified twenty-one indispensable qualities of a leader.[1] In what follows, I will try to address what I consider to be the core qualities, which are in essence somewhat of a distillation of a much larger group.

    I believe that leaders are decision-makers, and the most successful ones are those with a characteristic called vision which provides them with a crystal-clear view of the world around them. They gather the available data, carefully analyze it, and when they have digested every aspect, they make a decision—and it is their decision. Once the decision is made, every ounce of energy is applied in an all-out blitz to make the decision the right one. The force they are able to create within their organization is a result of the charisma they possess. This inherent quality tends to transform the entire workforce into a cohesive, enthusiastic, and therefore powerful group that is committed to achieving the goal at hand. The decision may be revisited later, but only to assess any mistakes or viable corrections.

    In addition to the exhilaration that attends the pursuit of a worthwhile goal, the leader also carries the burdens of responsibility, loneliness,

---

1. Maxwell, *21 Indispensable Qualities*.

weariness, and frustration. The leader must shoulder the total responsibility of the effort. He alone is responsible for the decision, and all the ramifications that result as a consequence of it. If the decision turns out to be a good one, he is a hero; but if the decision turns out to be bad, he is the goat.

There is much truth in the following sayings: "Nothing ventured, nothing gained." And "Behold the turtle, he makes progress only when he sticks his neck out."

When we stick our necks out to set the pace, we quickly discover that the crowd is no longer with us. We are out in front, and it can be lonely out there. However, we cannot lead the pack from within the pack. The leader sets the pace by stepping out in front; however, he has to stay in front. While this position can be exhilarating, it is also often weary due to the continuous struggle to stretch the organization to do more and more.

Finally, leaders are almost always frustrated to some extent; because there simply is insufficient time and resources to pursue all their goals. Regardless of how hard and how long they work, they just cannot do everything they believe needs to be done. This is particularly true of Type A's and can lead to health problems if not handled properly.

Although as indicated, there are numerous qualities that a successful leader should possess, and of that number let us examine some of the issues associated with four that appear to be fundamental and representative of the mix that should be in place. They are integrity, loyalty, confidence, and competence. Integrity, more than anything else, is the sine qua non for individuals in leadership positions. The person who lacks this quality cannot lead, because in general no one will follow. Integrity is the foundation of successful management, and it implies that there exists a strict system of ethics and values. It means that our modus operandi is based upon sound moral and ethical principles, which of course are an integral part of a Christian lifestyle. Honesty and trust are core constituents of integrity. When this quality permeates the system, trust is fostered both inside and outside the organization. Quite often, in order to be successful, management must be flexible; however, there is absolutely no doubt that there is a line beyond which they will not go. People who work in this environment feel as sure-footed as a mountain goat, because they can be completely confident that the structure will not shift beneath them. It is the leader who always sets the tone, and the operation of the entire organization will follow in concert. When that tone is generated by a sound sense of integrity, personal and business relationships can be established that will last a lifetime.

The successful leader leaves no doubt that he is loyal to both the goal that is being pursued and his colleagues that work with him to attain it. It is this loyalty that binds the members of the group into a cohesive whole. As important as this is for the successful leader, there is apparently no reciprocal agreement in the minds of those who work in the organization. In today's work environment, workers are extremely mobile, too.[2]

Changing jobs is simply a way of life, and most new hires today simply are not thinking along the lines of long-term employment in any organization. A high percentage of workers, while perhaps happy in their current organization, would leave at the drop of a hat if a better opportunity came along. This mobility is exacerbated by the almost universal use of 401k retirement plans, i.e., there is no retirement penalty in moving from one job to another because the retirement plan is mobile too. This mobility essentially destroys the link between loyalty and security, i.e., the successful manager cannot obtain loyalty by providing security. Thus, while the successful manager must exhibit loyalty, it would be foolish to expect it from the rank and file in the organization. As a result, the real contributors in the organization must see and understand the loyalty that the manager has for them via promotions and/or pay raises, while those who contribute less will have to be looked upon as expendable because their continued service cannot be guaranteed. This is a rather difficult situation, since while the successful manager should demonstrate complete loyalty to everything within his purview, he cannot be assured of it from those who work for him.

Confidence must be a fundamental part of the leader's repertoire, and the total belief in his ability to succeed in spite of tremendous obstacles has a magic quality about it. The leader must also instill this quality in his colleagues so that it runs wide and deep throughout the organization. Everyone must believe beyond any doubt that they can accomplish the task at hand. When the organization as a whole possesses a steadfast belief in itself, it finds that it can attack and conquer jobs which others would never attempt.

Integrity, loyalty, and confidence together shape and mold the organization, with the leader at its head, into a flying wedge with awesome potential. And the final ingredient needed to realize that potential is

---

2. See Stillman, "Employee Loyalty Is Dead."

competence. Competence, when possessed by the leader and his followers, is the quality which activates the flying wedge and blasts it forward in a manner which optimizes performance.

Successful leaders envision the future, and within it, the organization's optimal position. Once the vision is established, it must be articulated throughout the organization, goals set, and a plan devised to marshal the organization's troops and resources into a coherent force which focuses the energy on the proposed target. While assessing the performance of those in their charge, they are continuously coaching and encouraging them to perform at their best. When for any reason, an individual does not perform as required, he must be removed, in a clean and gentle manner when possible, and placed in a position that more nearly matches his specific talents and interests. This entire process is not a one-shot deal. The successful leader must keep reassessing the plan and apply whatever mid-course corrections are necessary to stay on target.

In order to perceive and understand the reality of the situation, the leader, through careful listening, receives prodigious amounts of information. Then, as in target identification, they must separate the crucial information from the chaff. Once all the pertinent data that can be gleaned is known, the leader's directions are clear and decisive and are based upon self-confidence and sound judgement. As a general rule, the decisions must be made in the presence of conflicting viewpoints, and thus within the leader's environment, ambiguity and uncertainty are norms. The effect of these two norms can be minimized if the leader works in a coherent fashion to establish and maintain good communication within his organization. The astute leader can be certain that all the data required to make an intelligent decision on any issue will be known if he encourages everyone to say exactly what he thinks. In this environment it is considered to be perfectly acceptable to question another's ideas in order to present another point of view. Attacking another person in the process is a bad strategy, i.e., to disagree without being disagreeable. Once every possible ramification of the issue has been carefully examined, the leader is then in a position to make a decision with all the facts concerning the case before him. This is a very effective style of leadership, because if everyone has contributed to the decision, he will generally work very hard for the things he has helped to create.

The leader occupies the pivotal position. As such, their inherent characteristics must include a high level of energy, a flexible outlook, good judgement, the stamina and foresight to take risks, and the ability to motivate others. Because he sets the direction and the pace, he is in charge, and if the whole organization is not moving forward as it should, he is the one the company's Board of Directors will replace.

Two of the primary factors which have a crucial impact on business today are the global scope of the marketplace and the speed with which advances in technology are being utilized. Both of these factors have a significant effect on competition, and therefore the effective leader's watchword is innovation, their fixation is quality, and their operational banner is change.

In order to remain viable and competitive in this ever-changing world, the Renaissance leaders at every level must constantly think in terms of evolutionary and even perhaps revolutionary transformations. If they have "run the diagnostics" and are thoroughly versed in the organization's capabilities and potential, they are in a position to explore and understand how they can enhance their operations through changes in areas such as personnel, new technology, or simply refocusing to attack new markets.

In addition, through thoughtful introspection, successful leaders have an excellent understanding of their own strengths and weaknesses, and surround themselves with people whose talents complement their own. For example, Matthew Ridgway, the nineteenth chief of staff of the United States Army, has said,

> The leader's flame that burns so bright in battle is not his alone. It comes from the interplay of his forces and those members of the team. Both contribute essentials that produce leadership.[3]

The leader's operational characteristics define the manner in which the organization functions. With a well-defined goal and his mind's eye constantly focused upon it, the winning leader expounds a basic philosophy that is always consistent and characteristically upbeat. He is the head cheerleader for the whole organization, and his positive approach sets the mood. When this is done, the whole organization tends to adopt this approach, and the relationship between the leader and his followers becomes a positive feedback system which directs the organization's energy toward accomplishment of the goal.

While maintaining the proper focus by constantly reminding the team of the goal, the successful leader attacks every stage with an enthusiasm that is contagious. The leader's actions are decisive and his

---

3. Rankin, "It's Worth Quoting," quote 49.

decisions are an optimal balance between an ideal and something that is realistically attainable. Although the decisions may not be popular, they are clear, well-thought-out, and in the best interest of the organization.

There may be times and circumstances that dictate a leadership style that can best be described as "my way or the highway." Information that cannot be shared or an unreasonable timetable that must be adhered to may force a more dictatorial fashion of leadership. While this may not be an ideal working environment for anyone, and personnel could be lost in the process, the circumstances may be such that the leader is left with no other option. Hopefully, this is a short-term exercise, and the good will that has been a hallmark of the operation will be remembered, since in today's volatile working environment in which loyalty is a scarce commodity and opportunities abound for good workers, this change from a more benevolent environment to one that is more hostile could produce irreparable damage.

While leaders define the goal, it is the senior management beneath them who are charged with the responsibility of executing the plan necessary to achieve it. These individuals should be carefully chosen and always the very best people available. Authority is then delegated to them to manage the effort to the best of their ability. These individuals are then backed to the hilt unless the leadership discovers that their parade is completely out of phase with the leadership's directions.

The individuals who are charged with executing goals are quite often also involved in setting them. It is impossible to overemphasize the importance of selecting the right people for this task, since if these individuals are chosen correctly, there is a high probability that they will find a way to marshal the people and resources to achieve the goal they have played an integral part in establishing.

Selecting the proper people to implement a goal is extremely important. I recall, when I was in school, some of my friends who were naval cadets told me a story that was going around about Admiral Hyman G. Rickover. Admiral Rickover was considered to be the father of the US nuclear navy. At that point in time, the program was in the development stages, and there was a special opportunity for young naval officers to get in on the ground floor. So, Admiral Rickover would interview each person who had applied to join his development program for naval nuclear propulsion. The interview took place over lunch. In one case, Admiral Rickover sat down with one officer, and after a few minutes, the lunch was served. The young officer immediately picked up the salt shaker and put some salt on his food. Without hesitation, Admiral Rickover told the young officer, "You can't work for me." The young officer was stunned; after all, they had just sat down to eat. Admiral Rickover told the officer, "You have not tasted that food, and therefore you do not know whether it needs salt or not." The young officer had made a quick decision based upon no data, and unfortunately it was a fatal one. The interview had come to a screeching halt. They finished lunch, and each went his separate way.

Poor leaders who are somehow able to hang on leave a bad taste in everyone's mouth and a negative impression on the organization. For example, when I lived in Tennessee a friend of mine told me about a retirement party he had recently attended for a manager in his organization. He said that he had just joined the department and did not know the man well, but the scuttlebutt indicated that the man was neither liked nor respected. My friend said that he was amazed at the number of people who turned out for the event, and it was a lively one. While mingling in the crowd he realized that for some reason he had not seen the honoree, so he asked one of the people in charge of the event where he was. The answer he obtained for this seemly straightforward question was "Oh heavens man, we did not invite him."

Winning leaders seem to exhibit an uncanny ability to get out of the maze. They appear to be very lucky. Not so! At least not in the sense in which the term is normally used. They create luck, and they do so by removing as much risk as possible through strategic planning and excellent personnel. With their principles fixed, they operate as an efficient adaptive control system, constantly adjusting plans in order to optimize the path to their goal.

It is unfortunately a truism that if we get our head above the crowd, we are going to be attacked. Therefore, a winner must not only have the qualities and operational characteristics we have already discussed, but in addition, he must possess a large dose of self-confidence, which helps protect him from the criticism he will undoubtedly receive in the pursuit of an unpopular, yet worthwhile, goal.

Leaders are forever pounded with problems, and the higher they are in the organization, the more problems they see. The continuous battering will eventually wear down those individuals who are not tenacious and resilient. The successful leader instinctively exhibits an ability to absorb the shocks and bounce back with determination to succeed in spite of adversity. These people are survivors with a shock absorber personality. Nowhere is this more clearly demonstrated for many of us than in the home. As parents try to create and maintain a value system for their children, their authority is continuously challenged, and they are besieged with requests and problems that run counter to their basic philosophy. Although it is undoubtedly very hard, those parents who absorb the shocks and disappointments and press on with a positive mental attitude to hold the line on the rules they have established are the ones who will win not only for themselves, but for their children as well. Parents who break under what must seem like incessant pounding will unfortunately form in their children behavior patterns which may retard or prevent their development as productive human beings. The following saying by Klaus Balkenhol, the German equestrian and Olympic champion, when paraphrased, would seem to apply here.

> There is a difference between being a leader and being a boss. Both are based upon authority. A boss demands blind obedience; a leader earns his authority through understanding and trust.[4]

I keep a copy of the following words of Theodore Roosevelt, the 26th President of the United States, handy so I can refer to them often.

> It is not the critic who counts, not the man who points out how the strong man stumbled, or where the doer of deeds could have done them better. The credit belongs to the man who is actually in the arena; whose face is marred by dust and sweat and blood; who strives valiantly; who errs and comes short again and again; who knows the great enthusiasms, the great devotions; who spends himself in a worthy cause; who at the best, knows in the end the triumph of high achievement; and who, at the worst, if he fails, at least fails while daring greatly.[5]

I have found these words to be very inspiring. They serve as a constant reminder to me that "when the going gets tough, the tough get going."

Creating the Proper Environment

The creation of an environment in which people work in a spirit of mutual support and respect is very much a matter of attitude. If the leader places the general welfare of the team on par with the importance of

---

4. Balkenhol, "Quotable Quote."
5. Roosevelt, "Theodore Roosevelt Quotes."

achieving the goal, then every member of the organization is treated as a worthy individual, deserving of personal respect and dignity. Although the leader sets the course and the pace to achieve the goal, it is the team players who follow him that do the bulk of the work. Thus the successful leader creates a climate such that everyone in his organization will work as hard as they can and be happy doing it. Although team players can be forced to perform under adverse circumstances and against their will, rarely does this modus operandi produce optimum results.

When our oldest daughter, Geri, was about ten months old, I was trying to feed baby food to her one night. She did not like the green beans, so I would put green beans in the bottom of the spoon and cover it up with applesauce. It only took one mouthful of that combination for her to realize what I was doing, so she refused to open her mouth again. Knowing that I could not fool her again, I took the brute force approach. I loaded a big spoon with green beans and tried to force it into her mouth without hurting her. Regardless of how much I tried, she resisted. All the sudden she leaned back and opened her mouth wide. At that moment, I rammed in a spoonful of green beans. I was so intent on forcing my will that I did not realize she was in the process of sneezing. One second later I was completely covered with strained green beans.

It is often hard being a slow learner. A critical report to be prepared by a group I headed was due for a staff meeting on a Monday afternoon. The group had explained to me that because of the complexity of the problem, the report would not be ready until Monday morning. In retrospect, that really would have been sufficient time for me to digest it and be prepared to present it later that day. However, I forced the issue and politely insisted that the report be ready the previous Friday instead. Big mistake. Friday afternoon I got the report all right; however, it had not addressed all the issues. I spent a significant part of my weekend finishing what the group obviously had planned to do early on Monday morning.

In order to stretch the organization and move it forward we have to take calculated risks. The history books are replete with stories of armies that succeeded against great odds because there was no way to escape. The commander had burned all the bridges behind them. In so doing he provided his troops with an enormous motivation to succeed since there was no reasonable alternative. In this frame of mind, people arise to the challenge and exhibit tremendous inner strength and an unusual capacity to accomplish what might appear to be insurmountable.

In the pursuit of almost any endeavor, mistakes are going to be made. It is absolutely imperative that the leader ensure that the working environment is a mistake-tolerant one. Mistakes are simply a glitch along the learning curve and should be treated as such. They support growth and creativity, and therefore we should simply learn from them, so they are not made again, and get on with the task in progress. The real failures of this world are not those people who get knocked down, but rather those who fail to get up. It is virtually impossible to traverse an error-free career path. For example, as addressed earlier, few would question the enormous success of Thomas A. Edison. He had about a thousand patents, and his fundamental contributions will serve mankind for all time. However, he probably made ten thousand mistakes. If someone had browbeaten the daylights out of him for his mistakes, I might be writing this book by candlelight.

As leaders, we must create a positive environment, and we can do so in a number of ways. At the outset we must insist on discipline. Leaders are the symbol of justice and order and have to maintain discipline for the benefit of the whole organization. It is the leader's responsibility to establish the guidelines and enforce them in a fair and equitable manner. In addition, we must exhibit and instill in those around us a positive, no-knock, mental attitude. This is critically important, because in any given situation the team will take its cue from the leader. If something goes wrong and the leader reacts in a positive and humorous mode, everyone will follow suit, and the situation will be quickly corrected in a spirit of cooperation. However, if the leader reacts in a negative manner, wading into the situation with a meat axe, everyone will run for cover and start pointing fingers at one another in an attempt to divorce themselves from the problem. It is difficult to solve a problem when everyone is running from it.

A good friend, Angel, worked as a hostess in a nearby restaurant. During one day at lunch, the kitchen failed to keep pace with the orders, and the patrons were beginning to ask if they would ever see the food. Instead of trying to lay blame at everyone's feet, causing a negative attitude to permeate the entire staff, Dan, the manager, went into the kitchen, and while exhibiting concern, asked if they had an order for a chicken croissant. He knew all too well they had this order; in fact, they had several orders for that item alone. He asked if there was something he could do to move the kitchen into high gear. The cooks realized quickly that there were serious problems that needed to be addressed immediately. So, they shifted into overdrive and eliminated the bottleneck in short order. Dan was delighted with this change in performance, and a potentially explosive situation was solved in an amicable manner.

Now suppose that instead of taking that tack, Dan had immediately launched into a tongue lashing of the waitresses because of the poor service. The waitresses would have immediately blamed the cooks, and the positive working relationship between these two groups, which makes everything flow smoothly, would have been severed instantly. If Dan had then marched into the kitchen and began an attack on the cooks, they would have immediately tried to make a case for their innocence to avoid his tirade. Note that while the accusations are flying everywhere, no one is working on the chicken croissant. All the energy is going up in heat, and none of it is going toward making the sandwich.

The creation of a negative working environment has one serious consequence for leaders who fall into this trap. The best employees leave—because they can. Good competent people are always in demand, and they encounter very few problems in moving from one place to another. As indicated earlier, this situation is exacerbated when people work with a mindset that if things don't work out good for me here, I will just leave for a better place. Guess who does not leave? The poor employees—because they can't. Who wants them? Leadership can be very difficult when you are left with the dregs of the group, because they can create more problems in five minutes than you can solve in five months.

While it may be difficult, everyone should be treated in a fair and equitable manner. We simply have to resist the temptation to refuse to work with those people who tend to drive us nuts. Extreme care should be exercised when correcting or reprimanding them, and the process should involve the use of a rifle and not a shotgun. In other words, we should focus our attention directly upon the specific troublemakers and try to correct them. Never spray the innocent with corrective schemes. It is very unfair and also demoralizing for a person who is doing a good job to be splattered with corrective actions simply because they worked closely with someone who exhibits poor performance. This is an important point, and therefore let me provide some examples of what I mean.

In an organization composed of several people, one of the employees is doing a poor job, and he is never on time for work. Other employees may not always be on time for work either, but in contrast to the poor performer, they stay late because they are very conscientious and want to do a good job. If the manager is a weak leader, rather than confronting the individual who will probably be late to his own funeral, the manager makes a rule that anyone who is not on time for work will have his pay cut. What are the consequences of this rule? Because the manager lacks the guts for a head-on confrontation, they have now made all the good employees mad, and as indicated this is the group who will encounter little difficulty in finding better employment. The individual whose performance is substandard probably assumes that since the rule affects everyone, they are not the real problem.

As another example, consider the manager who has two people working for them. One is a good, solid performer and the other couldn't work their way out of a wet paper bag. On payday, the manager calls in the two employees in and gives them their paychecks. However, as he gives the check to their good employee, he asks that employee if he thinks he really deserves the check. The purpose of this obtuse action is to try to get the bad employee to realize that perhaps he isn't doing his job well. Well, what do you think? Does the bad employee get the message? No! What does happen, however, is the weak manager has made the good employee so mad that he could split a railroad spike with his teeth. This type of approach is almost guaranteed to send the good employee to the Help Wanted ads.

As indicated in more ways than one, reprimanding someone can, and should, be done in a humane and Christian manner. The reprimand could follow the same guidelines issued by Mike Kolen, a former American football player, in a different context, i.e., the advice given to the chicken that wanted to lay an egg on a busy highway—"do it quick and lay it on the line." Don't wait for the fat lady to sing to get back to business as usual. It is not necessary to walk around mad all day. Don't worry, your employee will not easily forget your corrective comments.

Regardless of how we accomplish it, we must somehow, some way create and maintain an environment that encourages everyone to do their best. As indicated, failure to do this can have awesome consequences. Within the proper environment, people flourish. Individuals who love their work have boundless energy for it. For example, there have been times in my own career when I would have been willing to pay my employer to let me do my job (if I could afford to do so). In the wrong environment, the cadre becomes lethargic, absenteeism increases, employees act as though their get-up-and-go has got-up-and-gone, and the situation maintains a downward spiral until something breaks. The analogy that exists between business and home with regard to these environment issues is both striking and phenomenal. When children are estranged from their parents or become involved in any one of a myriad of immoral or illegal acts, the basis for their actions can usually be traced to the absence of a Christian environment which supports their proper growth and development.

Finally, unless we are convinced that the organization is operating in a suboptimal mode, an excellent rule of thumb for the work environment is contained in the phrase, "if it ain't broke, don't fix it." We may not even thoroughly understand the nature of all the forces at work and the complex interaction of the people involved in making an organization run smoothly and productively. What we perceive to be a better way may not in fact be a better way. Can you imagine for a moment an air brush salesman standing beside Michaelangelo in the Sistine Chapel, telling him, "Hey man, there is a better way?"

Hiring and Placing Personnel

The following quote by Theodore Roosevelt, the twenty-sixth President of the United States, applies here:

> The best executive is the one who has sense enough to pick good men to do what he wants done, and self-restraint enough to keep from meddling with them while they do it.[6]

Smart leaders instinctively know that their success is critically dependent upon the people who work under their supervision. If at all possible, they hire the best people available, and if for any reason they cannot hire them, they hire people who have a demonstrated potential to become the best. In this manner winning leaders surround themselves with the smartest and most competent people they can find. They hire these individuals into a position that matches their talents and interests with the position requirements. If a leader does this one thing extremely well, as a general rule, their other problems will be minor ones.

I once had a sign in my office that read "Nothing is impossible—if you don't have to do it yourself." I love the humor in this sign. However, more and more I am convinced of the underlying truth of this expression. When we have surrounded ourselves with the best talent we can find and matched their work with their interests, almost anything possible can be accomplished.

6. Roosevelt, "Theodore Roosevelt Quotes."

In the early seventies, I became the head of the Electrical Engineering Department at Auburn University. At that time, I was absolutely convinced that microelectronics would have an enormous impact on our area for decades to come. I was so sure of this that I told my colleagues in the department that we needed to develop this area in our department. Many, if not all, of my fellow faculty members, who were all very kind and highly intelligent professors, thought I was hallucinating. I had just been promoted to run the department and here I was talking like I had lost my mind. These professors were really smart, and they did not question the importance of the area but our ability as a land grant university in the State of Alabama to obtain and maintain the resources which would include competent and experienced people, space, utilities, and the specialized equipment to design, fabricate, and test the tiny integrated circuit chips, all of which would cost a small fortune and require thousands of square feet of space. For example, a modern facility, such as those operated by Intel Corporation, cost thousands of dollars per square foot, and the total cost is many billions of dollars. Today the individual transistors that are the building blocks for the electronic circuits have a feature size of five or six nanometers (one meter is approximately one yard, and one nanometer is equal to one billionth of a meter). Thus the laboratories in which the circuits are made must be ultra clean. A tiny dust particle is capable of damaging a circuit.

Our facility would not need to be anywhere close to a modern production facility, such as one run by Intel Corporation. After all we would not be cranking out integrated circuit chips like jelly beans. Nevertheless, the difficulties in establishing a microelectronics laboratory in our environment appeared to be absolutely monumental. So, my colleagues had every right to question my sanity. I told them that I understood their reticence, but if they could not help, please stay out of my way.

I began by trying to hire good people with expertise in this area. I was able to convince several people to join us in spite of the fact that what is now known as the Alabama Micro/Nano Science and Technology Center was only a gleam in my eye. Once these people were in place, my job was to help them generate the support they needed. We worked together to generate contracts and facilities. We sent our graduates to microelectronics companies and asked them to help us get the equipment at their company that was being replaced with new equipment as the technology changed and developed. The equipment that was being replaced at companies like Texas Instruments was perfect for our laboratories since we were not in a production mode but rather making small quantities in the process of educating our students. Today, the center is supported by six professors, serves to educate a large number of students at the bachelor's, master's, and PhD levels, occupies approximately twelve thousand square feet of laboratory space, and contains many millions of dollars of highly sophisticated equipment. At present, this facility is one of the best facilities of its type at any land grant school in the country.

The critical point here is that I had the right people in the right positions. I could not have done what they did, because I did not have the expertise and experience in this area. But I recognized the need for these people and sought them. They accomplished what had appeared to be absolutely impossible when first mentioned.

Unfortunately, I have known managers who surrounded themselves with incompetence. They apparently feel threatened by intelligent and energetic people. However, the price they pay for ensuring that they are the smartest one in their organization is a very high one. Jun-ichi Nishizawa, who is considered by many to be the father of microelectronics in Japan, is reported to have developed the following table, in which native intelligence is plotted against work ethic

	Very Intelligent	Dumb as a stick
Hard Worker	x	xx
Lazy	xxx	xxxx

The four blocks correspond to very intelligent/hard worker, dumb as a stick/hard worker, etc. The most damage is probably done by the person (xx) who creates so many problems by working hard while not having a clue what they are doing.

When a manager has surrounded himself with incompetent people, the issue is not what these subordinates can do *better* than him, but rather what these people can do *to* him.

There may be some isolated situations where this kind of environment can persist. However, in general it won't last long. As a rule, either the top management will realize that the manager who surrounds himself with inept individuals is not competent to be in that position and replace him, or simple economics will force the inevitable. Some managers employ incompetents to serve as a lightning arrestor. However, an individual employed in this capacity provides only a false sense of security, since in the final analysis, managers are always responsible for their organizations.

An individual who is promoted or otherwise inherits an organization will probably find a cross section of individuals within it. As Robert Frost, an American poet, has said,

> The world is full of willing people, some willing to work, the rest willing to let them.[7]

In a typical fashion not all of our colleagues may be competent or a pleasure to be around. Unless we have carefully and methodically selected those with whom we work, we may find ourselves interfacing with all kinds, and some of them may be a real challenge. Although they may be found in varying degrees, there are two types that typically present a real problem. The first type can talk and talk. They have opinions on everything, but are not really excited about doing anything. Their response to a call to action is to start up their mouth, which they normally do long before engaging their brain. They have little or no ambition, which is a terrible shame, since according to them, they are an authority on everything. Their value to the organization is seriously impaired by their affliction: too much talking, no actual work.

The second type of individual simply imitates everyone in the organization. They really don't know what is going on and quite often don't care enough to find out. They plod along, and provided their assignment is straightforward and devoid of pitfalls, they will just hang in there and follow the crowd. This person is best described by the expression I have been told was employed by a military officer on a subordinate's performance evaluation: "He is like the gyrocompass in the bowels of a ship—he adds stability to the organization, but nothing to its forward motion."

Winning leaders are always very careful not to hire or promote either of these two types of individuals, because they have a tendency to replicate themselves. They know themselves better than anyone else, and they apparently feel that there is safety in numbers. The organization that becomes top heavy with these individuals will eventually fail of its own dead weight.

Unfortunately, I believe there is at least one environment where incompetence can exist, and its effect may have far-reaching consequences.

---

7. Frost, "Robert Frost Quotes."

The environment is education. For example, in the university, department heads must be extremely careful in their hiring practices, because once a new faculty member is tenured it is almost impossible to fire them. Furthermore, when the department's faculty conducts a tenure vote, the least competent faculty members will vote to tenure these people because their own position within the group can be a lonely one.

Instead of these two types, whose primary contribution to the organization is a body with a temperature of 98.6 degrees Fahrenheit, the winners surround themselves with chargers. Chargers are very hardworking, conscientious, and loyal friends. They want to see the organization succeed and are willing to do more than their part to see that it does. When assigned a task, they diligently pursue it until it is completed in a satisfactory manner. These people are of enormous value, because they can be counted on to do it right the first time. These people remind us of the expression "if you want something done, give it to a busy person."

It takes time and considerable effort for us to thoroughly understand the people with whom we work. Through constant observation and continuous interaction with them we are able to gradually piece together the puzzle which defines both their normal operational characteristics and those that motivate change in their lives. If we know our colleagues well and correctly assess their strengths and weaknesses, we can often turn the lemons they carry into lemonades. Even the two types described earlier have inherent potential and can very often be judiciously placed in positions which accentuate their strengths and neutralize or minimize the impact of their weaknesses.

In general, everyone is good at something, and it is the astute leader who can devise a plan to place everyone in a position where they can contribute to the best of their ability. If a position within the organization cannot be found, then perhaps a swap of two individuals can be secured. If a swap is not a viable approach, then career guidance for the individual should be used to try to find some way in which to help them be as productive as they can be. If every positive approach seems to lead nowhere, it may simply be easier to change people than it is to change people. As the very insightful comedian George Carlin has said, "Just 'cause you got the monkey off your back, doesn't mean the circus has left town."[8] It is critically important to ensure that the worker bees are happy and

---

8. Carlin, "Just Cause You Got the Monkey..."

productive. It is here in the trenches that we have to win; because if we can't win here, we are not likely to win elsewhere.

Working Effectively with People

Motivating

Every business is a people to people operation, and exceptions to this are few and far between. Therefore, one of the primary functions of a leader is to motivate those people with whom they work so these individuals will not only perform their own duties to the best of their ability, but in turn effectively interface with others. The most effective motivators are those people who feel from the core of their being a special affection for those with whom they work. With a totally positive approach they administer a sense of purpose and instill the inspiration and enthusiasm to accomplish it. There is absolutely no doubt in the minds of their colleagues that the motivator is in total support of them, has their best interest uppermost in mind, and yet in return demands from them peak performance. Motivators intrinsically feel that their colleagues are magnificent and that it is a privilege and pleasure to help them achieve a position where they are not only highly productive contributors, but feel good about themselves and what they are accomplishing. The typical reaction that one's colleagues have to this approach is a reflective one in which they admire and respect their leader to the point that they will follow them to hell and back. In fact, when a highly charged interaction is developed, people can be inspired to achieve things they would never have believed possible.

As an outstanding role model, the leader employs the old Roman philosophy *exemplum docet*, i.e., the example teaches. Using this philosophy, the leader illustrates in a crystal-clear fashion what he considers to be proper performance, and high standards typically enlist high performance. In addition, in motivating another, it is advantageous to be able to see things from his point of view. Armed with this information, we are prepared to determine the most effective manner in which to encourage him to take action, i.e., why would he want to buy it, sell it, rent it, repair it, etc. A better understanding of the situation makes cooperation easier, and it is undoubtedly better to have him working *with* you as opposed to working *for* you.

Ironically, the leader is also a servant to those who work with them. If the leader is keenly aware of their needs and supplies them to the best of his ability, his troops will, in turn, be more productive. The technical problems are often the easiest to solve, since they are governed by the laws of chemistry, mathematics, and physics. It is often the personal interface between the leader and their colleagues that governs the amount and quality of work, as well as the speed at which the work is done.

When communicating with our colleagues it is very important to ensure that everyone understands precisely what is being said, i.e., be direct, concise, and concrete in providing directions. Never talk in parables. While Jesus Christ used this form of communication very effectively, in today's environment some people will misunderstand by accident, while others will misunderstand on purpose. In order to remind myself of the importance of unambiguous communication, I have a plaque, the exact source of which is unknown to me, which says the following: "I know you think you understood what I said, but I am not sure you realize that what you heard is not what I meant." Every time I read this quotation I realize how carefully I should be listening to what others are telling me.

In working effectively with people, we should avoid criticism at all cost. It serves no useful purpose and simply forces people to try to defend themselves, even if they are wrong. If we use a more gentle approach of helping them and appreciating them, we gain far more. A study of the life of Jesus Christ indicates that he was not only positive and encouraging in his approach to teaching, but he was also a model of forgiveness. As Elizabeth Harrison, an American educator, has said,

> The men who are lifting the world upward and onward are those who encourage more than criticize.[9]

My dad was for many years the budget director for Air University at Maxwell Air Force Base in Montgomery, Alabama. He told me the story of one of the Air Force generals who, while visiting the base, was to be briefed on one of the programs at Air University by a young officer who was extremely knowledgeable on the subject. When the time came for the briefing, the general and his aide sat down in a conference room to receive it. Just as the briefing was to begin, the general looked up and the young officer was as white as a sheet and could not seem to open his mouth. The general instantly realized that the young officer was experiencing a terrible incident of stage fright, and without saying a word

---

9. Harrison, "Quotable Quote."

to him, turned to his aide and starting talking about the local weather. The general gradually brought the young officer into the conversation and managed to gently loosen him up. When it became obvious that the young officer was over his problem, which only took a couple of minutes, the general then asked that the briefing begin. The young officer did an absolutely outstanding job, and the general left knowing everything he wanted to know about the program. It was undoubtedly one of the kindest and nicest ways to handle the situation that I have ever heard. It was obvious to everyone who was aware of the situation why the general had all the stars on his shoulder.

Just imagine for a moment what would have happened if the general had displayed ignorance, acted foolish, and insisted the officer begin immediately. The young man probably would not have known his own name, what's more the content of the briefing. The situation would have deteriorated almost instantly, and there would have been no winners. Life is just too short for that kind of attitude, and people who operate in that manner are too little.

If we could only see things perfectly clearly, motivating our colleagues would be much easier. Unfortunately, things are not always what they appear, and therefore astute leaders look carefully before they leap headlong into situations. As a good example of what not to do, I recall an incident that occurred when my children were ages four, five, and six. John at age five had a gerbil that he kept in a glass fish tank. Periodically, he would shut the door to his room and put the gerbil out to run around on the floor. One night when I came home from a meeting, I did not see the kids. I asked Edie if they were in bed, and she told me that although they were in their pajamas, they were still playing in John's room. I could hear them laughing, and it sounded like they were having a wild time. What I saw when I opened the door was Laura standing aside laughing hysterically, and Geri and John were on the floor. John was sitting there with his legs spread out at a forty-five-degree angle, looking down at his crotch. Geri practically had her head in his crotch, and they were laughing so hard they were practically crying. I took one look at them, and even though I did not know what was going on, the situation looked bad. Without checking further, I snatched up John and Geri and spanked them both. They were furious. I had violated their sense of justice, because they were sure they had done nothing wrong. When they stopped crying, they showed me what it was all about. While John was sitting on the floor with his legs spread apart, the gerbil would run up one pants leg and peak out of the fly at Geri. Then he would run out the other pants leg and repeat the whole process. It was a riot, and I laughed so hard I could hardly see. I had to apologize to the kids, and I took them out later for an ice cream cone to help compensate for my failure to look before I leaped. However, having seen what the gerbil can do with their teeth, I asked John not to let the gerbil run up his pants leg again, so we would have the opportunity to carry on the family name.

Finally, as leaders, there are a number of social functions which add zest to the relationship we have with our colleagues. Such things as entertaining in our homes, sponsoring office parties at special time during the year, or simply attending a concert in which one of our colleagues plays an instrument, clearly indicates the genuine interest we have in them. While these activities cannot possibly substitute for a poor working relationship in an otherwise well-run organization, they add support to a positive working environment.

In addition, we should help our colleagues get promoted, if possible, and be happy for them when they do. If we are genuinely interested in their welfare, we will rejoice in their accomplishments and take pride in what they have done. As university professors, my colleagues and I are continuously in this mode of operation. We take pride in the accomplishments of our students, and hope that as many of them as possible will achieve fame and fortune far beyond anything we ourselves will ever experience.

Developing

The importance of developing talent is clearly stated by the following quote by Mary Rose McGeady, an American Roman Catholic Religious sister:

> There is no greater joy, nor greater reward than to make a fundamental difference in someone's life.[10]

In essentially every business, people are the most important asset. Simply stated, outstanding businesses are composed of outstanding personnel. Since we are rarely able to hire people who know it all or can do it all, as leaders, one of the most important functions should be the development of our employees—not only for the benefit of the organization, but for the benefit of the individuals themselves. If the positions under our direction are career enhancing, our dedicated employees will

---

10. McGeady, "Quotable Quote."

develop quickly and everyone will win. In fact, good leaders will help their high octane employees to excel, even to the point of surpassing their own positions.

We read in Mathew 25:14–30 that if we develop the talents we have been given, Almighty God will give us even more. However, if we fail to develop our talents, even if we have only very few, what little we have will be taken from us. The consequences of this parable are very serious. As leaders, we therefore have an important responsibility to do what we can to enhance the talents and careers of those individuals who are placed in our charge. This concept is very fundamental and does in fact extend from our families to the international scene. An example of this principle in action was the long-standing relationship between government and industry in Japan, where the Ministry of International Trade and Industry (MITI), which in 2001 became the Ministry of Economy, Trade and Industry (METI), provided very strong encouragement and outstanding support for the industries of that country.

In our attempts to develop those in our charge and thus enable them to function as effectively as possible, we must carefully examine the results of our efforts. As Peter Drucker, an American business consultant, has said,

> Most of what we call management consists of making it difficult for people to get their work done.[11]

We must recognize that no one is perfect and respect another's right to be different. The possibility that we can remake an individual in our own image or that of another is extremely remote. We simply must work within the confines of an individual's capabilities and personality. In that regard I am always amused when I hear a prospective bride announce that her fiancé needs some reworking and that she will change him after they are married. In general, the probability of that happening is somewhere in the sixth decimal place.

It is unfortunate that some people believe that delegating a task is an admission that they themselves cannot do the job. Not so! It is a way of developing our colleagues and often the most efficient way to get things done. However, once the task has been assigned, it is a mistake to try and micromanage it. As the leader, we tell our colleagues *what* to do, not *how* to do it. They may not do the job in exactly the same manner that we would have done it, but we did not have to spend the time on the task

11. Drucker, "Peter Drucker Quotes."

and were free to do something else. If the task is completed satisfactorily, accept it, thank them, and move on. By providing the individual assigned the task the flexibility to adjust as the solution progresses, we give them the opportunity to optimize the entire process. If, however, we take a tunnel vision approach, our inflexibility may preclude a viable solution. For example, Charlie Weaver, the former Chancellor of the University of Tennessee at Knoxville, tells the following story. A football coach, whose team was behind 12–17 with only a few minutes left in the game, had the ball on their own five-yard line. His first, second, and even third-string quarterbacks had been injured. So, he was forced to put in a quarterback that had never played in a varsity game. The coach figured that with his list of injuries, he would be lucky to survive the contest with only a 12–17 loss, and if he was not careful because of the location of the ball, the situation could get much worse. So, he called over the young, inexperienced quarterback and emphatically told him, "Now I want you to do exactly what I tell you—no variations. Go in there and run one play and punt." The first play went ninety yards. As they lined up for the second play, the coach stood on the sidelines in utter amazement. His team was in punt formation. As he stood there in a state of shock, the punter kicked the ball right out of the stadium. The coach went completely berserk. When the quarterback returned to the sidelines, the coach grabbed the young man and said, "What the hell were you thinking about on that last play?" The young man replied, "I was thinking that I must have the most ignorant coach in all captivity."

When possible and when appropriate it is helpful to have a career development plan for those with whom we work. Mentors can be assigned who keep them on track and guide their development. Under this plan, their behavior must be tracked to ensure that they are making progress. If the actual behavior differs from that which is desired, then the issues involved must be addressed quickly, fairly, and in a straightforward but considerate manner. If we are always honest, fair, and forthright in our dealings with those in our charge, they will not feel threatened or manipulated. The feedback provided should always focus on the individual's behavior, its relationship to performance, and perhaps the impact it has on the people with whom they work. Never, never attack the person, only the behavior. Once the problem behavior is explained and understood, it is generally advantageous to have the employee propose a step-by-step plan for correcting it. If the problem behavior results from circumstances beyond the work environment, e.g., troubles at home, then the correction procedures should involve seeking appropriate professional help.

Although problem behavior must be addressed directly, it should not be done in an abrasive manner. We must always remember that we are dealing with another human being who has feelings just as we do. If we always deal with the individual like we would want to be dealt with if the positions were reversed, we will always do the right thing.

When trying to correct problem behavior, we may encounter a variety of reactions. For example, an employee may simply refuse to change their behavior in the belief that he knows best. This is an unfortunate situation because it leaves us with few options. In order to maintain order, we may just have to penalize the individual. If penalizing them, e.g., demoting them, does not solve the issue, then separation is probably the best and final solution.

If the employee is conscientious and cooperative, but for some reason cannot do the assigned job, then perhaps reassigning him to a different task may make him more productive. It would be counterproductive to fire him if he is capable of contributing in another position, where his talents and interests can help move the organization forward.

Employees who are doing an adequate job, but are willing and capable of better performance, should be challenged and supported to improve. Extracting the best performance from such an individual, while encouraging and helping them, should yield the best performance in both the short and long terms. Praise and encouragement in a positive atmosphere will ultimately yield the best results.

As a general rule, we can facilitate an individual's improvement if we systematically do the following things. First of all, we must be sure that the individual understands the deficiency that exists between his current performance level and the desired performance standard. This deficiency must be explained in very specific concrete terms. Second, we must obtain the individual's concurrence that the area we have identified does indeed warrant improvement. This agreement ensures that everyone is working toward a common goal. Third, a milestone chart containing both intermediate and long-term goals must be developed. This plan serves as a vehicle for guiding development and maintaining it on the right track. In addition, the intermediate goals not only serve as checkpoints along the individual's progress trail, but they provide us with markers where we can praise improvement and encourage further development.

If we carefully and judiciously observe an individual's performance, we will have the proper vantage point from which to praise even the slightest improvement. An appreciation of every increment in this development should be of paramount importance to us. This feedback should be immediate, if possible, but at least a continuous part of our interaction with him. Never sit back and wait for an annual review. The feedback can be easily handled in a very simple manner. For example, we can stop by the employee's desk or catch them in the hallway and say "I believe you are really getting the hang of this work," or "I am really pleased with your progress," or "I sure wish I could clone you." These comments, although very short, have a tremendous positive impact on our employees, and if we are watching them closely, we will have many opportunities to say them forthrightly.

We should teach our employees to prepare for and create opportunities. We know that as our employees try new ventures of any kind, there will inevitably be setbacks and failures. However, in a failure-tolerant environment, these will only be glitches along the progress trail. We are well aware that this positive approach is very stimulating in their development, because our experience and logic tell us that the success of those people who simply wait patiently for their ship to come will wait patiently forever.

Since opportunities quite often originate with problems, as leaders we must not only be excellent problem solvers ourselves, but we must, to the extent possible, instill this ability in our colleagues. As a general rule, the strategy that yields the optimum solution to any problem contains the following steps. First, we must identify the *real* problem. This sounds simple, but in many cases it is not. When we have not properly identified the problem, time is simply spent treating the symptoms rather than the disease. For example, suppose we have an employee who is unable to perform simple mathematical calculations. We may identify as the problem a lack of skills in mathematics. However, that may only be a symptom, whereas the real problem may be that the individual has a case of dyscalculia. All the mathematics courses in the world won't solve this problem.

Once we are sure we have identified the problem, we should analyze every facet of it to determine all of its inherent parameters. For example, what causes it, and how does it manifest itself? Having thoroughly understood the problem, we can define the entire spectrum of possible solutions, and from this list we can select the best solution. This "best solution" is typically the one that optimizes some set of parameters, e.g., cost, growth, or time. The solution selected must then be implemented in a timely fashion. Once implemented, the final step in the process is to evaluate this implementation to determine if it is indeed a workable solution.

When our organization is called upon to attack a particular problem, it is normally advantageous to get as many people as practical involved and encourage creativity. Good ideas come from everywhere. It is dangerous, unless it simply can't be prevented, to compartmentalize projects too much, because people who can easily contribute don't, assuming it is not a part of their job responsibility. It is especially important for those key individuals who play an integral part of implementing a solution to be a part of the decision-making process. In general, people will work very hard to support in every way possible a solution they themselves derived, and there are times when these key players have come up with some rather unusual solutions.

I recall an incident that occurred in our family when the children were ages seven, eight, and nine. We moved from our first house, which was quite small, to a house that was essentially twice as big. Once we settled in the new house, it became obvious to Edie that it was going to take a lot of work to keep this house straight and clean. During the time of the move, Edie was attending a short course entitled: "PET—Parent Effectiveness Training." One of the things suggested in the course was to get the kids involved in working out problems. One night after supper we all sat down to talk, and Edie explained that since we were in a bigger house, it was going to be more difficult to keep up with the housework. She mentioned specifically the kids' clothes and toys. Then she asked the children for ideas on how we could all work together to accomplish this task. For a moment, the silence was deafening. We could tell from the expression on John's face that the wheels in his head were spinning fast. Finally, as if a bright light had turned on in his head, he said he had an idea. Edie was so pleased that this PET course was paying off and asked John to tell us what he thought we should do. His suggestion was, "Let's move back to the old house where Mama can do it all." I looked at Edie, and she was in a state of shock. When John saw her reaction, he realized that his suggestion was not really a viable one, so the kids starting talking among themselves, and they agreed that if they kept their own rooms completely straight and their toys picked up in the rest of the house, they could be of immense help. We all agreed and that became the plan. From time to time we had to remind the kids of the plan, but on the whole it worked fairly well.

In general, the ability to solve problems depends on a number of factors. However, there is one requirement that is absolutely essential. That factor is competence. There is no substitute for this one. We not only have to have it, we need to maintain it. This world marches on day by day. People change, technologies change, laws change, markets change, and therefore whether we recognize it or not, we are on a treadmill. Depending upon the area, some treadmills move faster than others; however, as a general rule we have to work hard just to stay in place, and if we want to get ahead, we have to go the extra mile. If you slow down or stop, your competition will run right by you. The corporation graveyard is replete with companies that failed to maintain the competence required to sustain their market position. Likewise, there are a number of people who, for one reason or another, have not kept themselves up to date, and in many cases the consequences have been disastrous. Therefore, one of the key ingredients in any development plan is the acquisition and maintenance of the competencies required to excel in our jobs.

An environment that supports development is generally one that is as free as possible of unnecessary stress. As leaders we normally have considerable control over the amount of stress that plays no positive role in the development of our employees. First of all, we must exhibit the qualities of a good leader, since poor leaders can cause enormous stress when they set a bad example, are not decisive, and lack direction. We should teach our employees to work smarter and more efficiently so that any extra time they contribute enhances their development.

In the development of our employees, we must not only require minimum work standards, but we must carefully watch the other end of the spectrum as well. The race horses can get overloaded and therefore overworked. This situation can eventually lead to burnout—a condition where there are no winners.

In the development of our workforce, we have to provide them with as much experience as possible. Experience is often more important than a basic knowledge of a specific area. The manner in which things actually work in the real world may vary slightly from what the theory would predict. It is interesting to note that experience is no panacea, since as Vernon Law, a Major League Baseball player, has said, "Experience is a hard teacher because she gives the test first, the lesson afterward."[12]

---

12. Law, "Experience Is a Hard Teacher..."

The Art of Listening

Some people just love to hear the sound of their own melodious voice. If necessary, they will bring up an item every month and talk about it for three weeks. Their opinions may not be supported by any knowledge or experience, they may not be the opinions of their management, their colleagues, or anyone else in the right mind. In addition, you may have no interest in wasting your time listening to these people; however, there are many situations when listening—very careful listening—is extremely important.

The effective leader should know as much as possible about the people, products, and services with which he deals. In fact, as he tries to stretch and move the organization forward, he may encounter areas he knows very little about. He must rise quickly on the learning curve and, in order to do that, he must be a good listener. If the communication lines are wide open and he is a receptive node on the communication link, he can be brought up to speed very quickly. He may have to question and probe; however, the mathematics associated with the optimal use of his physical system would seem to indicate that he should talk only half as much as he listens.

If there is an established rapport between the leader and his colleagues, those people who are in a position to help will do so. Leaders may in fact defer to them if they are convinced that their colleagues really understand the situation at hand, and their judgement is trusted. This is not abdication—this is smart business.

Unfortunately, there are occasions in which we *hear* people talking to us, but we are not really *listening* to them. The real information may be, in essence, subliminally transmitted, and only through careful listening will we receive it. Careful listening requires concentration, and only through it can we hope to acquire any information present in the data we receive.

Mental health professionals are the real experts in listening. Although psychologists, psychiatrists and therapists each specialize in dealing with such things as anger management, depression, and stress, they have one thing in common—these licensed professionals are all excellent listeners. They provide a safe environment in which to deal with a variety of issues, and they are trained to pick up on the slightest nuances. They glean information from conversations and interactions that the rest of us would miss.

While we may not be very good listeners, in a wide variety of circumstances, listening is actually an easy thing to do. For example, imagine yourself standing for some time with another individual or group. If there is a lengthy period when no one speaks, the situation seems awkward. If you will simply remain silent, someone will say something, sometimes anything, to break the silence. Therefore, if you listen, you can at least extract whatever information is transmitted.

On a number of occasions, I have had colleagues come into my office just to talk. They simply needed to tell someone what was on their minds, and I have tried to help in any way that I could. I provided whatever advice was appropriate, but more than anything else, I lent them a caring and sympathetic ear in a confidential environment.

For example, I recall a situation in which an individual stopped by to see me just to chat. However, within a few minutes the conversation quickly focused on a particular problem the individual was trying to deal with. He just talked and talked and talked. I am personally convinced there is a therapeutic quality inherent within a conversation in which a person is able to freely release the thoughts that disturb them. My conversation with this individual was really very minimal. I said things like "uh huh," "Gee whiz," and finally in an attempt to reassure him as best I could, I told him, "I just know that everything is going to work out right for you." When he left my office, to my absolute amazement, he said, "Well, I sure appreciate your advice, you have been most helpful." My advice! What advice? I just listened attentively and sympathetically. However, it was clear that I was there, and listening meant a great deal to this man.

If people believe they can trust me and that I have their best interest upper-most in my mind, there will be many occasions when I will have the opportunity to listen. I remember two other situations which impressed upon me the importance of listening.

One case involved a colleague with whom I worked. The man's father had just died, and he needed to talk to someone. We probably talked for ninety minutes, and it had nothing to do with our business, but it was extremely important to him, and therefore it was extremely important to me.

In another case, a man came in to talk about his daughter who was in the hospital. She was divorced with two kids. Although we talked for some time, throughout the discussion I had the impression the problem was minor until he made reference to taking care of the kids long term. If I had somehow missed the words "long term," I would have guessed from everything else that he said that her problems were routine. They were not, and he was much more concerned than he indicated. Once I realized the real situation, I offered to give active, rather than just passive, help to him if needed.

I believe very strongly that any individual who comes in to talk with me about anything deserves my undivided attention. As a result, I always request that we not be interrupted unless there is an emergency or some very unusual issue which simply must be dealt with immediately. In addition, I refuse to answer the telephone while I am talking to someone. I feel that interrupting my conversation to answer the telephone somehow says to the individual with whom I am speaking that the person on the telephone, who is as yet completely unknown to me, is more important than he is.

Through attentive listening we can assure ourselves that we have gleaned as much information as possible from the data stream. As we talk with people, they will give us clues to what engages them. This data is very important because it is difficult to motivate someone with a subject in which they have no interest. For example, I would not walk across the street to get a free ride in a helicopter. I am prone to motion sickness, and within minutes of becoming airborne I would undoubtedly be nauseated.

I know that in the past I have gotten a lot of personal feedback by listening very carefully. The feedback may be either direct or indirect. When people in your organization want to tell you they think you are on the wrong track, more often than not, they will do it indirectly or use some innuendo. Admittedly, some people will just walk up to you and blurt it out, and if there is good rapport between the two of you, this is just fine. However, most people operate in a more subtle fashion.

I can recall several occasions in which, without referring to my own plans which were well-known, people would tell me stories about individuals in situations similar to my own, that had done what I had planned to do, and it did not work out. Some of these conversations are so subtle that it appears that the individual is just passing the time of day—but he is not. He doesn't want to take a hard stand against my approach, since I may decide to do it anyway, and I might make it work in spite of another's failure in the same area.

In any relationship, communication is one vehicle by which we pass information back and forth. If the real information is coded, we may have to dissect the message in order to extract it. We may receive only little clues from the data we are sent. As a result, we may be left asking ourselves—what does this person really mean? What information is thinly veiled between the lines of the message? Listening attentively may also involve watching the person's facial expressions and gestures, the tone of his voice, or anything that will help us obtain the real information from the available data. I am not proposing that we operate as a therapist and analyze every conversation. Therapists do this for a living, are very good at it, and often refer to this mode of operation as listening with the third ear. Most of us are not trained to do this, and I am sure it would wear me out. However, if you feel that hidden within the message is some important information, it pays to look hard to find it.

Under many circumstances, failure to listen can be very costly. Corporations have failed to solve problems, develop products, deliver on contracts, and the like because they did not listen carefully to their employees and customers. Some of the more ambitious employees have left for new highly successful ventures because no one listened to them.

In business, listening to the customer is not only a polite and thoughtful thing to do, it is often an absolute requirement for success. After all, your own enthusiasm notwithstanding, what you think of your product, while perhaps interesting, is almost insignificant in comparison to what the customer thinks of it. It is the client and no one else who will ultimately determine whether your product is a success or not, since his perception is absolutely critical.

A number of major corporations have demonstrated that they understand the importance of customer feedback. Corporations such as AT&T and Weyerhaeuser would invite their customers in for a face-to-face, candid, and even critical discussion of their products, and encourage them to identify weaknesses and suggest methods of improvement. The entire focus of the initiative is "You are an important customer; please tell us what we can do to serve your needs better." This type of interaction not only improves products and services, but it builds a lasting partnership in which every participant is a winner.

I remember an incident that occurred when I was about sixteen years old that embarrassed me to death. I worked after school and on Saturdays at one of the major food stores in Montgomery. I had a small Triumph motorcycle that I used to ride to work. One day I was at the motorcycle dealership to buy some parts. I stood around waiting for the mechanic to finish checking out this brand-new motorcycle. There was only one other man, who looked like he was about forty years old, in the store and the two were talking about the new motorcycle. The shop was small, and I was standing with them waiting for the mechanic to finish what he was doing. When there was a lull in the conversation between them I asked the mechanic "Who's getting the new motorcycle?" The mechanic replied "This new bike was for Brock." I knew most of the kids in the city that rode motorcycles, and I knew Brock. On a wild scale of one to ten, Brock was a fifty. I also knew that Brock had been given a new motorcycle about six months earlier, and he had wrecked it. So, when the mechanic told me the new bike was for Brock, I just laughed. I had on my Mr. Know-it-all hat, and I told the mechanic, "I will bet you that he wrecks that motorcycle in less than three months." The man standing there with us said, "He better not." To anyone with bird brains, that would have been a clue. I looked the man straight in the eye and said "You don't know Brock." The man looked at me as though I had lost my mind and said "I ought to know him; I am his father." I immediately started looking around for the nearest sewer drain that I could crawl in to. I wasn't listening! The two guys had been standing right in front of me talking about that motorcycle. That incident had a profound effect on my modus operandi. I had learned the hard way that my foot does not really fit well in my mouth.

Praise and Reward

I have always been amazed at the things people will do in order to be recognized. For example, some criminals will go to great lengths and act in very bizarre manners in order to achieve some notoriety. Some people fantasize, while others will go completely insane to achieve it, if they are incapable of obtaining it in any other way. Behavioral psychologists are the real experts in this area, and they work to understand why we behave the way we do.

I recall at one point in my career that Floyd, who was a colleague of mine, came into my office to tell me what he had achieved on a particular project. I thought it was neat, and I told him so. But I had a facilities problem that was bugging me to death at the time, and I guess I was preoccupied with it. Floyd left, but within an hour he was back. He started talking about the results of his project again, and once again I complimented him on what he had done. However, the meeting on the facilities problem was scheduled to begin within a few minutes of his second visit, and I was unable to sit and talk for long. He left, but after the meeting was over, he was back again. Although he used a different approach, I realized as if hit in the face with a baseball bat, that he was talking about the same project again. I also finally realized what he needed, and it was painfully obvious that I had not supplied it. So, this time I did it right. He had done an excellent job, and therefore I just used one superlative after another, raving about what he had done and the impact it would have on our work. I found several different ways to compliment him on the same issue. He left my office happy as a lark, and this time he did not come back.

It is impossible to overemphasize the importance of praising good performance quickly and as often as possible. To obtain some idea of its impact we need only watch the reaction of parents when their children begin taking their first steps. Are the parents' reactions "That's no big deal!" or "I can do that!" No way, Jose! The parents act like the kid just won the Nobel Prize for walking. In response to their parent's encouragement, the kid tries to run instead of just putting one foot in front of another. We can all learn a lot from this simple example. We should praise good performance every time we see it, and if we don't normally see it, we should go searching for it. As soon as we find it—shout it! By reinforcing it, we can be assured of seeing more of it.

I sincerely and honestly compliment people at every opportunity and recommend them for awards, promotions, and any type of recognition every chance I get. People want to feel important, and if they have done something which merits praise, lay it on thick. This concept is not lost on the Madison Avenue crowd. Watch closely and you will see in advertising that the successful and important people buy certain products, wear certain brands of clothes, drive certain cars, eat at certain places, and so on. We are constantly encouraged to move up to first class or synonymously important class. Therefore, if we will simply find a way to make people feel important, we will be a success, because they will give us their very best efforts. As a simple example, I recall a lady who worked in one of the local stores where we traded on a routine basis. I had seen her on a number of occasions, but one day I noticed that she had cut her hair short. I am partial to short hair—my wife's hair is also cut short, and so I stopped her and told her she really looked nice with her hair cut short. I never even learned her name, which was a mistake on my part, since an interest in another's name is also a compliment. However, in response to my comment, her face lit up like a Christmas tree, and every time I saw her again she would always speak to me and ask if she could help me find some item in the store.

Sincere and deserved praise and appreciation is the universal oil that keeps the machinery in any organization running smoothly and effectively, and provides the impetus for even greater achievement. There is nothing like it, and therefore no substitute for it.

There are a number of ways that we can sincerely praise and show genuine appreciation. We can tell them, write them, or use body language if necessary. Using body language, we can smile or use some other gesture which indicates approval and appreciation. This is, however, an area where extreme caution must be observed. The modern "Me too" movement has drastically changed the dynamic in this area. Whatever you do must be done in a strictly professional manner with only the best interest of the individual being praised in mind, and there cannot be any suggestive overtones that someone could misinterpret or take out of context. I believe this movement has had a negative effect on our ability to appreciate our colleagues, and this is most unfortunate. However, because of its importance, we simply need to find a way to do this right. Some people believe that everyone with whom they interact views every situation in the same way as they do. There is absolutely no doubt that this is definitely not the case. As a trivial example, is the glass half empty or half full? Therefore, in addition to such things as body language, success in dealing with others is also dependent upon what social scientist David Livermore, in his book *The Cultural Intelligence Difference*, calls "cultural quotient or CQ." Individuals with a high CQ are able to work very effectively with people who have different cultural backgrounds. While a high CQ is a definite advantage in almost any situation, it may be a necessary requirement for individuals whose work involves personal interactions in a wide variety of venues, e.g., businesses with a clientele that includes people from all over the world, or those whose operations span the globe. Not understanding the customs and culture of another individual can have some serious consequences when a simple act or statement that appears to be straightforward and mundane actually offends the other individual. For example, several decades ago, I was involved in running an international technical conference in Xian, China. My PhD advisor, who was Chinese, worked with me on the conference. Because of the enormous amount of work involved, I wanted to give a gift to my counterpart in Xian, who was handling the local logistics. So, I planned to give him an expensive wristwatch, since that was a nice gift that I could easily carry on the plane. However, my advisor told me that while my idea was a good one, my selection was a poor one. He told me that in the Chinese language, the word "clock" is associated with an "ending" or "termination," which could be interpreted as the end of life or death. I had absolutely no clue this was the case. So, in my attempt to reward my counterpart for the work he had done on the local scene, I would have unknowingly offended him.

When I worked at Bell Telephone Laboratories, we were on a first-name basis with the kingpins of the organization. I personally appreciated very much their attitude. These individuals, who had hundreds of people under their supervision, did not need a crown and scepter or a four-foot peacock plume emanating from their heads to indicate to me how important they were. I knew it already, and I felt that their attitude in dealing with me on a first-name basis showed that they appreciated me. They would also schedule luncheons in which a vice president would talk to some of us and answer questions about anything that was happening in the business. If these very important and extremely busy people did not appreciate me, they would never have spent their valuable time giving someone as unimportant as I was the opportunity to pick their brains. We can praise our colleagues by recognizing their importance. While I served as head of the Electrical Engineering Department, I essentially took orders from the super professors in my department. Their contributions to our program were outstanding, and therefore I let them decide their own schedules and I would adjust our operations around their needs. I sincerely appreciated them, and as a result I worked hard to help them accomplish whatever they had in mind. These people operated as entrepreneurs, and because they were appreciated and given the flexibility to call their own shots, they did not have to go elsewhere or set up their own organizations; they were appreciated and rewarded right where they were.

The competent and secure leader can be very humble and concentrate on crediting those with whom they work for the success of the organization. It is the insecure boss who feels compelled to praise themselves—after all, they can't rely on anyone else to do it.

While writing one of my textbooks, I employed a student named Bill to do some drawings for me. He helped me to prepare diagrams, figures, and plots, because no matter how hard I worked, I just could not seem to get everything done quickly enough. In order to hit the publisher's production windows, I had to send all of the material to New York on a Friday, so they would have it the following Monday. On the day before the deadline to ship the material, Bill and I met to see exactly where we stood.

The way I had it figured, we were finished if Bill had done his job right. Bill brought in an enormous stack of figures. I examined his work, and it was absolutely outstanding. The proportion was right, the line widths were even and the figures were centered on the pages. Everything was neat as a pin. Bill was the greatest, and I told him so. I was just delighted, and I fell all over myself complimenting him. However, when we made the final check of all the figures, we found that I had forgotten to do the figures in two of the chapters, and that meant there was a total of sixty figures, that were not drawn. I should have had them drawn weeks before, but I was probably busy and forgot. When we discovered my error, I felt like committing hara-kiri. I had really screwed up this time. I was extremely busy the day we met, and I knew instantly there was not enough time to do what had to be done. So, I thanked Bill again so much for all of his work, but I told him that even if there were three of him, I wasn't sure at that point that we could meet the deadline. Bill asked me to give him the sixty figures and he would see what he could do. I told him that if it was possible for anyone to do it, it would be him. The next morning Bill came in with all sixty figures drawn. He had worked almost twenty hours straight to complete the task. I was astounded. If I had hung over a drawing board for that length of time, rigor mortis would have set in, and I would have been in that position for the rest of my life. Bill was really proud of what he had accomplished under extreme circumstances, and he wasn't alone. I practically came unglued thanking him over and over for his efforts.

It is so very important to give credit where credit is due. I have heard Dr. Charles Jarvis of San Marcos, Texas tell the story of a preacher who was talking to a farmer as he admired his farm. The preacher said, "It is a nice farm, brother, you and the Lord have here together." To which the farmer replied, "You should have seen it when the Lord had it by himself."

It is important for us to realize that our ability to effectively support and appreciate someone is often a function of our mutual rapport and the feelings we have for them. In turn, our feelings for them are often a measure of the distance between us. Interestingly, our measure is not only physical but mental, e.g., expressions such as "we are not on the same wavelength" or "I would not touch that idea with a ten-foot pole" have nothing to do with physical distance. And yet, they are an indication of how close we feel to another. As the distance between us shrinks, we become closer and finally we touch. Touching signifies an intimate relationship, and therefore has a very special significance. It is normally reserved only for those individuals with whom we have an affectionate interaction.

As leaders it is extremely important for us to understand the inherent power associated with touch. Because of its special significance we must never touch if it would be interpreted in any way, shape, or form as a negative action. There are a lot of very normal people who would consider the most casual touch as a violation of their space, and therefore not appreciate it at all. If appropriate, when we put our arm around someone or hug them, it has to be a very positive and supportive relationship; if not, it is pure deception. When done properly, it is one of the most significant things that can happen to an individual.

There is a very special and powerful magnetism associated with touch. It is important to the maintenance or our overall wellbeing. We are reminded of its importance in so many ways throughout our lives. At birth, doctors want mothers to hold their new babies close to them as often as possible. In doing so, the mother reassures the child that she is there and all is well. This closeness minimizes the impact of the transition which occurs when the baby is thrust from the completely intimate relationship of the womb. In the Bible we read stories of the people who were healed simply by touching the garments that Jesus wore. Before the famous consent decree that broke up the nationwide Bell System, they had invested millions in advertising with the slogan "Reach out and touch someone."

If we have a positive and supportive attitude, we will look for opportunities not only to reach out and touch someone for their accomplishments, but to reward them too. The reward can take on any one of a number of different forms. In the home environment, the reward may be a special meal, a later curfew, tickets to a special concert, or whatever is appropriate given the situation in the home. In business, the reward can be money, promotion, or perks such as use of a car or secretary and the like. In fact, it is always smart to provide as much incentive as possible. There have been numerous situations when this approach has paid big dividends. For example, consider the fundraiser who is very good at what he does. Given the choice between a fixed salary and a percentage of the money he raises, he will probably take the latter, because in that situation, the sky is the limit.

One of the most important results that can be achieved in an organization where people are genuinely appreciated is the establishment of an esprit de corps. The loyalty and pride we develop among the employees ensures that there is a sustained dedication and allegiance, not only to the goals of the organization, but to one another. In such a supportive environment, morale is high and the organization runs like a top, even when the leader is absent. The employees themselves, through peer pressure, which can be enormous, maintain the standards. Through their intolerance of poor performance, which if left unchecked would reflect on the organization as a whole, they guarantee that everyone is doing their best.

Edie and I have always agreed that it is too bad that we did not have a dog before we had kids. If we had, we would have been a lot smarter with the kids as they were growing up. Our dog does not respond to negative things, e.g., spankings, etc., anywhere near as well as she does to positive reinforcement. We have learned the hard way the power of a well-placed negative comment. Some of my Army buddies have even quantified it. They tell me that it takes at least one hundred "Atta-boys" to make up for one "Aw shit."

In the material that follows, let us employ the ideas and concepts put forth earlier to develop a winning strategy, which encompasses both happiness and success.

Part III

Putting it All Together

6

Looking out for Numero Uno

Time Management

OTHER THAN OUR GOD-GIVEN talents, time is the crucial variable that we have to allocate for accomplishing our desires and our goals. Each of us has the same 86,400 seconds in a day to spend as we choose. Our success is critically dependent upon what we do with those seconds. We can spend our time daydreaming or living in the past, or we can simply kill time through either poor planning or no planning at all. For example, when my daughter, Laura, was much younger, I noticed that she would drive to the mall to shop, return, and then later in the day, go back to the same mall to do more shopping. She could have saved some time, not to mention the automobile expense, if she had planned her schedule and bought everything in one trip. In her case, and I am afraid it is true of many teenagers, she seemed to have an inherent need to ride. My motto is, "If I want to kill time, with periods of relaxation notwithstanding, I work it to death." So, let's budget our time wisely and spend it developing and executing plans that will lead us to our goals. Remember, our goals may include shooting in the low seventies for eighteen holes of golf; hence our time does not have to be tied to business, but simply something that helps us develop some facet of our lives.

    I am always amazed when I talk to people who are in essence spending their time fantasizing and blaming others for their own situations. Some of them tell me they are waiting for their ship to come in. Notice that the accent here is on waiting, not working. If I know them well enough, I try to gently tell them that they will never see their ship in the harbor, simply because there are just too many of us who are working like hell to get our ships in, and there is no way without some effort that theirs will ever make it.

These same people quite often have a propensity for doing a job quickly, but not necessarily accurately, just to get rid of it. If they don't have the time to do it right, where in the world will they find the time to do it over? These people are invariably on a salary. If we could somehow manage to put them in business for themselves, even for a short time, it would change their entire attitude.

In order to aid us in accomplishing as much as we can, the accent should be on planning and executing in minimum time. Scheduling our affairs so that we can work problems for as long as possible within the required constraints allows our subconscious time to help solve them. I used to keep at least one three-by-five card in my shirt pocket all the time so that as ideas popped into my head, I could write them down before I forgot them. Now I can simply put them in my cellphone for viewing later. It is also helpful to sandwich small jobs within big ones in order to optimize our schedule. I recommend ordering the tasks you have to do by priority and doing the most important one first. I may even reorder the task list more than once a day. Reordering the tasks in real time permits me to optimize the schedule either because of additional data or new problems which have just surfaced.

There may be some tasks that I do not even address because of time constraints. If the deadline for a task that I have not had time to do comes and goes, and I could not delegate it, I just forget about it. If such a task becomes very important, I will be pulsed again and, at that time, it will probably have a priority high enough for me to allocate the time to get it done.

Finally, it is important to allocate some breaks within our work in order to clear and refresh our minds. These breaks may involve seeing someone in another office, getting a cup of coffee, checking email and phone messages, or essentially any other activity that is different from our current train of thought. If we are concentrating in a marathon fashion, we invariably reach a point where the law of diminishing returns takes over, and when this happens, we are actually wasting time if we continue to press on. In the extreme case, a fast burner can completely flame out.

We have to be smart in our dealings with others so that, while maintaining a congenial environment, we do not permit our colleagues to waste our time. One of the executives at NASA in Huntsville, Alabama, had a neat way of handling people who dropped in to provide an unsolicited memory dump. Under the carpet next to his desk he installed a switch which activated a buzzer at his secretary's desk in the next room. When he decided that some conversation had gone on long enough, he would, unknown to his visitor, activate the switch with his foot. His secretary would then pop into the room and inform him that it was time for his next appointment.

In time management, organization is critical. Through careful planning and scheduling we place ourselves in better control. By scheduling events in a realistic fashion we are able to manage our time as efficiently as possible, even in the face of uncertainties. It is normally counterproductive to try and cram more activities into a fixed time frame than is humanly possible to do, or in our haste to accomplish as much as we can, to ignore the importance of timing. For example, if I want to ask my boss for a raise, selecting the proper time is very important. Talking to the boss after he has gotten some good news is much more preferable to asking him after he has just been loaded down with bad news.

Organized management of our time means setting priorities, avoiding procrastination, and eliminating confusion. Do what must be done immediately and don't put it off, even if everything associated with the execution is not perfect. If our ducks are in a row, we will at least know where to find what we need. As a trivial example, my keys are either with me or on the dresser—never anywhere else. However, I know people who, before they leave home, locate their keys via a ritual which consists of systematically shaking all the clothes in the closet and listening for the jingle.

We minimize the time required to perform a task if we focus our energy on the particular job at hand and remove all extraneous tasks from our mind. Through this concentration of our energy, we bring to bear every faculty of our being, and therefore we are able to accomplish whatever is necessary in the shortest possible interval.

When communicating with another individual we should make every effort to do two things. First, while talking, be concise. Don't tell someone something using a thousand words what you could have told them with fifty. If the real information can be transmitted in fifty words, the other nine hundred and fifty are superfluous or redundant and a waste of time. In written form we often give two versions. For example, most lengthy reports contain what is called an executive summary at the front of the report, and this summary selectively outlines in just a few pages the pertinent information that is contained in the main body of the report, which may be comprised of hundreds of pages. The purpose of this summary is to present the key concepts and conclusions. Therefore, while the reader may not have time to read all the data that is contained in the entire report, they are able to learn quickly the significant features.

Second, when someone is talking to us, we must really listen carefully, not simply pretend to do so. If we try to timeshare our mind between the conversation at hand and other topics such as calculating our next move, we will not only risk missing the information that is blatantly obvious, but if there is a subtext present, we will undoubtedly miss it completely. Failure to understand the message the first time can not only result in a large and unnecessary time investment later, but if it is your leader's directions that you have failed to comprehend, you may be up to your neck in it praying that no one creates a wave.

If for any reason I have to work overtime, unless it is necessary to do so, I come in early rather than staying late. I am fresh in the morning, and my mind is quicker. Therefore, I am able to do more in less time. In addition, my appearance before working hours broadcasts the message that I am a hard worker, eager to do the job. After working hours, I am normally tired and therefore less effective. Staying late may leave the impression that I am unable to do my work in the time allotted.

Handle correspondence only once, if possible. For example, if I have or can quickly obtain all the data necessary to answer current correspondence, I do it immediately. If I set it aside and go back to it later, I will probably have to read it again in order to answer it, and therefore I have now handled it twice in order to answer it once.

It is always important to ensure that interspersed within our work time is time for rest and relaxation. In fact, one technique which seems to be an effective incentive in the optimization of our time is to reward ourselves with some pleasurable activity as soon as a difficult task is completed.

I believe that time is one of my most precious commodities and, as a result, I treat it with a great deal of respect. I have two plaques that I enjoy displaying. These plaques, which help me keep my thinking on track, contain the following sayings: "If you don't have anything to do, don't do it here" and "Blessed is the man who, having nothing to say, abstains from giving us wordy evidence of the fact." I don't know the origin of the first saying, but the author of the second one is George Eliot, the pen name for Mary Ann Evans, a novelist, essayist and translator.

Finally, it is critically important to ensure that time throughout the day is spent in prayer. Our Lord knows intimately our desires, the mechanisms we are using to accomplish them, and most importantly the best path to them. Therefore, time is managed in the most efficient manner when we are in constant contact with him and can receive the necessary guidance, together with mid-course corrections, if necessary. Why would anyone start a project, whether large or small, and completely ignore the help of God who knows before we do, from all eternity, the optimum manner in which to accomplish it? Taking advantage of the help that God can provide ensures that a task is seamlessly integrated within our schedule and performed in an optimum manner.

Stress Management

We come under stress for all kinds of reasons, and interestingly, what causes stress in me may not bother anyone else at all and vice versa. However, stress is typically produced by either overload, conflict or uncontrollable conditions. We may try to do too much in too little time. Deadlines may be too short or standards may be too high. We may try to be someone we are not, or we may simply be the victim of circumstances that are completely beyond our control. A definition of stress, with which many of us can personally identify, was seen on a recreation wall in an apartment complex in Montgomery, Alabama. That defined stress as "that confusion created when one's mind overrides the body's basic desire to choke the living daylights out of some idiot who desperately needs it."

Stress can have either a positive or negative impact on us. If we are unable to manage stress, our reaction is normally worry, anxiety, or depression, and if we let stress get to us, it can be absolutely devastating. It can cause all sorts of physical and mental disorders, including such things as ulcers, stroke, and heart failure. It is believed that it kills more American businessmen than hard work. However, well-managed stress can be a very effective mechanism for growth which, in turn, permits us to handle even higher levels of stress. The ability to handle stress effectively is often the litmus test for a leader. A comment that addresses this subject comes from Benjamin Franklin, Founding Father of the United States: "After crosses and losses men grow humbler and wiser."[1]

Although we all have our own particular threshold, if the stress level is too low, then our motivation and enthusiasm may be insufficient for good performance. At the other extreme, performance rapidly deteriorates because the stress is detrimental to our physical and mental

---

1. Franklin, "Quotable Quotes."

wellbeing. There appears to be an optimum range, however, which promotes growth and produces enthusiasm and excitement about what we are doing.

We are capable of reducing the stress in our lives, and we do so through action and attitude. Through positive action we can adjust our lifestyle to minimize the circumstances that zap our energy and negate our zest for life. By analyzing very carefully our daily routine we can identify the pressure points. Then through better planning and time management we can adopt a schedule that tends to minimize the hassles in our lives. I know that in my own case I have found that when my stress level goes off the scale, I have tried to cram four hours of work into one hour. We must somehow get as much control of our lives as possible, and planning is a key factor in accomplishing this task.

Sometimes it is possible to prevent stress by adjusting the ground rules. For example, if there is a quarter of a pie left to be split between two people, the rule that the one who cuts the pie into two pieces gets the second choice normally leads to a win-win situation.

Stress management is even somewhat dependent upon time management, which should include rest, relaxing activities, and time spent in communication with God. Too many of us tend to run in the fast lane of life, and we simply need some time, regardless of how little, to reset our emotional, mental, and physical systems. Although we often have to convince the Type A's that it is not a sin to relax, we all need some time to heal and be at peace. A good balance between our activities and rest and relaxation is a necessary condition for successful living.

It is unfortunate that all too often we wait until stress seems overwhelming and we feel a total loss of control before we return to the original source of all peace. In Matthew 11:28 we find the loving call, "Come to Me all who labor and are heavy laden, and I will give you rest."

When we release our problems to our Almighty and Loving Father, we can relax knowing that God will help us. After all, God is in charge. When we turn to him in prayer and listen for his guidance, he reveals ideas and answers to the issues that are troubling us. The release of our problems to God gives us a sense of security and well-being which permits us to approach our tasks with assurance and confidence.

The daily habits of our lifestyle also affect our ability to deal with stress. Food, which controls our biological structure, is the fuel for our internal engine. Like the fuels in our automobiles, our engines run better on some fuels than others. Through a proper diet, we can fortify the body and enhance its ability to withstand stress.

Exercise, which should be another part of our daily routine, strengthens the body, tones muscles, increases stamina and improves the cardio vascular system. If we are in good physical condition, we are less susceptible to emotional disorders. Some words of caution are, however, in order concerning our selection of a viable exercise program. If possible, make exercise fun and something we enjoy doing. However, if we are very competitive, it is important to ensure that the program we use does not induce, rather than help prevent, stress. The professionals in this area are capable of designing a program that will put us on a path to accomplish the desires we wish to achieve without causing injury or pain. If we are not accustomed to doing some type of exercise on a regular basis, it is smart to consult these individuals first to ensure that the program we adopt does not lead to other problems.

Our attitude is perhaps the single most important factor in our ability to conquer stress. As John Milton, the English epic poet, so eloquently stated in his poem, *Paradise Lost*, "The mind is its own place, and in itself Can make a Heav'n of Hell, a Hell of Heav'n."[2] Regardless of the actual circumstances, if we think something is bad, it is bad; and if we think something is good, it is good. Hence, we should always look for the bright side of everything. While it is impossible for us to control all the events of our lives, the one thing we can control is what we think about them. It is our perception of the impact of events on our lives that is really the crucial issue. For example, I have witnessed fender-bender-type accidents in which the individual who was hit simply stepped away from the accident and called the police. However, I have seen other people under the exact same conditions become completely distraught.

Our mental attitude has a dramatic impact on our physical system. Stress, tension and worry not only lead to ill health, but they tend to prevent recovery. Therefore, if problems exist, it may be impossible to cure the physical without first healing the psychological.

An area of research called psychoneuroimmunology or psychoendoneuroimmunology is concerned with examining the connections among the brain, the mind, and the body's immune system.[3] The results seem to indicate that our immune system is critically linked to our attitude.

---

2. Milton, *Paradise Lost*, 1.233–34.
3. See ylenfest, "Psychoneuroimmunology and the Mind's Impact on Health."

Therefore, a positive, can-do, hopeful attitude is not only an excellent deterrent to illness in that it actually helps bolster the body's immune defenses and thereby makes us more resilient and less vulnerable, but it is also a vehicle by which we can recover as quickly as possible if illness does strike.

With the proper attitude, our response to negative stimuli is controlled and our thoughts are channeled toward dealing with them in a manner which enhances our growth. In this mode we are more realistic in our expectations and goals. We do not set for ourselves goals that even Superman would have trouble accomplishing.

We should not expect everything in our lives to go right, because in general it won't. Most contracts are written with contingency clauses. Do you know why? Simply because there is quite often an excellent chance that everything will not go as planned. Do we really have any reason to believe that we are so much different than everyone else?

We should look at problems as challenges and not as threats. Problems are often opportunities in disguise. There are an enormous number of individuals who are millionaires today because they met a problem head-on and solved it. At the very least there is usually much to learn when addressing a problem with the proper attitude.

We should also remember that problems come in all sizes and that some are much more important than others. With that in mind, don't sweat the small stuff. So many times we cannot even remember what was causing us so much pain only a few weeks ago. If something does not fall into the "small stuff" category, we should figure out what is the worst thing that can happen, accept it, and then direct all of our energy toward improving this worst-case condition. As an example, if I believe that my performance on the job does not merit a raise in salary, and if not improved, may lead to my dismissal, then I should accept this fact and then direct all my energy toward collecting and analyzing data that will help me institute changes that will minimize the impact of this fact and ensure that it does not happen again. This is also a very important issue when raising children. You have to pick your battles carefully in order to do the best you can under what can often be difficult circumstances. For example, suppose the children don't want to go to bed on time because they want to surf the Internet. Although they can probably get by with less sleep, surfing the Internet on sites you are not monitoring could lead to trouble. So as a compromise, you might agree to let them stay up later to read a book, play a game, etc., even though you are opposed to the idea, but hold the line and refuse them access to the computer.

We must take action whenever appropriate. When we can do something to alleviate the situation, we should do it. It is not productive to sit around waiting for lightning to strike. Worry can be paralyzing, and it is unfortunate that too often people sit and worry about something instead of analyzing the situation and taking steps to correct it. There may be a variety of things that can be done. We may be able to delegate responsibilities if we are overloaded or seek help from a friend. If we are in conflict, we may be able to call upon our colleagues for advice or if the situation is severe there are professionals in this area that could help. For example, the members of the American Institute of Stress[4] and psychologists trained in such areas as hypnosis, biofeedback, or cognitive behavioral therapy can provide much needed help when expert help is required. At a minimum we can discuss the problem with someone we can not only trust, but will have our best interest at heart. This action alone is normally an enormous emotional release.

Stress can produce paralysis that effectively blocks the mechanisms needed to relieve it. In this case, human help may seem inadequate. However, we always have at our disposal the Divine Physician, who knows us intimately and therefore is in the best position to prescribe a cure.

I have known people who have gone into a particular job, one in which they were not really interested, because their parents wanted them to do so. I am sure their parents had only the best of intentions; however, their parents did not have to work at this job at least eight hours a day. This can be very stressful and normally ends in disaster. If we don't like what we are doing for a living, if possible, get out, and do it as quickly as possible. If we can find a job that matches our talents and interests to the job requirements, we will not only minimize stress and other problems, but we will maximize success.

We need to accept the things over which we have no control. No control means exactly what it says—*we* can't do anything that impacts the problem. Therefore, any energy we expend in stewing about it simply goes up in heat and is detrimental to our health and well-being. When this type of problem arises, we just have to resign ourselves to the situation and go onto to something else. As children, we read the following Mother Goose rhyme that applies so well in this context.

---

4. See https://www.stress.org.

> For every ailment under the sun,
> There is a remedy or there is none;
> If there is one, try to find it;
> If there is none, never mind it.

Sometimes we are unable to cope because we refuse to let go of the past. We hang on for dear life, constantly reminding ourselves of our mistakes. In these cases, we must let go and let God. Jesus Christ died for all of our sins, and therefore we can always start fresh. Our Lord certainly wants us to recognize our mistakes, learn from them, but then cut them loose. If we continue to carry them, we make a mockery of his death.

We should learn from the past, plan for the future, but live, live, live today. The past is gone. We cannot change it. God only knows the future. The only thing we have for sure is today, so let's make the most of it. Press on, do our very best, and look back only to learn from our mistakes. George Washington and Abraham Lincoln practiced this philosophy and each commented on it. George Washington, the first President of the United States, states that

> We ought not to look back unless it is to derive useful lessons from past errors, and for the purpose of profiting by dear-bought experience.[5]

Abraham Lincoln, the sixteenth President of the United States, expressed the idea this way:

> If I were to try to read, much less answer, all the attacks made on me, this shop might as well be closed for any other business. I do the very best I know how—the very best I can; and I mean to keep on doing so until the end. If the end brings me out all right, then what is said against me won't matter. If the end brings me out wrong, then ten angels swearing I was right would make no difference.[6]

Instead of worrying about something, let's just be concerned. There is a big difference between these two terms. Worry is a tight feedback loop, and when we worry the stress level builds up and the situation deteriorates. Concern, on the other hand, can activate positive planning which can then lead to some action that will minimize or alleviate the situation. For example, I developed back problems as a teenager unloading

---

5. Washington, "We Ought Not to Look Back…"
6. Lincoln, "Quotable Quote."

food trucks for a grocery store where I worked parttime after school and on Saturdays. At that time, we were considered subhuman if we could not catch a one-hundred-pound sack of potatoes rolled off the truck. Soon after the problems developed I would run for exercise; however, this exercise aggravated my back problems, and I had to stop running and start walking. During this period my problem became so severe that it was dominating my life. Instead of worrying about my deteriorating condition, I consulted the athletic trainers at the university, an orthopedic surgeon, and colleagues who had similar problems. After distilling all this information, I determined that surgery was my best option. So, I signed up for back surgery with the best surgeon I could find. After surgery I developed a strict regimen of exercise that would strengthen my back and have followed it religiously. My back problems can easily be reinstituted if I forget and try to lift something that is too heavy. However, by acting decisively and developing a modus operandi that will help me stay out of pain, I have avoided more problems and remained basically pain-free. Unfortunately, some of my friends with similar problems have been back in surgery a couple of times and still must deal with pain on a daily basis with no end in sight.

We can improve our lives if we focus our thinking on the good things in our lives and maintain our perspective and a sense of humor. We have to work hard at being in a stressful condition while we are recounting the many blessings in our lives or while we are laughing. Since it is absolutely impossible for us to concentrate on two things at once, let's attack stress with two kinds of power; humor power and horsepower. During periods of stress, we will temporarily forget the stress if we can laugh. Anything that makes us laugh gives us a break from stress and improves our physical and mental condition. It is an excellent mental tonic. On the other hand, if we become consumed with our work or some other endeavor, e.g., a hobby, we will be unable to think about some conditions that cause stress. As the Irish playwright, George Bernard Shaw, has stated: "The secret of being miserable is to have the leisure to bother about whether you are happy or not."[7] Therefore, if we can pace ourselves and seek help when appropriate, we can do much to reduce, if not eliminate, the stress in our lives.

One of the most beautiful poems I have ever read is "God's Footprints" by Ken Brown. It resides permanently in my office at home, and is a tremendous source of comfort in times of stress.

---

7. Shaw, "Secret of Being Miserable..."

> One night in deepest sleep, I dreamed,
> Upon the beach I walked.
> The Lord was by my side each step
> As quietly we talked.
> Then on the sky my life was flashed;
> Each vision was serene.
> Two sets of footprints on the path
> Were there in every scene
> But then I noticed in some scenes
> Of suffering, pain, and strife,
> Just a single set of footprints
> At the worst times of my life.
> "God, You said You'd stay by me
> In good times and in bad.
> Why then did You leave me
> Each time my life was sad?"
> "My precious child," God answered,
> "When your life had pain, I knew;
> The *single* set of footprints
> were the times I *carried* you."[8]

Coping with Change

Throughout our lives, the one constant is change. Sounds like a weird statement doesn't it? And yet with only a moment's reflection we realize how true it is. Change affects every aspect of our lives, and it is an ongoing phenomenon which we will typically encounter every day. Our biological structure is continually changing. We are affected by worldwide political and economic factors, our families, our jobs, and the weather, i.e., everything seems to be in a constant state of flux. It appears that every year the pace at which we live seems to quicken, and change seems to accelerate. One need only consider the advances that have been made in the phones we use to see just how fast things can change. The new phones are like computers with dual processors which can load apps that can do some absolutely amazing things. And more technology is added with each additional model which seems to come out annually. While young people adapt to the enormous changes that occur on a regular basis in the development of smartphones, older people have problems adapting. Many seniors typically use the device solely for the purpose

---

8. Brown and Brown, "In Deepest Sleep..."

of making a phone call. They are not even aware of what appears to be a list of endless changes that enhance the capability of the phone. These changes are embedded in the device or available to them via the Internet or Bluetooth technology, which supports a wide spectrum of uses that involve exchanging data between fixed and mobile devices, e.g., controlling smart locks or thermostats in their homes.

These types of changes and ones that are similar will continue to affect everything that we do. As a result, it is increasingly more difficult to maintain a stable position on terra firma. Therefore, in order to cope, we must learn to live effectively and comfortably in what is normally a chaotic world.

Although changes come in a variety of forms and in a wide range of intensities, from a personal standpoint, they seem to fall into one of two categories: those that we initiate ourselves and those that are forced upon us. Improving the status quo and solving problems are perhaps the dominant reasons why we initiate some change. For example, we may move to a different house or change jobs.

Changes we are forced to address are often more difficult to deal with, because we may have little or no control of the situation. In our efforts to succeed and win, failure or loss is a constant companion. In order to achieve anything, we must typically take risks, and if we take risks, there is always a finite probability we will fail. Therefore, change shadows our every move in our efforts to succeed.

The impact that change has upon us seems to be critically dependent upon our ability to deal with it and adapt to it. It is not surprising that our ability to cope is further dependent upon one additional factor—age. The young people of today have grown up in a time of rapid change, and therefore change is a familiar part of their environment. Their level of responsibility is typically low, and they have what appears to be an entire life time ahead of them to recover from any potentially catastrophic change. However, older people find themselves in quite a different situation. They typically have less time and energy to recover, and their level of responsibility is normally high. Hence, the loss of a job or a substantial portion of their savings, for example, may have some rather terrible consequences.

The manner in which we cope with change usually spells the difference between success and failure, and the three primary mechanisms with which we cope are a proper attitude, an ability to seize control, and the knowledge that Almighty God is with us. With a positive attitude, we are normally more resilient to any change. There is often some way to benefit from any change, and when it can be viewed as an opportunity and not a problem, there is the possibility that we can turn the lemon into a lemonade. A positive attitude tends to eliminate fear which can be absolutely devastating, because it incapacitates us and thus prevents us from bouncing back. However, our ability to adapt to change with change is an extremely important antidote. By simply adjusting our thinking to view changes from a broader perspective, we can concentrate on positive, rather than negative, aspects, thereby achieving the best in any situation. By continuing to focus our attention on our goals, we tend to minimize or ignore negative implications. For example, a woman after giving birth focuses upon the child and not the pain she has endured to bring her new baby into the world. Because the baby is so important, the pain must take a back seat.

We can always cope better if we can somehow step in and take control. In this mode we always have options, and therefore after carefully considering each of them, we can develop a method of attack. The key to an effective attack is constructive planning. The overall plan can be subdivided into short-term goals, which give us confidence as we progress. In addition, at each stage we can assess the tradeoffs which, in turn, focus our attack. Every goal typically has both positive and negative consequences, and we can achieve almost anything if we are willing to pay the price.

Suppose, for example, that we wish to accept a promotion in our company which would involve not only an increase in salary, but a move to another city. While we may view this move as an excellent opportunity, our family may not share our enthusiasm. In fact, our children may be completely hostile to the change. Moves are typically difficult for teenagers because they don't want to leave their friends. However, we can minimize the hostility and make the transition as smooth as possible if we carefully prepare every aspect of the move. For example, we can begin as early as possible ordering materials from the Chamber of Commerce, talking to people who have lived there or have family or friends that reside there. In addition, we can examine brochures with maps and pictures that describe living conditions, such as housing, weather, and the recreational activities afforded the people who live in the area. Once we have gathered and disseminated as much data as possible, then we can take the family there for a close inspection and examination. While there, we can meet with people in the schools and churches, as well as see houses and recreational facilities that are of interest to the family. If possible, it would be helpful to meet the families of people with whom we will work, and generally learn the area as best we can in the time available. Then when the move actually occurs, the family will adjust more easily to the change, because they are now moving to an environment with which they are quite familiar. In many cases such as this there is no silver bullet. We simply take every opportunity at our disposal to minimize the downside.

We may encounter change through some failure on our part. When this happens, if we deal with it in a positive and constructive manner, we can emerge from it a much wiser and more capable individual. If we perform a very honest analysis of the situation, assess what happened so that it is not repeated, determine what we can learn from it that will make us a better person, and if possible, find a way to correct it, we will eventually be successful. Winston Churchill, the former British Prime Minister, put it very succinctly when he said, "Success is going from failure to failure without loss of enthusiasm."[9] And Henry Ford, an American captain of industry and founder of the Ford Motor Company, put it this way: "Failure is simply the opportunity to begin again, this time more intelligently."[10]

Although there are literally numerous examples of failures leading to success by dealing with it in a constructive manner, perhaps one of the most profound, as we have indicated earlier, is the experience of Thomas Edison. He failed a thousand times in trying to invent the electric light bulb. Far fewer failures would discourage most people, but not Edison. He simply believed that it took that many steps to achieve success.

It is important to note that change leads to stress. This should not be a surprising phenomenon, since for many people, any disruption in the status quo can produce uncertainty and have consequences, some of which are central to a person's self-worth with far-reaching implications. For example, positive change, e.g., marriage, or negative change, e.g., divorce, can each cause physiological stress responses. When viewed from an organizational perspective, change can lead to feelings of anger, anxiety, betrayal, and vulnerability, to name a few. Leaders must be acutely aware of the implications that change can have in their organization and be prepared to address these issues up front in a positive and empathetic manner in order to minimize its effect.

9. Churchill, "Success Is Going from Failure..."
10. Ford, "Failure Is Simply the Opportunity..."

Finally, even though we may feel that the track upon which Almighty God has placed us seems to have a lot of high hurdles, it is our knowledge that he is with us every step of the way that is a most important ingredient in our ability to cope with change. God is constantly moving us forward, and regardless of how difficult change may seem, we have God's assurance that he will not place upon us a burden we cannot bear. The constant unfolding process of change in which we live, leads us to good. As stated in Philippians 3:13–14,

> forgetting what lies behind but straining forward to what lies ahead, I continue my pursuit toward the goal, the prize of God's upward calling, in Christ Jesus.

God is our anchor. When we turn to him in times of change for guidance, courage and strength, and then place our trust in him, he translates changes into blessings which show us the way to new ideas, new opportunities, and new prosperity. Therefore, we can approach change with great anticipation, secure in the knowledge that they are God-planned, God-directed, and therefore perfectly timed in accordance with the good he has in store for us.

Dealing with Adversity

In dealing with this topic, we should follow the advice of Pythagoras, the Greek philosopher and mathematician, who said, "Rest satisfied with doing well and leave others to talk of you as they please."[11]

Regardless of our position in this world, one of the hardest things we have to do is deal with adversity. Although none of us are immune from it, those who seem to catch the most flak are typically those people who get their heads above the crowd. The higher your head is above the crowd, the harder the wind blows, and when someone stabs you in the back, it is probably because you are out in front.

Adversity comes in all sizes and many forms. For example, your boss may micromanage your work. Perhaps you have refused to loan some individual something, or do someone's work for them because they insisted it was your responsibility. You may encounter people who are jealous of your position or accomplishments. If you have supervisory responsibilities, you may experience considerable adversity with people

---

11. Pythagoras, "Rest Satisfied with Doing Well..."

you have had to discipline, e.g., tenured professors. Just refusing to write a letter of recommendation for someone can lead to problems. There are myriad ways in which adversity can play a part in our lives, and of course adversity leads to—stress. This is unfortunately a common theme, and the adversity-stress connection is all too common.

I never cease to be amazed at some people in an organization who cannot find the time to work, but seem to have an incredible amount of time for minding my business or disrupting the organization in some manner. These disruptors are easily spotted and typically come in three sizes: regular, giant, and jumbo.

The regular disruptor is out of step with an incredibly large percentage of the population in an organization; however, it is okay because they may not be correct, but they are never in doubt. Individuals of this sort would rather be critical than correct. Instead of working hard to catch up to their colleagues, they devote their talents and energy to tearing their colleagues down to their size. They have no interest in positive actions, and while working with you, will simply look for your weaknesses and then attempt to exploit them. Their goals are usually negative, and they enjoy witnessing someone else go belly up. The notches on their guns represent the number of bodies they leave in their wake. Other than these typical characteristics, the regular disrupter has no special credentials. Thank God, most organizations eliminate these individuals whenever possible.

The giant disrupter is a more formidable adversary. Because of his position, he is much more difficult to deal with. Typical examples of giant disrupters are those individuals who operate like the regular disrupter, but in addition are owners of the organization, their relatives or close friends, or a government employee with so much seniority that they would be the last to go in any reduction in force or a tenured teacher. These individuals are fairly well protected, and in general, some not only hide behind it, but use it to their advantage.

While the giant disrupter can be a powerful force to reckon with, the potential of the jumbo disrupter is truly awesome. These individuals possess many of the features we have just described, but in addition, they are a religious fanatic. The Ten Commandments were not given to Moses, they were given to them, and therefore their interpretation is the only correct one. If you become their target because they dislike you or something you have done, they will bad-mouth you every chance they get by dumping poison about you to essentially everyone they meet. It is apparently their way of being a good Christian! For the life of me, I can't imagine what Bible they read, because mine speaks of God's love, mercy, and forgiveness.

Disrupters usually have an axe to grind. However, this is their problem. Confident and competent people do not tear down someone else in order to build themselves up. Disrupters appear to have something missing in their lives, and hence these people are to be pitied rather than despised. They are managing to waste one lifetime—their own, so don't let them waste another—yours. Simple economics or top management can normally be effective in negating the impact of a regular or sometimes giant size disrupter. Jumbos on the other hand, are difficult to control with anything short of dismissal.

From a leadership standpoint, we should do our best to make these disrupters as productive as possible. However, in this environment it is difficult to succeed with them every time. If we carefully study these individuals and their work habits, we may be able to learn things that will help us to work more effectively with them, to help them find their niche, and hopefully to excel in it. This exercise is unfortunately often like raising children. No one is trained for this act. We all ride the maiden voyage, and by the time we learn how to handle the situation correctly, it is too late, they are gone, and the cycle repeats.

The positive approach is the preferred way to address problems. However, when the individual refuses to respond to our best efforts, then we must bite the bullet. As Helen Keller, an American author, has stated, "The best way out is always through."[12]

When complaining or requesting corrective action, we can take one of two tacks depending upon the history of the particular situation. If the individual has done a good job in the past but recent performance is not up to par, we should first try to determine the cause of the current poor performance, devise a plan to correct it, and provide positive encouragement. However, if the individual with whom we are dealing is either a chronic problem or the type who will interpret any positive statement as a signal that everything is really okay regardless of what else is said, we must be very careful in the manner in which we address the issues. These disrupters often keep files which contain material that can either be used against someone else or for the purpose of protecting their own hides. These files, which may provide the exact location of the errors and offenses of others, may be useful to them if they are faced with dismissal

---

12. Keller, "Famous Quote From: Helen Keller."

or lawsuits. In general, this data collection process is easy for them because they don't waste a lot of time doing positive and productive work. Faced with these types of situations, while being as kind as possible, we may have to dismiss these disruptive, nonproductive workers. It is very important to deal with these individuals in this manner because they are like a cancer in the organization which could be transmitted to others, and in turn serve to exacerbate the problem.

There are so many situations where failure to bite the bullet at the earliest opportunity can mean that we have to chew it for the rest of our lives. Placing ourselves in a bad situation that seems endless can result in stress and often a lot of it, which in turn can lead to health problems, some of which can be devastating.

Only in rare circumstances is it easy for us to deal with adversity, and yet we find that we must often deal with it on a regular basis. We soon learn that we derive peace, not from the absence of conflict, but from our ability to cope with it. As the noted theologian, Reinhold Niebuhr, has stated:

> God grant me the serenity to accept the things I cannot change, the courage to change the things I can, and the wisdom to know the difference.[13]

Learning to Play the Power Game

There are basically two approaches to power; one is positive and constructive, and the other is negative and destructive. The most powerful people are winners most of the time, survivors all of the time, and smart enough to learn from their mistakes. These people possess an intangible quality through which people work effectively in concert with one another to accomplish some goal. They understand that responsibility is an integral part of power, and therefore they must enforce discipline; however, they do so effortlessly with an air of charm and grace. They have a knack for predicting how people will react to a given situation and through this somewhat clairvoyant quality, they are able to convince the troops that their goals are worthwhile and worth working for. They are self-confident, have industrial strength guts, and yet transmit power through people without making servants of them. They know that politeness is not a sign of weakness and that ambition and brutality do not

13. Niebuhr, "God Grant Me the Serenity..."

necessarily go hand-in-hand. Unfortunately, there are people who have somehow reached positions of power and never learned these things. We may get many things from these people, but what we really need is something very special—protection.

Damage prevention in a power action requires not only an understanding of the facets and ramifications that are the basis for the action, but a knowledge of how to effectively combat it. Although the hallmark of power is control, nowhere is it more visible than when people employ it to manipulate anything and everything at their disposal to get whatever they want. For these people, power is an intoxicant, the ultimate high. They have to have it, and once they have it they have to use it. The fundamental instrument in the exercise of power is fear. They make intimidation an art form to exploit another's insecurities. Some roam their territory like an efficient predator, often leaving carnage in their wake. They simply must control; and via this mechanism they achieve and conquer regardless of the consequences. In the extreme case, they will symbolically make us an offer we can't refuse with a veiled threat that a refusal from us would immediately trigger devastating consequences for us.

The *position* power that the individual possesses is a result of *what* we say that he is. For example, he may be president, manager, officer, doctor, lawyer, parent, teacher, etc. It is because of his position that he possesses authority and power. Such an individual may do such things as supervise people, allocate money, distribute materials, or enforce laws. This power, when used as a weapon, can be employed at home, the office, the club, the store, or wherever. Every place presents an enormous number of combinations of inputs and responses which are possible in the power game. The more ruthless the individual, the more havoc that can be wreaked from even placid situations.

It is unfortunate and indeed tragic that some power players feel compelled to operate in a negative mode. Their approach, which is completely out of phase with a positive, upbeat, forward-looking attitude, is often self-serving and generally lacks sensitivity and compassion for others. While it is distasteful to even discuss the manner in which these people operate, nevertheless, from a realistic standpoint, we must be able to detect and understand their actions in order to survive and even, perhaps, flourish in their environment.

In the work environment, power applied in a negative fashion can range from the ridiculous to the sublime and take any one of a number of different forms. For example, we may be shocked by someone's sudden irrational behavior, and in order to establish some form of normality, give in to his demands. We may be embarrassed by someone who, while withholding critical data, carefully leads us out on the end of a limb and then proceeds to methodically saw it off behind us. Or he may simply ask us no-win questions in public, such as "Are you still beating your wife?" I believe that some of the news media personnel have developed this tactic into a precise science.

In a display of power, some people always come late to meetings. In this manner they may completely ruin your schedule, but after all, that may have been their plan in the first place. Others will camouflage data so we can't understand it. They now have the facts, and all we have is an opinion. A manager may set unrealistic goals for an individual and then grind them into the carpet for failure to meet them. Some managers will provoke a confrontation just so they can flex their muscles in our face or create catastrophes by turning some slight problem of ours into a monumental calamity.

While some of these power exercises are blatant, others are quite subtle. For example, some people simply wonder about things. They wonder how the organization will function if the budget is cut by 20 percent. They wonder if the organization will be viable if they lose 10 percent of their personnel. Although their comments have absolutely no factual basis whatsoever, before they are through wondering, everyone within the organization is in a state of alarm anticipating imminent disaster.

I recall going to talk to an individual once who had a special chair for visitors alongside his desk. When I sat in the chair, I was practically reclining at a forty-five-degree angle and the seat was low to the floor. In this orientation, I was looking almost straight up at him, and he, in turn, was looking right down my throat. Although the man never said a harsh word, sitting in that subservient position made me feel very uncomfortable.

In order to insulate ourselves from the power plays that may be occurring around us, we must be prepared. At the very least we must understand our environment; what are the rules, personalities, forces, and risks that are involved. The more thoroughly we understand the nature of all the power relationships that can potentially impact us, the better prepared we are to operate effectively and securely within our surroundings. An understanding of what makes someone tick is often a prerequisite for developing an effective working relationship. In addition, at the outset we must recognize that the negative use of power is much too often a sign of insecurity, and in the extreme, paranoia.

Within any organization there is an information network and it pays not only to know the sources, but to ensure that you are one of the nodes on the network. With a true knowledge of the true power structure, which may in fact bear little or no resemblance to the actual organizational structure, we are able to recognize the difference between real power and simulated, or what is typically the illusion of, power. For example, I recall, that before the fall of the Soviet Union, Mikhail Gorbachev was unquestionably the most powerful person in the USSR. And what was his title? He was the general secretary of the Communist Party. Wait a minute—he's a what? A secretary of a party. This man who could wield enormous power with a worldwide presence is only a secretary! What about the president of the USSR? Most people didn't know who this individual was, and they didn't care, because he apparently had very little power.

When being confronted in a power play, there are a variety of tactics that can be employed to minimize the damage. If we are shrewd but congenial, we can often deflect the arrows that are aimed at us and in some cases even turn them one hundred and eighty degrees. For example, if we are under attack for some position we have taken on a particular issue, we can begin writing memoranda stating our position and the logic behind it, and send them to our boss with copies to everyone we deem appropriate. If there are no serious flaws in our analysis, we may generate a number of other people who think like we do. In fact, they may be able to add to our list of supportive arguments. This approach will tend to "head them off at the pass" or at least help to diffuse the force and thereby minimize its impact.

When asked a question designed to put us on the spot, we can answer the question with a question. If my boss assigns me a task and then asks when I will have it done, I can provide a date, or I can ask them for a date when they actually have to have it done. The latter approach should force the boss to name a date they can realistically defend. If the boss wants it too early, then he may appear to be someone who is incapable of doing his own job.

Another approach involves the use of the old cliché, "If you can't lick 'em, join 'em." In fact, when possible, call them and raise them. If the boss tells us that our work is sloppy, but we know this is not true and are convinced we are being jerked around, don't argue, agree. Then point out to the boss how the entire office is a mess. The facilities are old; the lighting is poor; the computers are ancient; there is an insufficient supply of paper, pens, and pencils; and the reproduction machines are lousy. If we can back up these statements and we handle this process very adroitly, we can go a long way toward convincing the boss that the entire office is substandard. Under these poor working conditions, we are certainly not out of line; however, the boss is in charge, and therefore, it is at least possible that the boss isn't doing his job well either.

These tactics and some like them may or may not work depending upon the circumstances. In some cases, they may work just fine and in others not at all. However, when we are convinced that we are being treated unfairly, it is worthwhile to look for ways to deflect the attack or at least minimize its impact.

We have to always remember that the real power that an individual enjoys is critically dependent upon the respect that everyone has for him. While there is, in general, a strict chain of command for directives and policies within an organization, the flow of information can completely circumvent that chain. The flow of information may take some rather devious paths; however, as a general rule, it is not difficult to get information from the shop floor to the upper management, completely bypassing the chain of command. Therefore, if the boss is a real problem, this message can be transmitted up, too. The threat of good people leaving the organization or some other action that threatens productivity may not result in the removal of the problem individual, but it will certainly tend to keep him in check.

Perhaps the best defense against position power is a good offense called *personal* power. In sharp contrast to position power, personal power is *who* we are. Our personal power resides in the culmination of all the personal qualities we possess, e.g., our integrity, self-confidence, positive mental attitude, judgement, ability to work effectively with others, competence in our work, the ability to turn the lemon into a lemonade, and empathy for our colleagues. Personal power is a state of mind and spirit, and as a result it is an ageless asset.

There is incredible power in being good at what we do and trying to do the right thing. As a case in point, consider what came to be known as Irangate in the summer of 1987. Congress held hearings on the diversion of funds from arms sales to Iran to the Contra Freedom Fighters in Nicaragua, which was in direct violation of the Boland Amendment. In what the television ratings at one point proved to be the best soap opera at the time, witnesses were paraded before a committee composed of representatives from both the House and the Senate. The central figure in the investigation was Marine Lt. Col. Oliver North, who was the action man on the National Security Council staff. Ollie, as he came to be known, could "make it happen," and it was he who orchestrated the whole operation. Whether you agree or disagree with what he did is not the issue here. What is interesting from the present perspective is an analysis of the power play that took place. On one side was Lt. Colonel North and his attorney, Brendan V. Sullivan Jr. Colonel North appeared in his uniform with an array of medals and ribbons on his chest. He was neat and clean and looked like a red-blooded all-American boy. On the other side were the distinguished members of the House and Senate Investigative Committees with their counsels. This array of Congressmen represented some of the most influential and powerful people in the United States. Ollie and his attorney were outnumbered at least ten to one. From the outset, many people believed that the main objective of the whole opera was simply to provide the Democrats with an opportunity to find some mechanism to "knock off" one of the most popular Presidents in recent history, who just happened to be a Republican. Whether this is an accurate portrayal of the proceedings or not, the questioning of Colonel North certainly gave credence to that philosophy. However, in the interrogation of Colonel North, some of our national leaders forgot something—they forgot to be polite. It would not have cost them anything. They could have asked the same questions. Instead, to many who watched the proceedings, the interrogators appeared to be mean-spirited and totally unprofessional in their questioning. The whole tone of the questioning appeared to be "Let's give this guy a fair hearing and then take him out and hang him."

On the other hand, Colonel North admitted that he had diverted funds to the Contra operation, but argued that he believed that he was following the wishes of his superiors and doing what he believed was in the best interest of the United States. It appeared that he truly believed that he was doing the right thing, and while his critics might have been appalled at what he had done, they had to admit that he was an ardent patriot and an extremely capable individual.

As the power play developed before a national television audience, Colonel North skillfully answered the questions in such a way that Congress was depicted as wishy-washy and apathetic, while he in turn was simply supporting God, motherhood, freedom, and the best interests of the United States. There were clearly many people in the country who were absolutely dismayed by his actions. However, his performance before Congress struck a resonant chord in a large segment of the American people and the resultant nationwide support he received was incredible. "Ollie Mania" became a phenomenon. He started receiving fan mail and letters of support. People started collecting money for his defense. At one point, a group blacked out the letter "H" in the huge sign overlooking Hollywood California so that it read "Ollywood". Letters to national magazines referenced our pompous politicians and called Ollie a precious national resource. The leaders at large US corporations wrote to the *Wall Street Journal* stating that they would be very pleased to have someone like Colonel North on their staff, and an undertone supporting a Presidential pardon quickly began developing. It was an outstanding example of personal power that struck the inner core of the hearts and minds of millions of Americans.

In mid-September of 2020 another excellent example of personal power was exhibited on the national stage when Justice Ruth Bader Ginsberg died. President Trump was then given the opportunity to nominate a third member of the Supreme Court. The speculation surrounding Justice Ginsberg's successor began immediately. Within what appeared to be a matter of hours, the focus zeroed in on Judge Amy Coney Barrett. Although she had never served as a judge prior to 2017, in that year President Trump asked her to leave her position as a law professor at the University of Notre Dame to be nominated for the US Court of Appeals for the Seventh Circuit.

In filling the Supreme Court vacancy, President Trump had said that he would like to nominate a woman, and there were about a half-dozen excellent candidates. However, as a result of her national prominence achieved in the confirmation hearings for the Seventh Circuit, Judge Barrett quickly became the front-runner. In Judge Barrett President Trump had one of the most brilliant and battle-tested jurists in the nation, having only recently survived the hearings for the seventh circuit. She was for many reasons an ideal candidate. She had impeccable credentials, a record of outstanding achievements and a towering intellect. She had graduated first in her class at Notre Dame Law, which was also significant since the sitting justices of the Supreme Court were all Ivy League graduates. She served as a law clerk for Justice Antonin Scalia and served with distinction as a professor at Notre Dame. Following her tenure at Notre Dame, she went on to become one of the most respected federal appellate judges in the country. She was a Catholic mother of seven, two of whom were adopted from Haiti and another one with Down's Syndrome, and she was unapologetically pro-life.

When Judge Barrett's nomination became official, the Democratic Party and the liberal media that has for years operated as the party's marketing wing went apoplectic and with good reason. First of all, Senate Republicans announced they had the votes to confirm President Trump's nominee. Second, Judge Barrett was viewed by many to be the polar opposite of Justice Ginsberg.

Before the hearings had even begun, the onslaught of attacks began on late night TV shows. Judge Barrett belonged to a group called "People of Praise," which the liberal news media appeared to classify as a cult. Organizations like Planned Parenthood, the National Organization for Women, NARAL and the ACLU joined the battle immediately. However, with the hearings of Justice Kavanaugh still clearly in mind, Senator John Kennedy from Louisiana said in essence that he hoped that these hearings would not degenerate into the "freak show" that characterized the Kavanaugh hearings.

While Senator Kennedy's comments could have been prophetic, the hearings did not turn out to be a "freak show." As the hearings unfolded, Judge Barrett's demeanor was calm, cooperative, and peaceful. While the Democratic Senators meticulously crawled over notes to read their questions, Judge Barrett sat on the hot seat with *no* notes. Every question was answered clearly and concisely, except the ones pertaining to possible cases to come before the court in the future, which she refused to answer by quoting what came to be known as the Ginsburg rule, i.e., no hints, no previews, no forecasts. While the Democrats were content to let Justice Ginsburg use the rule, they found it completely inappropriate for Judge Barrett to apply it. Although Judge Barrett stated that she wanted to be forthright and answer every question as best she could, she would follow Justice Elena Kagan's comment during her confirmation hearings and would not grade precedent or give a thumbs up or a thumbs down.

The key issues for the Democrats were of course well-known in advance. All they wanted was someone on the Supreme Court who would, among other things, preserve the right to an abortion, save Obamacare, eliminate the Second Amendment, and support gay marriage. With that agenda in mind, Judge Barrett's nomination must have been absolutely terrifying.

As the Democrats launched their attacks, much of which was designed to appease their base, they went after Judge Barrett's faith again, having already done so in her hearings for the Seventh Circuit, in spite of the fact that such consideration is unconstitutional. In a full-blown attack

Looking out for Numero Uno

on her family they even looked into the Haitian adoption proceedings to see if procedure was followed, in order to find something, anything that could damage her nomination. Judge Barrett knew that this process would be distasteful and excruciating, but she and her family chose to endure it because of their belief in the rule of law and their desire to be of service to the nation.

Although several days had been set aside for the hearings, they could have been concluded in short order if Judge Barrett had pledged unwavering support for abortion and Obamacare, was willing to criticize the Second Amendment and support gay rights and open borders, prior to the hearings. However, abortion was the Democratic litmus test, and Judge Barrett was on record opposing this ruling. This fact alone caused the pro-abortionists to oppose her nomination. After all, how could someone with seven kids, two of whom were adopted, support abortion? In addition, the fact that the two adopted kids were black also meant the race card, which is always a favorite in the Democratic deck, was essentially useless. Furthermore, she admitted to owning a gun. It is interesting to speculate just what the Democrats on the committee believed they could accomplish going into the hearings facing someone of her enormous stature with outstanding credentials.

However, the Democrats were not without plenty of firepower. They had the liberal news media, which could be counted on to provide only the Democratic Party's view of any issue and distort the facts to make them look legitimate, if necessary. The Democrats also had social media, i.e., Twitter and Facebook. In fact, Congress is exploring the monopolistic power of these platforms because these communication tools are not only very effective but they can unilaterally block any information from appearing on their sites that does not support the Democratic Party's position. With all this formidable support, the Democrats lacked one key ingredient: the Senate votes, and of course they were the only thing that mattered for the ultimate outcome.

In order to demonstrate to the Democratic base that they were fully committed to using the hearing to inflict as much damage as possible, not only on Judge Barrett but President Trump as well, they asked the same question from different perspectives in an attempt to catch Judge Barrett with conflicting answers. When they could not get any traction on the trick questions, which were typically political and had absolutely nothing to do with legal philosophy, it became clear that they were dealing with someone who exuded personal power and was much too smart to fall into one of their traps. At that point, the questioning took an unbelievable turn when Senator Mazie Hirono asked Judge Barrett if she had sexually assaulted anyone. The question was not only outrageous, but in fact ridiculous, since such behavior if found by the Democratic detectives would have already been on the liberal news media twenty-four-seven nonstop.

In what must have been an act of total desperation in their inability to even create a sliver of doubt that this was an extraordinarily capable candidate who would indeed be confirmed, the Democrats began immediately threatening to pack the Supreme Court, give statehood to Washington, DC and Puerto Rico, as well as anything else they could think of which would ensure that they would be in control forever. It was clear that they would lose this battle, and there was nothing they could do about it. So, rather than operate as disappointed professionals, they resorted to other tactics. At one point, Senator Schumer stated that if Judge Barrett's nomination went forward, he would go nuclear and said "nothing is off the table next year." When that threat was treated as a hot air balloon, he tried numerous tactics to shut down the Senate in an effort to derail the confirmation. Since Judge Barrett's qualifications were undeniable and the Democrats were careful never to address them, it became clear that the Democrats simply wanted someone who would produce the political results they wanted.

There were polls taken during the hearings and they indicated that support for Judge Barrett kept rising as the week progressed and this increase was found among Democrats, Republicans, and Independents. In fact, even the late Justice Ginsburg's clerks agreed that Judge Barrett was "a woman of remarkable intellect and character."

In spite of their losing position, the Democrats should have come away from the hearings satisfied that Justice Barrett would approach all cases with an open mind and set aside her religious beliefs in making decisions. She clearly stated that in every case she would follow the law and the rules that bind justices. After all, it is the Senators, not the Supreme Court justices, who make the law.

In the final analysis, Judge Barrett's combination of intellectual power, an outstanding record of achievements, an impeccable personal history, and a virtual army of people praying for her, was just too much for the Democrats to circumvent or overcome. As Judiciary Chairman Lindsey Graham stated, Judge Barrett had not only "punch[ed] through a glass ceiling, but a reinforced concrete barrier."

Her nomination was voted out of the Senate Judiciary Committee on October 22, 2020 and confirmed by the full Senate on a vote of 52 to 48 on October 26, 2020.

While we may have seen personal power employed by others in a number of situations, the most important thing about it is that each of us has it. As a general rule, and I don't think there are many exceptions, each of us can do something better than anyone else, and we bring our personal power to bear in an optimum manner when we match our talents and interests to the job.

An important and often extremely critical element of our personal power is judgement. We must be able to correctly assess any situation and the surrounding circumstances in order to determine an effective strategy in which to operate. If we misjudge our environment or the forces active within it, our plans may be doomed from the outset. As a case in point, consider President Reagan's nomination of Judge Robert Bork to replace Justice Lewis Powell as an associate justice of the Supreme Court in the summer of 1987. In Judge Robert Bork, the Republican administration had one of the most brilliant jurists in the nation with impeccable credentials. He was a conservative and therefore presented President Reagan with an opportunity to overhaul some of the nation's liberal policies. Justice Lewis Powell, on the other hand, was a moderate who might vote either way on close decisions.

When Judge Bork was nominated, the political prognosticators believed that he would indeed prevail, but not without a fight. The administration, however, made some rather damaging tactical errors, but more importantly, they completely misjudged the entire situation. Looking back at the situation from a historical standpoint, it appears that the Republicans should have known early that this nomination was in serious trouble, if not absolutely unwinnable. Although the Democrats had warned President Reagan upfront that they would produce a solid block against Bork's nomination, what had to be one of the most damaging events was Democratic Senator Ted Kennedy's speech on the Senate floor which summarily condemned Judge Bork in front of a nationally televised audience. This was a textbook example of personal power. Although Judge Bork denied Senator Kennedy's accusations, it did not seem to matter. The speech was extremely effective and in a sense represented the first nail in Judge Bork's odyssey.

As the battle for confirmation evolved, his opposition managed to package him in such a way that even the conservative right-wingers would not support him. In addition, the Republicans misjudged the new Southern politician who, to a large extent, had been placed in the marble swamp by black votes. Furthermore, they failed to realize that even the white voters were unwilling to address once more the civil rights issues.

The Republican's ineptness in the process was met by an opposition that had a different and quite formidable agenda. The civil rights, labor, and pro-women organizations threw everything against Judge Bork. Much of the rhetoric was undoubtedly exaggerated, but they covered him with bad news like Kudzu covers Alabama. Millions of dollars were spent on ad campaigns opposing him, and before the liberal interest's groups and lobbyists were finished, they managed to place in the minds of our citizens the thought that Judge Bork was essentially somehow akin to a villain.

Judgement was the key, and the lack of it in this case meant that the Republican Administration was outgunned and outflanked. Their failure to correctly assess the situation even prevented them from administering an antidote. Any attempt was for them unfortunately not retroactive; it was too late and the die was cast. The situation deteriorated quickly into a fiasco on a roll call vote of forty-two to fifty-eight.

If we have great personal power, we are practically invulnerable to someone who is operating from position power. The person using position power may be able to wound us in some way, but is absolutely impossible to strike a critical or fatal blow. Ironically, personal power is not only the engine that propels us forward to accomplish our desires and goals, it is also a shield that protects us from adversity.

The more of the very best of ourselves that we can apply in any situation, the less we abdicate to someone else who, by employing position power, tries to make us less than we are. For example, if we are an excellent accountant, bricklayer, carpenter, salesman, teacher, or whatever, those who supervise our activities have very little power over us. Whether we realize it or not, as a general rule, the success of our boss is tightly coupled to our own. It is virtually impossible for them to be successful unless the people in their organization are successful, and every astute leader is well aware of this fact. Every time I think of this coupling relationship, I am reminded of the statue I have seen of two nude Greek wrestlers. One of them, who appears to be in control, is holding the other horizontally over his head. From this position he can obviously throw the other wrestler in any direction. However, he has this pained expression of uncertainty on his face, because the other wrestler is holding him by the testicles.

If we are really good at what we do, the organization needs us and we are a real asset to it. If the leadership of the organization is not smart enough to understand and appreciate our worth, then more than likely we are better off elsewhere. If we do not give others permission to intimidate us, they cannot do it. It is impossible to be intimidated unless we allow it, and people who know they are good at what they do, never permit it. Interestingly, position power, as a general rule, can be taken from us. However, our personal power, which has been given to us by Almighty God, is inherent in our being; we have it at all times and can apply it in any relationship.

People who employ their personal power simply expect great things to happen and, in general, they do. At our very best we are awesome, and it is critically important that we not only realize this potential, but apply it in our daily lives to every relationship and every situation.

Building a Strong Faith

Consider the following quote from Hebrews 11:1: "Faith is the realization of what is hoped for and evidence of things not seen." Faith is a spiritual force and as such often appears as a mystery. Because of its nature, we may not completely understand it, nor is it necessary that we do so. It is only important that we know beyond any doubt that it is a force of enormous potential and that it works. Thomas Aquinas, philosopher and priest, says the following:

> To one who has faith, no explanation is necessary. To one without faith, no explanation is possible.[14]

Faith has both active and passive components. When used in the active mode, we take the appropriate action to ensure that all the conditions are right to bring about some event in our lives, i.e., we do everything *we* can do to make it happen. The passive component of our faith is composed of both perseverance and patience. We continue to press on in spite of any obstacles, and we have the patience to wait for the perfect time for Almighty God to act. Richard M. Devos, an American billionaire and co-founder of Amway, stated it very simply when he said,

---

14. Aquinas, "To One Who Has Faith..."

> The only thing that stands between a man and what he wants from life is often merely the will to try it and the faith to believe that it is possible.[15]

Although faith is an inherent quality which, like a muscle, gets stronger the more we use it, its genesis for each of us, typically lies in the great trials we encounter throughout our lives.

God has made us like palm trees. We can whip in the wind of the hurricanes of life, even to the point that we are doubled over; however, as long as our roots are firmly based in faith, we cannot be swept away. It is only when we permit the worldly forces to weaken our grip that the tentacles of faith tear loose, and we tumble with every strong external impulse. Faith is a force of unimaginable power, and therefore if we really work for something and have faith, we will find a way to make it happen.

It is through faith that we connect our minds and hearts with the awesome power of the Almighty and through prayer that we communicate to him our needs. We can be certain and confident, because of our faith, that Almighty God will hear us and provide us with the good that we request. As stated in Matthew 21:22, "Whatever you ask for in prayer with faith, you will receive."

Through the Almighty power and presence of God, we are capable of absolutely amazing accomplishments. When we deny all doubt and adopt the passage from Philippians 4:13, "I have the strength for everything through Him who empowers me," that which we affirm over and over through faith is inextricably drawn to us. The stronger our faith, the more powerful is the magnetic effect. Matthew 17:20 states it well in the following passage:

> I say to you, if you have faith the size of a mustard seed, you will say to this mountain "Move from here to there," and it will move. Nothing will be impossible for you.

In order to achieve our desires through faith, we must work in concert with Almighty God. His miracle-working power in the spiritual realm is channeled through, and works in conjunction with, our human endeavors. When we have traveled along the straight and narrow path of obedience and gone the last mile to the limits of our ability, then we can turn to Almighty God and know beyond any doubt that he will do what is best for us.

---

15. Devos, "The Only Thing That Stands..."

When Moses led his people out of Egypt, he found himself caught between the Red Sea and the advancing Egyptian Army. He had followed God's orders to the letter, but now with no visible means of escape he was helpless to do more. He had done all that he could do. It was now time for Almighty God, the God of Moses and us all, to act. Moses was absolutely certain that God would somehow extricate them. The waters divided, and his people walked the sea bed to safety.

An examination of these events illustrates a number of salient features. We note, for example, that when Moses was told to lead the people out of Egypt, Moses did not tell the Lord that it would be a lot simpler if he would just pick up everyone and bodily place them on the other side of the Red Sea. On the other hand, God did not tell Moses in advance that when the time came he would part the Red Sea so that Moses and his people could walk to safety, and then he would close the path and annihilate the Egyptian Army. No! There were lessons to be learned then, and for us, there are lessons to be learned now. God seems to operate like the electronic doors we encounter in the stores. They do not open in anticipation of us, they open only when we are directly in front of them. Therefore, if we see the door closed and fail to approach it, the door will not open. By failing to go to the very edge, we can miss the saving power of Almighty God.

The tangible benefit we derive from a strong faith is the capability to live in peace, free from fear, secure in the knowledge that God, who is mightier than any challenge we could possibly face, is always with us to guide us and support us. The Bible addresses this issue in a clear and concise manner in Deuteronomy 31:8:

> It is the Lord who marches before you; he will be with you and will never fail you or forsake you. So do not fear or be dismayed.

God is always with us, in fact it is impossible for us to be where God is not. This knowledge, together with the fact that Our Lord is *the* power of the universe, provides us with a sense of confidence and fearlessness. As Carlo Caretto, an Italian Catholic writer, states in "Letters from the Desert,"

> The thought that the affairs of the world, like
> those of the stars, are in God's hands—and
> therefore in good hands—apart from being actually
> true, is something that should give great
> satisfaction to anyone who looks to the future with
> hope. It should be the source of faith, joyful

> hope, and, above all, of deep peace. What have I to
> fear if everything is guided and sustained by God?
> Why get so worried, as if the world were in the
> hands of me and my fellow men?
> And yet it is so difficult to have genuine faith
> in God's action in the affairs of the world. To
> refuse to believe it is one of the gravest
> temptations to which we are subjected on this earth.[16]

Knowing that our real security is firmly based and centered in faith, we rise every day to meet the wonderful blessings that God has prepared for us. God's good for us can manifest itself in any one of a number of different ways. We may get a raise, a new job, a better relationship with our colleagues and superiors. We may even be miraculously cured from a deadly disease, or saved from imminent disaster. God reigns supreme and therefore as stated in Mark 9:23, "Everything is possible to one who has faith."

As children, when threatened, we hid behind our mothers, confident that we were safe and secure. As adults, we find safety and security in such things as family, friends, knowledge, laws, and wealth. However, these things are nothing in comparison to the incredibly awesome power of Almighty God. It is like comparing a thimble of water with the combined volume of the earth's oceans. Therefore, through a strong and vibrant faith, we can live our lives in the knowledge that God has the perfect answer for our every need, and he will work with us to achieve for us our highest good. The following passage by Patrick Henry, a Founding Father of the United States, says it well:

> I have now disposed of all my property to my family. There is one thing more I wish I could give them, and that is the Christian Religion. If they had that and I had not given them one shilling, they would have been rich; and if they had not that, and I had given them all the world, they would be poor.[17]

There are times, of course, when we wish and pray for God to take some action and provide the help we need to satisfy some desire or accomplish some task. Our problems may be large or small, and our requests can range from soup to nuts and cover essentially all the aspects of our lives. When God does not answer our requests in the manner we

---

16. Caretto, *Letters from the Desert*, ch. 4.
17. Henry, "Founding Father Quote #687."

have chosen, it does not mean that he did not hear us. He is closer to us than our breath. Failure to obtain the things we have asked for can be very disheartening and cause us to believe that God has refused to give us what we believe is in our best interest. Of course, the catchphrase here is "what *we* believe is in our best interest." We may believe that we know what is in our best interest, but our omnipotent God knows *exactly* what is in our best interest, and it may be a far cry from what we think. Furthermore, God knows the future, and there is no doubt that we don't.

I know there have been several occasions in my life when I wanted something, and prayed diligently to receive it. However, God did not grant my request, and I was horribly disappointed. Later, I learned why. If I had gotten what I wanted, I would have put myself in a very bad position, one I could not even imagine at the time of my initial request. However, God has the long view, and his actions are always aligned with our best interests.

I always have requests in to God. I never cease asking him for help in essentially everything I do. Some of my requests he answers, and others he does not. In addition, it is difficult to wait and wait for God to act. However, God's time is not our time, and God's ways are not our ways. Therefore, although it is often very difficult to do, we simply have to put our hope and trust in God and know beyond any doubt that the creator and sustainer of the entire universe has the capacity to do, and will do, what is best for us. In the meantime, the suggestion made by President Ronald Reagan, the fortieth President of the United States, applies "Live simply, love generously, care deeply, speak kindly, leave the rest to God."

# 7

Winning as a Way of Life

Positive Mental Attitude

ATTITUDE IS A KEY component in winning. Consider the following statement by Robert Collier, an American author.

> We can do only what we think we can do. We can be only what we think we can be. We can have only what we think we can have. What we do, what we are, what we have, all depends on what we think.[1]

There is tremendous power in our attitude, and because of the enormous control that it exhibits over our every action, it is extremely important that our attitude is positive. While this is easy to suggest, it is often very difficult to implement. I know that I have had to work very diligently on this issue myself. Although I make no claim of being completely cured, I have experienced the baptism of fire. One event in my life produced a possible chain reaction, leading to a sequence of at least several negative consequences. I was really concerned and started looking for, and indeed expecting, these negative things to follow. Guess what? They did! One by one I found them all. In Mathew 7:7, we read "Seek and you shall find, knock and it shall be opened to you." Well, I sought them, and damned if they were not there.

I recall that many years ago, I attended a short course at MIT. The course was taught by an individual who was not particularly brilliant, but he was very self-assured. He simply exuded confidence and was very intent on getting his message across. During the course one of my

---

1. Collier, "We Can Only Do What We Think..."

classmates asked a very good, but difficult question. I could tell instantly that the instructor did not know the answer. I remember thinking that I could not wait to see how he was going to handle this situation. However, the instructor began with a straightforward analysis of the question. He kept talking about every aspect of it as he assimilated all the issues that surrounded it. As he continued, he kept eliminating the extraneous points until he finally arrived at a logical conclusion, which we all had to agree was unquestionably correct. I was amazed. I am absolutely convinced that if he had approached the question with a negative attitude, he would have thrown in the towel immediately, or his negative attitude would have persuaded him that he was unable to solve the problem. I believe beyond any doubt that our subconscious works with us to solve problems as long as we provide the impetus for it by maintaining both a positive attitude and the will to succeed. As Napoleon Hill, an American author, has said,

> Through some strange and powerful principle of mental chemistry, which she has never divulged, nature wraps up in the impulse of strong desire, that something which recognizes no such word as impossible, and accepts no such reality as failure.[2]

Winners inherently exhibit a positive mental attitude. This personality trait, which gives them a bold and optimistic approach to life, colors everything they do. Because of their attitude, they generate a myriad of ideas and, perhaps more importantly, they put these ideas into action. Napoleon Hill stated it very succinctly when he said, "Whatever the mind of man can conceive and believe, the mind of man can achieve."[3] Ideas are the genesis of our actions. If we conceive of an idea, really believe in it, and work at it, it will come to pass. As Winston Churchill has said, "The empires of the future are empires of the mind."[4] With a positive mental attitude, we find a way to succeed; because we will not take "no" for an answer. We never even think about failure; in fact, the word "no" is not a viable part of our vocabulary. What others would call failures are nothing more than a glitch on the road to success. While a bold and optimistic approach is, in itself, no guarantee of success, it we don't try, we cannot possibly win. We are all in complete control of the way we think, and therefore we need to take a positive approach and work to make our

2. Hill, "Through Some Strange and Powerful Principle..."
3. Hill, "Whatever the Mind of Man..."
4. Churchill, "Quote."

dreams come true. To quote Charles F. Kettering, an American inventor, engineer and businessman,

> I have found that if I have faith in myself and in the idea I am tinkering with, I usually win out.[5]

Life is a game of inches. Quite often just a little more makes an enormous difference. Therefore, the individual with a positive approach, a can-do attitude and the killer instinct is the one who will win. For example, if you ask someone to run a quarter mile track as fast as he can and time him, and then later tell him his running time and ask him to run it faster the second time, he will typically do so. It is amazing that, as a general rule, we seem to be capable of doing just a little bit more.

In general, the individual who works just a little harder or a little longer or a little smarter will come out on top. As an analogy to demonstrate the importance of a small difference, do you realize that water heated to 211 degrees Fahrenheit is just real hot water, but water heated to 212 degrees Fahrenheit is steam, which is used to drive turbines which, in turn, drive generators which produce electricity.

If we predict our success and then expect it to happen, the results are amazing. To illustrate this point, consider the performance of Babe Ruth. In a critical inning the bases were loaded and there were two strikes against him. In a prediction of what was about to happen, he stepped out of the batter's box and in such a way that everyone could see, pointed the bat at deep center field indicating he would knock the ball out of the park in that direction. Within a matter of seconds, the ball went sailing into the center field stands.

We must very carefully select what we want, because if we believe it, imagine it and work for it, we almost always achieve it. If opportunities in some area exist, we will find them with a positive mental attitude. Quoting Winston Churchill,

> A positive thinker sees the invisible, feels the intangible, and achieves the impossible.[6]

The benefits we obtain from a positive attitude are enormous. Our attitude not only influences our own actions, it influences the actions of those people with whom we come in contact. Our attitude is like a beacon to them. For example, if we come home at night down in the dumps, we

---

5. Kettering, "Have Faith in Your Ideas."
6. "26 Positivity Quotes on Thoughts," quote 3.

in essence throw a dark shadow across our entire family. In this manner, unknowingly perhaps, we drag them down with us, and their problems will, in turn, seem magnified by our attitude.

In sharp contrast, however, a positive outlook is a very refreshing influence that adds zest and vitality, not only to our own lives, but others as well. People who display such an attitude have a certain charisma about them. They are fun to be with, and others enjoy doing things with them whether it is work or play. Their upbeat approach tends to make everyone's problems seem smaller.

The power derived from a positive attitude not only influences people to follow us in some endeavor or support our position on some issue, it is a solvent that dissolves the obstacles that hinder working relationships. It promotes health and happiness in us and all with whom we come in contact. As such, it is a formidable shield against stress and illness. In addition, it gives us both energy and confidence to accomplish whatever task is at hand. There is a powerful, yet unknown, force which supports this attitude, and people who won't take "no" for an answer usually end up getting a "yes."

Winners never pre-qualify anything with a negative attitude, e.g., "I'm not smart enough to . . .". In addition, they do not apply a negative attitude to anyone with whom they come in contact. For example, if you tell your kids that they are stupid, they will start acting stupid. Their subconscious tells them, "Hey, we are stupid, and we should start acting that way." I recall playing cards with a very good friend of mine. We were partners and got along great, but he was somewhat of a "klutz." During this particular game I was kidding him while recounting events of our past in which he seemed to be totally uncoordinated. Within minutes it became his turn to shuffle the cards. They went in fifty-two different directions. As he reached for the cards, he knocked over a glass of coke. In an attempt to prevent the coke from rolling off the card table, he leaned forward to catch it, and as he did, he lifted the table, and the entire contents of the table landed in my lap. Well, I asked for it. In fact, I begged for it. I told him he was a "klutz" and he simply proved that I was right. Never again!

Since our internal "thinkostat" has significant control of our behavior, we must concentrate on maintaining an optimistic attitude. We are what we think we are, and therefore we should continuously remind ourselves of all of our good qualities. When someone else acknowledges these qualities, we should simply be gracious and thank them.

Through a positive attitude, we can view our environment as a dog would a meat market. God has created a world with a myriad of opportunities; therefore, if we will simply do our best, our probability of success is extremely high. The very foundation of our ability to win is our attitude. It is completely independent of luck or education. There are unfortunately a lot of lucky and educated people who are hooked on drugs or alcohol.

We help people by encouraging them to project a very positive self-image, because the world tends to reflect our attitude back to us. I know in my own case, there have been occasions in which I took a chance, started a project, and assumed that somewhere downstream I would manage to circumvent all the obstacles in my path. In essentially every case, and sometimes in a miraculous manner, most if not all the necessary ingredients fell into place, and I was able to accomplish whatever I set out to do. On the other hand, whenever I have been too cautious, because of fear or doubt, I have seen someone else, who was less cautious, achieve what I had planned to do.

Fear is a tremendous negative force. Its enormous power was vividly illustrated to me as a child. Normally, I cannot remember a dream for two minutes. I don't recall all of the details of this particular one either; however, I remember in that dream I was so afraid that I could not move. I tried but I couldn't. I tried to scream for help, but when I opened my mouth, nothing came out. That incident is burned into my memory. I finally woke up in a pool of sweat.

If we possess a positive mental attitude, we do not exhibit fear, but rather concern, and this concern, coupled with our attitude, leads to the search for a viable solution to whatever is troubling us.

Winners instinctively deal with adversity in a direct manner. They learn from mistakes, and the quicker the better, since they are nothing more than a part of their education. In general, they try to anticipate problems and plan for them. However, when setbacks occur, they do not rattle a winner's cage. Winners simply refocus their goals and steer a steady course toward them.

I believe that for many of us the fundamental basis for a positive mental attitude is religious faith. It is the belief that each one of us is a child of Almighty God, and that in his infinite love and mercy, he will help guide us if we will do our part. Through our faith, mighty forces come into play that couple directly with our own efforts to provide us with everything we need to succeed. Those of us who have that faith find that we are never able to live beyond our capabilities, and that our faith leads to boldness, which leads to accomplishments, which finally leads to success.

The following poem, "Thinking," by Walter D. Wintle, states the case for a positive mental attitude very well.

> If you think you are beaten—you are.
> If you think you dare not—you don't.
> If you'd like to win, but you think you can't,
> It's almost a cinch that you won't
> If you think you'll lose—you've lost,
> For out in the world you'll find
> Success begins with a fellow's will,
> It's all in the state of mind.
> If you think that you're outclassed—you are,
> You've got to think high to rise.
> You've got to be sure of yourself before
> you can ever win the prize
> Life's battle doesn't always go
> To the swifter and faster man
> But sooner or later the man who wins
> Is the man who thinks he can.[7]

So, regardless of whether your goals are large or small, attack them with the confidence of a four-year-old in a Superman T-shirt.

Steadfast Belief in Ourselves

The following quote by John Stuart Mill, a British philosopher, provides insight on this topic: "One person with a belief is equal to a force of ninety-nine who only have interests."[8]

Our success is critically dependent upon the faith and trust we have in ourselves, because if we don't think we can—we can't. The absolute belief that we will be a success is like a catapult that propels us beyond those who are not convinced beyond a doubt that they will indeed succeed. It points the way through the maze in which we live. Like night vision glasses it permits us to see what others cannot, and in addition it triggers the unseen power that somehow automatically opens the doors before us. Through this steadfast belief in ourselves, we know that we will succeed, even though we may not know exactly how it will be accomplished.

7. Wintle, "Quotable Quotes."
8. Duggleby, "So What Is Coaching," para. 5.

Confidence is the all-important ingredient, and with it we make a habit of success. Rather than tell ourselves why we can't succeed, we are completely confident that we can, should, and will. With a forward-looking attitude, we learn from our mistakes and continue to build from strength to strength. Ann Landers provided some very sage advice on this subject when she said,

> If I were asked to give what I consider the single most useful bit of advice for all humanity, it would be this: expect trouble as an inevitable part of life and when it comes, hold your head high, look it squarely in the eye and say, I will be bigger than you. You cannot defeat me.[9]

What we believe is very important, because *we are what we believe*. Others take their cue from us, and they see us as we see ourselves. Therefore, it we don't think we are worth a damn, why in the world would anyone else? After all, no one knows us as well as we know ourselves. There are always a host of reasons why we cannot do something, e.g. we are either too young, too old, have insufficient education or are in poor health. If we look hard enough, there is at least one good reason why we shouldn't do something. In fact, people who do not believe in themselves devote a great deal of time and energy to manufacturing an air-tight excuse. Imagine that; working hard to derive a reason to be a failure. Their goal is to put themselves in such a position that whenever a challenge arises, their first thought would be, "Oh, poor, poor, there is just no way anyone could expect me to . . ."

When we really believe in ourselves we find a way to meet challenges no matter how hard we have to look. The circumstances will never be perfect for anything. Winners succeed in spite of adverse circumstances. If the problem is trivial or everything is perfectly aligned, then a child could solve it.

We can learn from others, and what we learn can strengthen our belief in ourselves. However, we must be careful to calibrate our advisors. If they are moving up on a fast track and are genuinely interested in our welfare, listen carefully to what they have to say. On the other hand, if they are going nowhere in a real hurry, their advice is probably not worth our consideration. The only good advice you get from a failure is how to fail, and do it in style.

---

9. Landers, "If I Were Asked..."

The mechanisms for achieving success are only developed in those individuals who unquestionably believe that they will be successful. Wishful thinking just won't get the job done. In fact, wishing seems to inherently imply that someone else is going to do it, and that they are responsible for our success.

Our attitude plays a central role in our success and is an outward sign of how we think. As Peter Marshall, a Presbyterian minister, has said,

> Give to us clear vision that we may know where to stand and what to stand for, because unless we stand for something, we will fall for anything.[10]

What we think is a function of what is stored in our subconscious, and it, in turn, is like a magic genie. This extremely competent and powerful slave devises a scheme to carry out in an efficient manner whatever we believe. Then all we have to do is execute. For example, if I want to make a million dollars and believe beyond any doubt that I can, my subconscious starts generating ideas and plans that will help me do it. It does not execute them; I have to do that. However, it does lay the groundwork and point the way. I may have to work very hard to execute the plans which unfold as I proceed, but make no mistake about it, as I work toward the goal with a can-do attitude, my subconscious will keep generating creative solutions that keep me headed in the right direction.

In contrast, if I tell myself that I can't make a million dollars, then my magic genie, in complete obedience, starts setting up all the roadblocks that will absolutely ensure that I don't become a millionaire. Even if someone came to me with a fool-proof scheme, the genie would convince me that I am too young, or too old, or not smart enough, or not in good health, or not capable of working hard enough and so on ad infinitum. My little genie would follow my instructions to the letter and find some way to block even a possible attempt.

My subconscious just follows my thoughts with absolute obedience. Therefore, if I have a can-do, forward-looking, positive attitude and fill my subconscious with these kinds of thoughts, I have a virtual army working for me. Thus a firm belief that I can do something triggers the subconscious to unleash the creative energy and produce the constructive thinking necessary to find a way.

When memory is loaded with positive, can-do thoughts, a self-induced brainstorm can produce some rather phenomenal results. Wild

---

10. Marshall, "Give To Us Clear Vision..."

ideas can often be solutions to some very sticky problems. We may be able to make drastic improvements by breaking the paralysis exhibited by the traditional status quo—we have been doing it like this for years—approach. People who cling to this stagnant environment are not contributors, since in many cases a trained monkey can do it "the way we have been doing it for years". The world is changing every day, and only a moment's reflection is needed to validate this comment. The modern cell phones are an excellent example and, as we have indicated earlier, each new version brings with it a list of new features. Your competition is changing, so you had better change, too. Corporations, through their investments in research and development, work very hard to outstrip their competition with a more capable and less expensive product. All a company has to do is decide that its product can't be improved, and the next thing it sees up ahead will be the rear ends of its competition.

It all boils down to what we think, i.e., the ideas and concepts we have planted in our subconscious. From an operational standpoint, the actual scenario unfolds something like this. I think I'm _____. My subconscious begins working to make me _____. I act like _____. Other people observe me and they think I'm _____. Therefore, they treat me like I'm _____. The cycle repeats and the whole situation escalates in a manner to provide positive reinforcement. There is tremendous potential in this approach, and since the awesome power inherent in this activity works whether we are trying to do some routine, trivial task or a gigantic one, for God's sake let's *think big*. And we have every right to think big because we have at our constant disposal the master controller of the universe.

Is the approach we have delineated a surefire panacea? Of course not. In all that we do, we need to be realistic. I have had lower back surgery. Is it possible for me to be a world-class weight-lifter and lift the world record of five hundred eighty-two pounds? No. Even attempting something far less would send me directly to the hospital. Can we expect a paraplegic to compete effectively in a cross-country race? No. We could provide an entire litany of situations in which the desired result would be impossible. There must be at least some way to accomplish a goal or we are simply banging our heads against a wall with no hope of success. In the process of attempting some impossible goal, however, we may make some progress, but the progress we achieve will have to be considered our success in these situations.

Think Big and Take Action

The Irish playwright George Bernard Shaw states that "The man who listens to reason is lost: reason enslaves all whose minds are not strong enough to master her."[11] Isn't it interesting that when we ask a young child what they would like to be when they grow up, it is not uncommon for the child to respond with "President of the United States" or "Governor of the State". And yet, what kind of encouragement do they often receive? In too many cases, people will tell them, "you're naïve" or "that is not realistic" or "you can't do that." Why? How could these people possibly know that some thirty-five years hence, they can't achieve this goal? After all, somebody is going to assume these offices, and why not this child! Do you suppose that all of these "advisors" are clairvoyant? That possibility is too remote to even warrant casual consideration. We can say with certainty, however, that the kid's unsolicited brain trust is low on confidence, but loaded with negative advice.

If we tell a big thinker that one day they could be somebody or do something, regardless of how difficult the challenge may appear, they will not suppress these desires or goals. In fact, they will probably attempt to determine just how they could be accomplished. However, tell the same thing to a small thinker and what happens? He will probably respond with a list of reasons why these things can't be done and why he shouldn't even try to consider them. In addition, the attitude of these small thinkers is often that of an omnipotent physician who is trying to treat some poor devil who, while suffering from illusions of grandeur, is at least slightly off-center.

Unfortunately, small thinkers are everywhere. They feel inadequate and therefore they are often miserable. Hard work is not a part of their repertoire; therefore, they are jealous of anyone who is willing to put in the effort to get ahead. These individuals are characterized by an "I can't" attitude, and they would be absolutely delighted to inoculate us with it. Hence, it is to our advantage to give them a wide berth, since their group is continuously on a campaign to increase their membership.

We avoid negative thinkers for the same reason we avoid poisonous food. Our bodies are made up of what we put in them. Our minds are no different. Therefore, our total environment, which supplies our mind food, should be completely controlled, if possible. We should try very hard to constantly be under the influence of positive, enthusiastic

---

11. Shaw, "Man Who Listens to Reason..."

individuals who think big. If we continuously associate with these forward-looking people, how could we ourselves be anything else?

Big thinkers are not necessarily brilliant, but they are definitely not content to forever ride in tourist class. They never sell themselves short; in fact, they continuously stretch and strain to achieve beyond the limits of their ability. Never satisfied with the status quo, they are perpetually on the lookout for ways to improve and capitalize upon any situation. They operate on a macro, rather than micro, scale and they are an effective team leader and/or team player. They clearly see beyond their own area of responsibility and are keenly aware that if the other end of the boat is torpedoed, there is the very distinct possibility that they will be underwater soon. It is only fitting that those people who worry about the big picture and have a sincere and unselfish interest in the whole operation, be the ones destined for the executive suite.

Those individuals who are capable of operating effectively in the rarefied air at the pinnacle of an organization are typically upbeat in every aspect of their lives. When asked how they feel, they answer, "Fantastic." When asked how they are doing, they respond, "Just great." Since they are homo sapiens, the probability that they are always "fantastic" is zero. However, what happens when the subconscious is told that it is "fantastic?" It goes to work to make them feel "fantastic," and through positive reinforcement they become "fantastic." In addition, these individuals are extremely well focused, and their concentration is fixed on the goal. As such, they don't sweat the small stuff. These things don't matter to a big thinker, because they are nothing more than a nit and not worth valuable time.

Big thinkers are outstanding students in the sense that they learn something positive from every negative experience. For example, my brother Mike tells the story he had heard of the very successful executive who was interviewed on the occasion of his retirement by a young reporter. The executive was asked to explain the secret of his phenomenal success. He replied that it all boiled down to two words, "right decisions." The interviewer, anxious to learn how these decisions were made, asked for an explanation. The man replied that the answer could be explained in one word, "experience." Intrigued by the utter simplicity of the great man's success strategy, he continued to probe and asked, "How did you get the proper experience?" Without hesitation, the old gentleman responded that the reason could be stated in two words, "wrong decisions."

Big thinkers have an enormous advantage, because quite often there is so little competition.

People who think big expand their horizons through imagination. Through their inherent vision they see things, not only as they are, but also for what they can become. Sometimes it is only a matter of scale. For example, the basic aerodynamic principles are the same whether we are building a model airplane or a large passenger aircraft. In other situations, it is a matter of visualizing things from a broader perspective. For example, finding multiple uses for a product can send the sales of the unit right through the roof. Perhaps the obvious example of a device that originated for one function and has morphed into one with numerous functions is the cell phone. This device was originally developed to permit telephone conversations without a hardwired connection to the telephone network, and the early versions did just that. However, today, the device is in essence a handheld computer with vastly expanded functionality, capable of performing as an alarm clock, camera, music player, recorder, financial calculator, road atlas, etc., which has become so popular that there are billions of these devices worldwide. Another example is radar units. Radar that was typically employed in defense systems and aircraft landing systems at airports is now being employed in self driving/autonomous vehicles. Each vehicle may require several of these devices, which will cause their sales to skyrocket because of the tremendous number of vehicles produced each year.

For people in positions of leadership, thinking big has awesome consequences, since one of the most effective means to learn is through imitation. Children imitate their parents and workers imitate their supervisors. Our subordinates reflect our attitude back to us; and therefore, we have to think positive and think big so these subordinates will also.

Leadership and big thinking go hand in hand, and nowhere is this more prevalent than in the case of entrepreneurs. As an example, consider the history of Bill Gates, who as we all know is the cofounder of Microsoft Corporation and one of the wealthiest people in the entire world. He proved himself to be one of the most brilliant people in the industry. He was energetic, persistent, and a big thinker with a vision to look beyond the present and into the future. Through his technical genius and business acuity, he convinced IBM to adopt his software, which guaranteed that it would be used on millions of IBM machines, but in addition, it would be a requisite component for every IBM clone. His success story is well-known and history has documented the manner in which this very wise and astute individual judiciously led Microsoft to the number two position in IBM's extremely competitive and volatile industry. Prior to what became known as Black Monday, October 19, 1987, Bill Gates' stock was worth approximately one billion dollars. An individual unfamiliar with Bill Gates' success story would undoubtedly assume that it would take a lifetime to accomplish what he had done. However, in 1987 Bill Gates was only thirty-one years old.

A more recent example of big thinking is Mark Elliot Zuckerberg, the American technology entrepreneur, who cofounded and led the development of Facebook. The company was launched from his dorm room at Harvard. Although the company originally targeted college campuses, it became so popular so fast that it became a worldwide phenomenon within a few short years. The company went public in 2012, making him an instant billionaire at the age of twenty-eight.

The ability to extrapolate the present into a myriad of possibilities in the future not only enhances our own lives, but can be employed as a successful strategy to enrich the lives of others. Think for a moment of the tremendous accomplishments that are made by those people who are working in areas such as drug rehabilitation. The impact that these forward-looking and dedicated people have on the lives of addicts is absolutely phenomenal. In some cases, people who have lived an almost subhuman existence have, through a very positive support system, been miraculously changed into a very productive and useful human being. The importance of such a metamorphosis is immeasurable since it is impossible to put a price tag on a human life.

Unfortunately, things don't happen just because we think about them, even if we think big. They happen because we do something about them. Action is the real horsepower behind our thinking. All success-oriented people are action-oriented. Their action leads to achievement, which breeds confidence, which leads to more action, then achievement, etc. These winners are bold. They do not sit around waiting for some kind of harmonic convergence in order to act. No attempt is made to try and eliminate all the problems in advance, instead they are attacked and defeated as they surface. Every worthwhile endeavor has unknown risks and uncertainties. The key is to jump in and force the conditions to align themselves for success, and as Christians we can do this with confidence, knowing that Almighty God is our source for help and guidance.

It is somewhat a paradox that the genesis of our inability to act is often fear, and yet we conquer fear by acting. Indecision and procrastination fuel our fears, and if left unchecked, the fear level rises. As fear increases, we are able to generate even more reasons not to do something. As the situation escalates, we are finally convinced that the smart move is to do nothing.

It is absolutely tragic to listen to people say "had I only followed through on the idea to _____," or "If I had just played my hunch on _____." Yet deep down in the fiber of our mind, we believe that "he who hesitates is lost." We make progress only when we stick our necks out. I recall the first time I jumped off the high board at the local swimming pool. The diving board was probably only twelve feet off the water, but from where I was standing, it appeared to be one hundred feet. Once I summoned the courage to jump, every subsequent jump was a piece of cake. Prior to the first talk I gave before a large crowd, I was extremely nervous. Even though I was well prepared, just the thought of having a sea of faces staring at me was frightening. However, within fifteen seconds of the time I opened my mouth, I was fine. Even now, I find the same situation exists in writing. I can think of all kinds of ideas, but they only really gel into coherent thoughts when I start typing.

When our oldest daughter, Geri, was very young, she was awakened by a nightmare. It had scared her, and she was crying when Edie tried to comfort her. Edie held Geri in her arms and told her it was only a bad dream. That was an unfortunate choice of words, because Geri was then convinced that we had a "bad dream" running around the house, and what's more, we could not even see the thing. Edie could have talked until she was blue in the face trying to explain this "bad dream" to Geri. Instead, in an authoritative manner, Edie grabbed the broom and started rigorously sweeping toward the back door. She told Geri she was going to sweep that "bad dream" right out of the house. When she reached the back door, with one final heave, out went the "bad dream." Edie very confidently slammed the door, shut it, and locked it. Geri's expression reassured Edie that the issue was no longer a problem.

Be the Best That *You* Can Be

Vincent T. Lombardi, the famous American football coach says the following:

> The quality of a person's life is in direct proportion to their commitment to excellence, regardless of their chosen field of endeavor.[12]

At one time in the recent past, the recruiting slogan for the US Army was "Be all that you can be." It did not say, "Be all that someone else can be." This latter slogan would be ridiculous, and yet it is amazing how many of us try to be all that someone else is, and we make ourselves miserable in the process of trying. Each of us is unique. Our mind, our body, our complete history of experiences from the day we were born is different from anyone else. How could we possibly be anyone other than ourselves? Regardless of our destination, the worst trip in the world we can take is the one in which we try to be another individual. If we could somehow manage to be someone else, it would represent for us personal suicide. The one thing we have that no one else has, our own uniqueness, would be lost. Hence, we must strive to be the best that *we* can be, and remember that God created each of us to occupy a special place in the mosaic of humanity.

We can optimize our own performance by maximizing our strengths and minimizing our weaknesses. In a straightforward manner, we march to our own tune. We live for ourselves and not for what others think of us. We live our own lives rather than having another live our lives as well as their own. Regardless of whether we are Type A or Type B, as a general rule, we will set the stage for being our best if we exhibit a positive mental attitude and achieve a match between our environment and our own talents and interests.

Success is essentially the result of realizing our maximum potential in the position we are in.

Mother Teresa, i.e., Saint Teresa of Calcutta, says it this way:

> In this life we cannot always do great things. But we can do small things with great love.[13]

People who are capable of achieving their goals typically fail if they refuse to give it all they've got. And unfortunately, some people, who would otherwise be very successful, are unable to do so because of some handicap resulting from physical, mental or emotional problems. These individuals must think of success in relation to what they are able to

---

12. Lombardi, "The Quality of a Person's Life…"
13. Mother Teresa, "In This Life…"

achieve, given their circumstances. The television ads that demonstrate success at St. Jude's Children Hospital would seem trivial to a normal child. However, for the children there, the simple things they have achieved represent for them an extraordinary, monumental, and almost unbelievable success. Clearly, success must be viewed with a fundamental reference point in mind and the consideration of at least a somewhat level playing field.

People who are capable of being successful in their environment fail only when they refuse to give it all they've got. Rudyard Kipling, the English poet and novelist, expressed it well when he said, "We have forty million reasons for failure, but not a single excuse."[14] In addition, quoting Abraham Lincoln, "Always bear in mind that your own resolution to succeed is more important than any other one thing."[15]

If we expect more and organize ourselves to achieve more, we will get more. We cannot be our best unless we are totally committed. We must exhibit an innovative and aggressive approach, and possess the drive, discipline, and vision to plan and execute. Failing to plan is tantamount to planning to fail, for only the prepared deserve to be confident and thus successful. Success-oriented people seem to operate under the philosophy that it is infinitely better to attempt something great and fail than to attempt nothing and succeed. People who never make a mistake are the real failures, because they never attempt anything worthwhile.

Confident people with a strong self-image work very effectively with their colleagues, because they are not afraid to share the power of their position, responsibilities, or the glory achieved as a result of the work done together. They know that mistakes will be made, but when they are, the world will not end. They will all learn from them and then keep on keeping on. Their basic approach is that it is better to have some things done imperfectly than to have nothing done perfectly. Hence, the critical issue is our willingness to jump into the breech and give it a shot. As Thomas A. Edison has said, "If we all did the things we are capable of doing, we would literally astound ourselves."[16] As a corollary to this statement, we will also find that it is amazing what a group of dedicated individuals can accomplish when they are not concerned about who does what and who gets the credit. In business, one of the most exhilarating

---

14. Kipling, "We Have Forty Million Reasons..."
15. Swisher, "Resolution to Succeed," para. 3.
16. Edison, "Quotation Details."

feelings we can experience is achieved by doing whatever we do and doing it to perfection. There is nothing like it, and the drug that produces that feeling has not been invented yet. When we are at our best and we know it, regardless of our position, we are on top of the world.

In order to be our best, we have to be willing to work at it, and we must have the courage to stick our necks out. As Ralph Waldo Emerson, an American philosopher, said,

> Do not be too timid and squeamish about your actions. All life is an experiment. The more experiments you make, the better. What if they are a little coarse, and you may get your coat soiled or torn? What if you do fail, and get rolled in the dirt once or twice? Up again, you shall never be so afraid of a tumble.[17]

Everyone who competes is a winner. The losers never attain the courage to enter the contest. Winners may have setbacks, and at times, they may fail. However, the characteristic that sets them apart is that they get right back up and try again.

Winners are tough, and they exhibit a resilience which permits them to bounce right back. They expect to win because they have earned the right to do so. Regardless of their size or sex, they are awesome, because they possess a tremendous amount of personal power. This personal power gives them the feeling that they are essentially invincible. They have the confidence of a Black Belt karate expert who is bullied by some mere mortal.

As Charles Schwab, the founder of a stock brokerage company that bears his name, has said,

> A man can succeed at almost anything for which he has unlimited enthusiasm.[18]

People who exhibit this enthusiasm live by the adage, "The difficult we do immediately, the impossible takes a little longer." These people continuously push and stretch themselves. They have found by experience that they really did not know how much they could accomplish until they were moved by some strong emotional stimulus to do it. I recall as a child being told about a man who worked at a zoo. One day when they were moving a lion from one cage to another, the lion got loose. When the workman saw the lion free, he went straight up a flag pole. No doubt

---

17. Emerson, "Do Not Be Too Timid..."
18. Schwab, "A Man Can Succeed..."

if, before this incident, someone had asked the man if he could climb the flag pole, the answer would have been a resounding "no."

When we are the best that we can be, we find ways to do things that otherwise would seem impossible. When we think we have exhausted every possible avenue, we find that there is at least one more approach. Quite often in order to guarantee success, we make commitments that have no means of escape, and in doing so, force ourselves to achieve incredible performance. For example, history has recorded that the Spanish commander Hernán Cortés scuttled his ships during the Spanish conquest of Mexico to force his men to conquer, because this action left his men with no way to escape.

It has been said that necessity is the mother of invention. If we persistently forge ahead expecting a breakthrough, we vastly increase our chances of obtaining one. If a positive mental attitude is a consistent part of our character, we can and should apply it, not only to the most important and major situations of our lives, but to each and everything we do regardless of how dramatic it is. A positive mental attitude is a powerful tool in problem solving, and its power is in no way controlled by the size of the problem.

We get out of life exactly what we put into it, and we put in the most if we are the best that we can be. The following verse by Jesse B. Rittenhouse, an American poet, illustrates the point,

> I bargained with life for a penny
> and life would pay no more.
> However, I begged at evening
> when I counted my scanty store.
> For life is just an employer
> who gives you what you ask.
> But once you have set the wages,
> then you must bear the task.
> I worked for a menial's hire
> only to learn dismayed,
> that any wage I had asked of life,
> life would have willingly paid.[19]

---

19. Don'tgiveupworld, "Introspective Poem."

Working Like Hell

I don't know who said it, but a phrase which describes the case for hard work can be stated as follows: *All things come to he who waits, if he works like hell while he waits.* Determination, dedication, and persistence are three of the common threads and perhaps the most visible characteristics of a winner. Successful athletes are an obvious example of the results that can be achieved through hard work. For example, before one of the NBA playoff games in 1986 between the Boston Celtics and the Houston Rockets, the radio and TV announcers arrived early to set up their broadcast equipment. Although the game would not start for three-and-a-half hours and the stadium was like a giant tomb, they quickly learned that they were not alone. Larry Bird was already on the court working with a ball boy as several janitors watched. Larry was standing outside the three-point circle, shooting one ball after the next. As the janitors counted them off, Larry shot twenty-six baskets without a miss. Guess who won the NBA's Most Valuable Player award that year? Does Larry Bird have talent? Absolutely! But Larry is great instead of just good because he works like hell.

As Henry Wadsworth Longfellow, an American poet, has said,

> Perseverance is a great element of success. If you only knock long enough and loud enough at the gate, you are sure to wake up somebody.[20]

If we just keep plugging and are optimistic in our approach, the chances of achieving our goals are extremely high. Every path we take may not be the right one, and we may end up on a number of dead-end streets, but if we continue to work hard with a positive mental attitude, we will almost assuredly get where we are going.

One of my best friends, and an outstanding colleague, is a real entrepreneur. Bill is a dedicated, hard-working individual who has a diversified portfolio of operations. One of the areas he handles is unusual real estate deals. Because of his expertise, the banks call on him to help them settle deals that are extremely difficult to solve. His most potent weapon in closing one of these deals is persistence. He is a very tenacious negotiator. In a marathon manner he continues to discuss the deal, analyze alternatives, generate new ideas, and propose solutions until he has finally found the proper mix that is agreeable to everyone involved. Through

---

20. Longfellow, "Perseverance Is a Great Element..."

perseverance, in spite of any and all obstacles, he is able to obtain a compromise solution that would otherwise seem completely intractable.

Success-oriented people are willing to work long hours whenever it is necessary to do so. They seem to be driven to succeed, and find the chase to be an exhilarating experience. They earn the right to be successful, because they are willing to pay the price. However, the price can, at times, be very steep. That is why in general, it is not always sufficient to just work hard, we must work as smart as we can. There is no doubt that intelligence and information can be traded for plugging away at the goal with determination and dedication without the benefit of critical data. As a trivial example, a person would have to sail around the tip of South America in going from the Pacific to the Atlantic, if they don't know that the Panama Canal exists. While winners find the pursuit of a worthwhile goal to be exciting, it is a lot more fun if they can operate with as much data at their disposal as possible as they work to achieve it.

Quite often, hard-driven Type A personality types have to be extremely careful. It is one thing to achieve a goal and quite another to do so and ruin your health in the process. To label someone a success, who has ended their quest with serious medical problems, seems to violate the basic definition.

From a different point of view, I recall attending an award ceremony many years ago, when the recipient of the highest award, as a part of his acceptance speech, thanked his wife for raising their children. He had apparently devoted every waking moment to the development of this scientific breakthrough. As a result, it appeared that his children were raised without the benefit of their father's guidance, and now these children were out of the house and gone. It seemed that he had missed the time with them, and of course, that time could not be recaptured. Was this gentleman a success? Certainly, the results he achieved would definitely be considered a wonderful success; however, his family may have thought of him somewhat differently—and that is not success. That is a tragedy.

Some people have the attitude that we have to be a genius to succeed. However, as Thomas A. Edison said, "Genius is one percent inspiration and ninety-nine percent perspiration."[21] Success is not so much a matter of raw brainpower, as it is a judicious use of our personal power coupled with a determined will to succeed. Winners stretch and push themselves. They

---

21. Edison, "Genius Is One Percent Inspiration..."

try to accomplish a little more each day. They put pressure on themselves, and therefore, external pressure is superfluous because they are their own worst critic. No one could work them as hard as they work themselves.

One of the reasons for their success is that they are *in the stream*. They are so completely immersed in their activity that essentially everything going on in and around their area passes directly in front of them. They examine all opportunities, and once they have selected their goal, they pursue it with a vengeance. These aggressive individuals exhibit the attitude expressed in the statement by author and columnist Lewis Grizzard:

> Life is like a dogsled, if you ain't the lead dog, the scenery never changes.[22]

Just knowing what to do is not sufficient. To be successful we must act. As Will Rogers, an American humorist, has said,

> Even if you are on the right track, you will be run over if you just sit there.[23]

Everything in the world will eventually belong to those people who keep working at it rather than waiting for the sky to open up and drop it in their lap. People who wait very quietly and piously for the Good Lord to throw them a miracle are going to quietly and piously rot. As someone told me: The meek may inherit the earth, but they are going to have to work like hell to get title to it. The word "meek" is actually a translation, and in this context it refers to an assertive, but kind and unselfish person.

In Matthew 25:14–30 we read the parable of the three servants. The master was leaving on a trip, so he put the servants in charge of his property while he was gone. Two of the servants invested the money they were given and doubled it. The third servant buried his master's money in a hole in the ground. When the master returned, he asked for an accounting of their work. The master was obviously pleased with the first two servants and praised them. He told them that since they had done so well with small amounts of money, he would put them in charge of larger amounts. However, when the master learned what the third servant had done he took the money from him and gave it to the others. He then made the following critical statement:

---

22. Grizzard, "Life Is Like a Dogsled..."
23. Rogers, "Will Rogers Quotes."

> For to everyone who has, more will be given and he will grow rich; but from the one who has not, even what he has will be taken away. And throw this useless servant into the darkness outside, where there will be wailing and grinding of teeth. (Matt 25:29–30)

It is both interesting and informative to examine one of the fundamental reasons for the prowess Japan displays in the worldwide industrial markets. The reason is simply stated by the nation's historic ethic, "Senyu Koraku," which when translated essentially means *struggle first and enjoy later*. This principle of conduct, which governs their daily lives, is instilled in them from childhood where they attend school five-and-a-half days per week. The work ethic is so strong that the Japanese labor force has typically worked an average of four hundred hours per year more than their counterparts in the United States.

The following statement, which has been altered slightly, is often used in a negative sense, but for the workaholic they are the words on the banner they carry,

> I have done so much with so little for so long, that now I will try to do everything with nothing in no time.[24]

However, hard work does not always translate into longer hours. Long hours by themselves don't always pay dividends. Sometimes we reach the law of diminishing returns, and then we are only wasting time. The trick is to make time count, not count time. Successful people typically work like hell to begin with; however, through experience they learn to work smarter and more efficiently. Through organization and the delegation of authority and responsibility, their time is more productive and they get more accomplished by doing more work in fewer hours. Through this approach, they are in a position to relax and spend more time with their families and friends. Although for some of us it is an extremely difficult lesson to learn, a balanced life generally improves, rather than detracts, from work performance.

A beautiful example of just one of the many people who have risen to become a super success is Estée Lauder. She came into this world in Corona, Queens, New York, the youngest of nine children. What began by selling face cream to friends and neighbors was catapulted into an international business, headquartered in New York, that employs about forty-eight thousand people. Her secret: she had a goal, believed in it, was

---

24. See "We Have Done So Much..."

excited about it, and worked like hell at it. She was, however, a balanced individual. She was a super saleswoman who took time to relax, was devoted to her family, and through her numerous charitable contributions, returned to Almighty God much of what he had given to her. Among her awards was the Presidential Medal of Freedom, given to her in 2004.

Turning the Lemon into a Lemonade

Another hallmark of a winner is an inherent interest in, and ability for, turning the lemon into a lemonade As Henry Ward Beecher, an American clergyman, has said,

> It is defeat that turns bone to flint, and gristle to muscle, and makes a man invincible, and forms those heroic natures that are now in ascendancy in the world. Do not then be afraid of defeat. You are never so near victory as when defeated in a good cause.[25]

The winner instinctively knows that throughout life there are going to be a number of setbacks; however, they are also aware of the fact that within a problem there is tremendous potential. In other words, problems are not sudden death, but rather instant opportunities. Problems, if attacked with a positive mental attitude, can be a vehicle for improving our own competence, enhancing our position, making money, helping others, or some combination of these things. Winners don't dwell on the negative by cursing it; they concentrate on reversing it. In so doing they find that quite often trouble is nothing more than a blessing in disguise.

I recall many years ago when funding for the space program began decreasing, some of the NASA engineers, recalling the events that followed the launching of Sputnik, would say, "What we need is another Russian spectacular."

Winners simply refuse to throw in the towel. They are like shock absorbers and bounce right back. As the Chinese philosopher Confucius has said,

> Our greatest glory is not in never failing, but in rising every time we fall.[26]

The threat of some failure often brings out the very best in us. As we have previously indicated, "Necessity is the mother of invention." In

---

25. Beecher, "It Is Defeat that Turns Bone to Flint…"
26. See "Motivational Quote."

many cases it is the super successful individual who has found a way to solve some tremendous problem.

Looking at every lemon as a potential ingredient for a lemonade is not always simple and easy to do. However, the ability to do this is usually the first step in a series which leads to accomplishment. As George Bernard Shaw has said,

> People are always blaming their circumstances for what they are. I don't believe in circumstances. The people who get on in this world are the people who get up and look for the circumstances they want, and, if they can't find them, make them.[27]

There are a number of things we can do to aid us in this transformation involved in going from a lemon to a lemonade. If we are trying to get someone else to do something, one of the best things we can do is to make it their idea. If we can somehow plant the idea in their head, as it grows and they become interested in it, all we have to do is help and be as supportive as possible. There is scientific evidence to support this basic concept. For example, trying to get someone to change their mind on some particular position can range from non-trivial on the one hand to essentially impossible on the other. Blaise Pascal, the seventeenth-century philosopher, proposed a technique that is now gaining traction with leading modern-day psychologists. Pascal suggested that prior to disagreeing with another individual, first point out the ways in which this individual is correct in their thinking, and then help them discover by themselves another point of view, which is of course the position you propose. Professor Arthur Markman, who is a psychology professor at the University of Texas at Austin, says that modern thinking supports this approach.[28] A frontal attack usually causes an individual to double-down and freeze their position, which simply makes the encounter worse. However, if areas of agreement can be discovered first, then the other individual is more likely to begin to look at the situation from a broader point of view. Once there is cooperation in examining the issue, then it is possible for the other individual to realize and adopt another position, which could then lead to agreement.

In general, however, regardless of what we are trying to accomplish, we will achieve the best results if we have a coherent method of attack. One such method involves the following items: have a goal that is simple,

---

27. Shaw, "People Are Always Blaming Their Circumstances..."
28. See Goldhill, "Philosopher's 350-year-old Trick."

somehow achievable, and clearly stated. If achieving the goal requires the assistance of another individual, examine both the goal and the method of accomplishing it from their point of view, i.e., can he be motivated in some manner to aid in achieving the goal? We must often convince the other person to take the risks necessary to achieve the goal, and make an estimate of just how far we can push the situation before we call it quits. The following simple examples are a part of my own past history and serve to illustrate various scenarios for achieving the desired results.

While we were living in New Jersey, my oldest daughter, Geri, was three years old. At that age Geri was still sucking on a pacifier. We did not want the kids to suck on anything, but if they had to use something, we preferred the pacifier to the thumb. In sharp contrast to the thumb, we believed at some point in time we could take the pacifier away.

One day when Edie and the kids were shopping, Geri saw a pair of red shoes that she wanted. She asked Edie if she could have them, and Edie told her that we would talk about it and let her know. That night while Edie and I were discussing the red shoes, the thought occurred to us that perhaps we could use the red shoes to turn a lemon into a lemonade. We decided we would tell Geri that she could swap the pacifier for the red shoes. My brother Mike is an orthodontist, and he had continuously warned us of the potential problems with her front teeth if she continued to suck her pacifier or her thumb. So we wanted to get rid of that pacifier as soon as possible. We realized that Geri might not be as excited about this idea as we were, and that we would have to somehow convince her that this was a good deal. This goal was also a little risky since Geri could forget about the pacifier and just start sucking her thumb. However, we decided that if push came to shove, we could always return her pacifier.

The next day when we initiated the attack, we concentrated on the red shoes. We talked about how nice they were, and how good Geri would look in them. We really made a production of it, and any wallflower watching the proceedings would have thought we were casting for a Broadway play. Once we were sure we had peaked Geri's interest in the shoes, we started talking about what things she could wear with them. Finally, we pointed out that she would not look good in those new red shoes with that old pacifier in her mouth. At first Geri did not see any reason why the pacifier would not be an excellent match. However, we kept pushing our point, and when we felt that she was at least leaning in our direction, we told her that we were sure that she could swap the pacifier for the red shoes. That was a really tough decision for Geri, but Edie and I just kept a positive approach while Geri decided what to do. Finally, she agreed to the swap, and so as soon as we could, we went to pick up the red shoes. While Geri was not looking, I paid the saleslady for the red shoes. Geri gave the lady her pacifier (which the saleslady returned to me), I brought it home, hid it in a closet and fortunately never had to get it out again.

When our son, John, was sixteen, he bought a motorcycle with money he had earned while throwing newspapers and working part-time in stores. Even though it was a small motorcycle, not suitable for highway use, I had tried unsuccessfully to convince him not to buy it. There had been a number of motorcycle accidents just prior to the time he purchased the bike, and I was really afraid for him to have one. Although he rode the bike for approximately eighteen months, I never felt good about it, and I was continuously looking for a way to get rid of it.

During the summer prior to John's senior year in high school, we took all the kids to Fort Walton Beach, Florida for a vacation. While we were there, John met some girls from Meridian, Mississippi. They invited him to come over for a visit before school started, and he agreed to go. He did not have the money for a bus ticket, and I wouldn't give it to him, so he started working at odd jobs to earn the money for the bus fare. We did tell John, however, that we would be happy to pay for one long distance call to make all the arrangements for the trip. A week or two before he was going to leave, I noticed that he was on the phone an awful lot. I just assumed he was talking to his friends in town. When the time to leave arrived, we put John on the bus. Since the girl's parents were not told about the invitation, what happened on the trip was an almost unbelievable adventure in itself, but suffice it to say, he returned several days later safe and sound.

About three weeks later, as football practice was beginning, we received our monthly telephone statement. When I opened it to pay the bill, I could hardly believe my eyes. There were several pages listing long distance calls, and essentially every one of them was to Meridian, Mississippi. When I added up the calls, with the exception of one large one which I had agreed to pay, the total was a little more than seventy dollars. That figure was even more than the bus ticket. As soon as I gathered my composure, I started trying to figure out what I was going to do to him for this. The more I thought about it, the more I believed that this was a blessing in disguise. I knew that John owed me about seventy dollars. I knew that football practice was starting, and that John really wanted to play. I also knew that he was broke; however, he had one marketable asset—that motorcycle! All the sudden it was my turn to feel good, and his turn to sweat.

When John came home that day I sat down with him and showed him the phone bill. I reminded him that I had agreed to pay for one call and that I had deducted the biggest one from the total bill to cover the cost of the call to set up the trip. Then I told him that I would have to pay the bill within two weeks, and that from my perspective he had two choices: he could forget about football and get a job, or he could sell the motorcycle. John did not like either alternative. I held my ground, asked him to think about it and let me know what he decided to do. While he thought it over, I reminded him that he had talked before about saving his money for a car. We also discussed the fact that this was his last year to play football. I thought I knew what he would do, but I was never really sure. I had backed him into a corner, and that is always a risky venture with a teenager. After what appeared to be much soul searching, John decided to sell the motorcycle. I was delighted. A couple of weeks later, he sold it for more than he had paid for it. I got the money for the phone bill, John got the start on a savings account for a car, but more importantly somebody else was riding that motorcycle.

While I was still a graduate student at the University of Tennessee at Knoxville, Edie and I had two kids in diapers and one on the way. We were living from hand to mouth in West Knoxville when the University built some new married student housing, called Taliwa Court. It was not only new, it was cheap. As soon as Edie and I realized that these new apartments were under construction, I went to the University Housing Office to get our names on the list. I remember that it was a Friday afternoon, and the office was almost empty. I sat down to talk to a young lady who was in charge of taking applications for the apartments and assigning families to them. After I completed the application, I asked her if we would be assigned a particular apartment at that time. Although she was very polite, she went to the filing cabinet and pulled out a stack of applications that would have choked a hippopotamus to death, and she put my application at the end of the file. She indicated that our chances of getting one of the apartments was somewhere around the sixth decimal place. I felt like someone had just drained all the blood out of my body. As I lapsed into a state of depression, I thanked her and left.

Two days later, as I was combing the pages of the Sunday edition of the Knoxville News Sentinel, I saw the young lady's engagement picture.

I recognized her immediately. As I read the announcement, it occurred to me that she might like to have an extra copy of it and, in addition, she might be able to offer me some advice that would aid me in finding other cheap and suitable housing.

The following morning, I went back to see the young lady at the housing office and took her engagement announcement that I had neatly cut from the newspaper and placed it in the kind of plastic folder that is used for term papers. I told her that I had recognized her picture and thought that she might like to have an extra copy. I then explained my urgent need for a suitable place to raise the Irwin tribe, and asked her if there was any advice or help she could give me. For what was probably only a couple of seconds, but seemed like ten, she just stared at me in a very unusual manner. I could tell that her brain was in overdrive, but I could not tell what she was thinking. Then, without saying a word to me, she went over to the filing cabinet, opened the folder with all the applications for Taliwa Court, and moved my application from the very bottom to somewhere up near the front. Then she turned to me to announce that after reexamining (and reshuffling) her files, she was absolutely confident that we would easily get an apartment in Taliwa Court. I thanked the young lady so many times that she was embarrassed to be in the same room with me. My original probability of getting an apartment in Taliwa Court was absolutely nonexistent, and all of the sudden I was a shoo-in.

There are times when the lemon is simply dropped into our laps, and we have to plan our attack in real time. I encountered such a situation at work with a colleague named Frank. Frank and I had worked together for only a short time. However, in that time I had learned that he was a very competent individual. He was a nice guy, and I got along with him well. I also learned that he was a little like nitroglycerin, i.e., it did not take much shaking to set him off.

I had assigned him a particular task to do. It was not easy, but it was right up his alley. I will probably never know all the circumstances that rattled his cage this particular day, but when he came in to see me, I knew the instant he walked into my office that he was livid. He had apparently walked up and down the hall working himself into a frenzy and then came rolling into my office to explode. He started complaining about the task I had given him in addition to all the other work he had to do. The words were flying at me like bullets out of a machine gun. He wouldn't shut up long enough for me to talk to him. The longer he talked, the louder he got. I had to somehow get him to stop blasting away at me. Since I was only permitted to respond in monosyllables without escalating the confrontation to a shouting match, I decided to take the opposite tack.

I remained very calm, and as he got louder, my short statements became softer. Within perhaps a minute or two, he was almost screaming, and I was down to a whisper. All of the sudden, as if he had been hit in the face with a baseball bat, he must have realized the enormous difference in volume that existed in the room. I was sitting there calmly whispering to him, and he was screaming at me like a raving maniac. I think it was the instant he realized what this conversation would have sounded like to an outsider, that he calmed down to the point where I could talk to him. When I got a chance to talk, I explained to him that I knew he was busy, and I also knew that the task I had assigned him was not easy. However, every task he was assigned had been done extremely well. He was first class, and I needed someone of that caliber to solve this problem. Finally, I told him that if he felt that he could not handle the task, I would understand. But that would be the easy way out. I had selected him because I knew he was better than that, and I was sure he could do a better job than anyone else I could select.

When he left my office, he said he would think about it. I didn't hear another word about it for about ten days. At that time, he walked into my office calmly, but beaming with pride. He had completed the task, and he had done his usual outstanding job. Now it was my turn to scream, and I did a lot of it. I fell all over myself complimenting him, and I told everyone else I could find what a super job he had done.

In thinking of this story, I am reminded of the following quote by Robert Louis Stevenson, the Scottish novelist,

> You cannot run away from a weakness; you must sometime fight it out or perish; and if that be so, why not now, and where we stand?[29]

Although we can be dealt a lemon in any one of a number of different ways, quite often lemons arise because of our own weaknesses or failures in some endeavor. Our reaction to any loss, however, foreshadows our ability to win later. Instead of blaming others or circumstances, playing a martyr or victim, or simply getting mad, successful people learn from every setback or defeat. Mistakes can be milestones in our careers if we face them, analyze them, and derive a plan to correct them. They are

---

29. Stevenson, "48 Inspiring Quotes."

simply a component of our education, and the winners won't make the same mistake twice.

Constructive self-criticism can be a very effective tool in our development. Suppose for a moment that a member of our family has mysteriously died and we ask the physician what happened. If their response is "Well, you know, we win some and lose some," we would be absolutely incensed. Not only is the comment hurtful, insensitive, and apathetic, it contains no information, so we don't know how to prevent it the next time.

Many winners have a basket full of failures. How can they possibly advance, achieve, or succeed at anything without risking failure? Success and failure are inextricably joined. Since winners and losers are both failures at times, it is important to note that the difference between them is that winners learn from their failures and keep right on until they fail into success. They seem to instinctively understand, as Michael Korda, the British writer, states,

> The freedom to fail is vital if you're going to succeed. Most successful men fail time and time again, and it is a measure of their strength that failure merely propels them into some new attempt at success.[30]

With a positive mental attitude, winners seize control. They never rely on their horoscope or biorhythms, and they couldn't care less if Jupiter is aligned with Mars. They are intent on success, and one way or another they will succeed. As William Hazlitt has pointed out,

> A strong passion for any object will ensure success, for the desire of the end will point out the means.[31]

Successful people hang tough and exhibit tremendous "staying power." For example, as we have indicated earlier, Thomas Edison failed so many times that anyone else who did not possess his persistence would have folded their tent and given up after only a few thousand failures. Not Edison. For him a failure was simply the process by which he eliminated a number of possibilities.

Imagine for a moment a stock investor who is consistently right 75 percent of the time. Do you realize that while that individual is failing one out of every four times, he is more than likely making money hand over fist?

30. Korda, "Michael Korda Quotes."
31. Hazlitt, "Strong Passion for Any Object..."

8

The Ultimate Strategy

The Balancing Act

THERE IS AN IMPORTANT message in the following statement by Samuel Brengle, an American author:

> The final estimate of men shows that history cares not an iota for the rank and title a man has borne, or the office he has held, but only the quality of his deeds and the character of his mind and heart.[1]

Although the terms are often used interchangeably within the context of positive achievement, in the general sense there is a subtle, and yet important, difference between success and winning. For example, by placing a bet, I can win a lot of money in a lottery; however, as the famous British writer H. G. Wells has said, "The only true measure of success is the ratio between what we might have been on the one hand, and the thing we have made of ourselves on the other."[2]

Note carefully that this statement makes no reference to comparing ourselves with others, and there is no mention of the acquisition of material possessions. However, success as defined here, requires discipline, which in turn is the key to balance. Success costs, and we have to pay the price; unfortunately, it is not cheap. Through discipline we gain control of our lives. We are free to choose from among a myriad of opportunities with which life presents us, and through a disciplined approach, we are able to match our talents and interests to the opportunities at hand.

1. Brengle, "One of the Outstanding Ironies..."
2. Wells, "H. G. Wells Quotes."

When we view our lives in a global sense, it is impossible to overestimate the importance of balance. My mother used to tell me, "All work and no play makes Johnny a dull boy." However, I was a slow learner. I used to beat my head against the wall, trying desperately to accomplish something. Finally, when I became absolutely exasperated and went on to something else, I realized that the next time I looked at the problem, it did not seem quite as difficult as it appeared to be initially. I recall having to counsel my oldest daughter, Geri, for working too hard. She was a senior in electrical engineering at Auburn University and was studying her brains out. In a tearful dialogue, she confided that she wasn't having any fun. She literally lived from one exam to the next. I told her about my own similar experience, and then together we devised a plan for her to study more efficiently while simultaneously spending more time doing other things she enjoyed. Under the new plan, life became more enjoyable for her, and she did at least as well in her classes as she had done before.

I am absolutely convinced from numerous personal experiences that the balanced approach to life is best. I am not advocating that we grind our business activities to a halt. Absolutely not. I still work like someone driven, but I don't do it all the time.

In this highly technological world scientists and engineers are perhaps the best prepared to contribute to the fundamental developments which are capable of radically changing the way in which we live. Think for a moment of the advances in communication, electronics, medicine, and transportation, to name only a few of the obvious ones. While there is no doubt that these technologists are successful in their field of interest, the executive suite is normally filled with individuals who not only possess an appreciation for technical expertise, but are also balanced by interpersonal skills and business acumen.

An unbalanced approach normally results from the application of tunnel vision. We are so committed to some course of action that we have no peripheral vision at all. As a result, trouble can be brewing all around us, and we don't even know it is there. In extreme cases some people become so determined to win at something that they don't care what they have to do to achieve it. I recall one day being a passenger in an automobile with a driver, who, because he was completely frustrated by the driver ahead of us, said jokingly (Lord, I hope he was joking), "I am going to pass that automobile ahead of us if I have to kill everybody in this car doing it." That extreme approach could have very serious consequences.

On the other hand, I have met numerous people who are not only extremely successful captains of industry, but upon close examination have found that they are devoted to their family and also major contributors to religious and civic organizations. Their activities are so wide and varied that if I were involved in their endeavors, there would need to be three of me. In fact, from interfacing with very successful people, I have learned that while they are occasionally and judiciously forced to say no, in general, they willingly give of themselves, their time, their wealth, their love and support.

Variety is the spice of life, and there are myriad activities that can be pursued in order to enhance our lifestyles. We can join clubs or groups of people who enjoy the same kind of things that we do. We can do something as sedentary as reading or as active as sports. We might find tremendous fulfillment in the community by helping make it a better place to live, or in the church by helping needy families or organizing religious education activities. The list of possibilities is almost endless.

If we find ourselves in a rut, we can get out of it by organizing our time so that we always spend a portion of it in leisure, or something other than our main thrust that we feel is worthwhile. In addition, we must not become so wrapped up in any set of activities that we completely ignore our health. After all, it is a fundamental precursor for practically everything else that we do. Diet and exercise are perhaps the two critical variables that we can control, which have a significant impact on our health posture, and therefore must be given priority because they are a necessary and integral part of our balanced approach to life.

Even within the limited sphere of any one particular aspect of our lives, balance remains critical. While this concept of balance has wide application, the lack of it is perhaps most visible in those individuals who not only strive for, but believe they can achieve, perfection. The dedication and perseverance required to strive for perfection are marks of a successful individual. However, the absolute belief that perfection can be achieved is a tragic mistake. Perfectionists strive valiantly for a level of achievement that is often unrealistic, and pursue their goals with such irrational intensity that the slightest error is catastrophic. They believe beyond any doubt that if they work long enough and hard enough, they can achieve perfection in what they do. However, because they are unrealistic in establishing their goals, they guarantee failure. In an attempt to compensate, they work harder, the level of intensity rises, and the number of failures increases. The ultimate results are self-doubt, depression, and panic, which taken in total can be absolutely devastating. For example, I have known students who were extremely intelligent and maintained a straight A average for years. However, in what appears to be a tragic act of desperation, they dropped out of school because the inherent pressure to continue to perform at this high level was too intense.

The non-perfectionist, on the other hand, makes certain that his goals are high, but realistic, and his standards are at least somewhat comparable to others in similar situations. He learns from his mistakes and those of others, and is satisfied with his best performance, whatever it is. As a result, he is not only balanced, he is in control.

Since the balance concept should extend to every facet of our lives, it must be applied to our families as well. For example, it is just as important to be a personal success as it is to be a business success, and sometimes it is even harder. Our families deserve their fair share of our time and interests too. If we are not truly interested in them and don't devote time and energy to them, look out. There is a school of thought that subscribes to the idea that children demand discipline, and it they don't get it in the home, they will eventually get it on the street. Therefore, within a positive and upbeat framework, one viable strategy for dealing with children encompasses the following: reward good behavior, punish major misbehavior, and don't sweat the small stuff in between.

Whether we realize it or not, our children are continuously watching and learning from us. We are teachers, and we set the standards whether we like it or not. Many years ago I heard a popular song, the thrust of which I will never forget. It struck a resonant chord in my brain every time I heard it. If you are a Type A personality, you will find it thought-provoking at the very least. The song is entitled "Cats in the Cradle," it is sung by Harry Chapin, and can be heard on YouTube Music. The lyrics provide a very sobering, and for some tearful, message. It is unfortunate that there are times in our lives when the number of opportunities to get it right are limited, and when they are missed, recovery is almost impossible.

If we don't achieve a balance in our lives, we are going to have to accept the consequences, for as we sow, so shall we reap.

On one of my trips to Japan many years ago, a female tour guide, who was also a mother, told me about a national survey that was conducted there at that time. If I understood her correctly, she said that this survey indicated that the mothers, although devoted to their children, were less enthusiastic about their husbands. Apparently, the husbands spent just enough time with the family to have a family. The Japanese government was carefully studying the results because of their serious overtones, but many believed this situation would be hard to combat because of Japan's historic work ethic.

Raising children is an extremely important task, and the consequences of doing it poorly can be devastating. However, some people get so wrapped up in every minute detail of their children's activities that I am afraid that their lives will be absolutely boring when their youngest child leaves the nest. Some parents continue to remain closely involved in their children's activities after the children have left home. This closeness is normally good unless the parents have refused to cut the umbilical cord and are in essence preventing their children from emerging as their own persons. However, regardless of one's passion in life, e.g., family or business, or anything else, an unbalanced approach will normally lead to some kind of personal, social or medical problem.

Finally, true balance in our lives is impossible without a link to the source of all supply—Almighty God, and it is through prayer that we link our mind with the Mind of God. When we align our thoughts and activities with the God Mind, we receive the guidance and strength necessary for the achievement of any good. As it is stated in Isaiah 58:11,

> Then the Lord will guide you always and give you plenty even on the parched land. He will renew your strength, and you shall be like a watered garden, like a spring whose water never fails.

After all, health, happiness, prosperity, like any good, is a divine idea which emanates from God, and therefore, is an integral part of his plan for us.

Our entire world is always in a quasi-state of instability. Changes occur daily that impact essentially every aspect of our lives. However, our operating system must remain tightly coupled to the Divine Mind, for God is our stable platform, and it is only through Him that we can ever really achieve a balanced life.

The Proper Perspective

The theoretical physicist, Albert Einstein says the following:

> Many times a day I realize how my own outer and inner life is built upon the labors of my fellow man, both living and dead,

and how earnestly I must exert myself in order to give in return as much as I have received and am still receiving.[3]

Albert Einstein was obviously very capable of enormous achievement, and his labors will live on as hallmarks of science. However, as we strive to succeed and leave our mark upon the world, the dominos will not always fall as we had planned. It may appear to us that inequities exist all around us and that justice is not served in our lives. When these thoughts invade our minds, we must remember that we are always in the care and keeping of Almighty God, and his plan for us is only good. Well-known to him, but veiled from us is the road ahead, and along that road the interplay of our lives with those of others. In addition, God's loving justice is an underlying principle that continuously works in and through us, and is therefore one of the foundation pillars of our existence. Through prayer we stay in-tune with God's will, which for us is always manifested through the guidance he provides. Fundamental to that guidance is the call in Matthew 7:12 to love and help one another: i.e.,

> Do to others whatever you would have them do to you. This is the law and the prophets.

Corrections required in the lives of others will be supplied by Almighty God, and even he waits until the last chapter of life is written before he administers the final justice. Our part in life is not to judge another. As stated in Luke 6:37,

> Stop judging and you will not be judged. Stop condemning and you will not be condemned. Forgive and you will be forgiven.

We may think that another's load is light in comparison with our own, and that it would be easy for us to do what is required of them. However, the same is true for us. What we consider to be a terrible burden may be handled with ease by someone else. How could we possibly know all the circumstances that surround another's action. Even to "walk in his moccasins for two weeks" could never allow us to understand the imprints of a lifetime that have influenced his life. We can only lead him to God and let him make the necessary corrections.

In administering his justice, he may teach us things we could not learn in any other way. For example, he may give us a dose of our own medicine to illustrate that it can often be a bitter pill to swallow. Several

---

3. Einstein, "Albert Einstein Quotes."

decades ago, I was part of a team running a technical conference at MIT. One of the people we had to work with was absolutely obnoxious. Those of us working with him learned that he was so obtuse that we could not even insult him. However, I got so frustrated with him at one point that I did insult him, and I did it in front of the whole team. It was a bad scene, and I should not have done it.

A couple of days later when I returned home I had to attend a meeting chaired by one of the administrators, several layers above me in the chain of command. I was not prepared for the meeting, and I made a comment that displayed my ignorance in full bloom. In response, the chair metaphorically sliced me to pieces. I am sure my face was several shades of red, and I was belittled in front of my colleagues. Since I had just returned from the trip, I remember thinking, I asked for this, it's payback time, and in his infinite wisdom, God delivered.

However, Almighty God is a just and loving God and nothing, absolutely nothing, is beyond his reach. All power belongs to him. For those who remain close to him, the implications are utterly astounding. We should be ecstatic, bold and fearless, secure in his strength, with the absolute conviction that victory is never beyond our reach.

God's constant loving presence is a stabilizing force which tends to combat the tyranny of modern life. Our lives seem to be fashioned around deadlines and drop-dead dates, the mere sound of which invokes feelings of constraint and vulnerability. Many of the things we do tend to have foreboding overtones, and failure to maintain the proper perspective can lead to feelings of coming apart at the seams. While striving to be a success, we must also guard against taking ourselves and our life's encounters so seriously. If we view encounters as a life and death struggle, we will be depressed a large part of the time because we simply will not win every encounter. However, if we maintain our perspective, we will view a setback as nothing more than a ripple on the smooth path of our forward progress.

It is indeed the rare individual who does not encounter one problem after the next along the road of life. In fact, most of us would be lucky if we could just have the problems occur in tandem rather than in parallel, so we could address them one at a time. Regardless of the number of problems or the frequency with which they occur, we can avoid stress, which often accompanies them, if we remind ourselves that God is always in charge, and in spite of the problems which surround us, all is well. Almighty God's continuous message to us is love and laugh. When we display a sense of humor and look on the bright side of every situation, our entire system is revitalized and energized. As clearly stated in Proverbs 17:22,

> A joyful heart is the health of the body, but a depressed spirit dries up the bones.

Even while trying to do the will of Almighty God, we are going to make, what we believe to be, mistakes. They are not mistakes. We learn by mistakes, and the wisest among us learn our lessons quickly. The suffering and pain that often accompany our errors are never accidental. They are the means by which God teaches lessons that support our growth. Sometimes the lessons to be learned are extremely difficult, but remember that it is only at very high temperatures that we transform raw ore into steel.

Sometimes our training must be severe so that we are prepared for the life Almighty God has planned for us. The training may even lead to shame of oneself; however, we must learn to view it as nothing more than an integral part of our development. Therefore, we must never dwell on the sins of the past and look back only to learn from them. Instead, press on, eyes firmly fixed on the goal. Today, right here and now, is the beginning of the rest of our lives.

How many times in life have we wished for and planned for some event which did not happen, only to realize weeks, months, or perhaps years later that it would have been a mistake, and sometimes a terrible one?

Real estate is a hobby of mine, and I continuously watch for deals anywhere I go. Many years ago, a new development was being planned in an area that I visited from time to time. This looked like it would be an upscale development with waterfront lots. I was really interested in buying one of them as an investment. The initial selling price was high, but it appeared to me that the cost would only increase with time as houses were built there. However, I would really have to go out on a limb to buy it, and it would put a real strain on my finances. As I tried to make this deal work, there was always some problem in completing it. As soon as I solved one problem another would appear. Finally, I just gave up and forgot about it. Several years later, I was again in the area and learned that the value of this property, and those around it, had decreased substantially. If I had somehow been able to buy this lot, I would have had trouble making the payments, in addition to losing a lot of money. God knew this was a bad deal, and I am convinced he kept setting up roadblocks to ensure that I was unable to make it work. We must realize that our vision is so limited that it actually distorts the actual situation.

When we do not get an instant answer to our prayer for help, it does not mean that God has not heard our request. Like a loving father carefully watching over every aspect of our lives, God knows and wants to help. However, we are not hermits. Our lives are so intertwined with those of others that it takes time to devise a plan that not only will reconcile our need, but everyone else's as well. God is the only one capable of deriving an optimal solution, since he is the only one who knows all the parameters. Remember, with him, all things are possible, and his desire for us is always our highest good. In 1 Thessalonians 5:17–18 we read,

> Pray without ceasing. In all circumstances give thanks, for this is the Will of God for you in Christ Jesus.

When our troubles, whatever they may be, seem overwhelming, God is the one place we can always go for shelter from the raging storms of life. Deuteronomy 23:29 states, "The Lord is your saving shield, and his sword is your glory." In him, we find faith, hope, and love, and worry and fear cannot exist with these three.

Jesus' message to us on worry can be found in Matthew 6:25–32.

> Therefore I tell you do not worry for your life, what you will eat [or drink], or about your body, what you will wear. Is not life more than food, and the body more than clothing? Look at the birds in the sky; they do not sew or reap, they gather nothing into barns, yet your Father feeds them. Are not you more important than they? Can any of you by worrying add a single moment to your life-span? Why are you anxious about clothes? Learn from the way the wild flowers grow. They do not work or spin. But I tell you that not even Solomon in all his splendor was clothed like one of them. If God so clothes the grass of the field, which grows today and is thrown into the oven tomorrow, will he not much more provide for you, O you of little faith?
>
> So do not worry and say, "What are we to eat?", or "What are we to drink?", or "What are we to wear?" All these things the pagans seek. Your heavenly Father knows that you need them all.

Jesus knows that the more we worry about a problem, the more unfit we are to deal with it effectively. Therefore, like Moses we have to go forward, without concern, certain that when we reach our "Red Sea" the waters will part and we will achieve that for which we strive. In steadfast obedience to his direction we must let go and let God. As Loretta P. Burns so eloquently states,

> Like children bring their broken toys with tears for us to mend,
> I brought my broken dreams to God because He was my friend.
> But then instead of leaving Him in peace to work alone
> I hung around and tried to help with ways that were my own.
> At last I snatched them back and cried, "God, how can you be so slow?"
> "My child," He said, "what could I do? You never did let go."[4]

Someone said that hindsight is 20/20, and although it is usually impossible for us to see clearly the path that lies ahead, in many cases we can look back upon the path traversed and remember the manner in which the pieces have coalesced to form the mosaic which represents our lives. When we do this, we find that there have been many crucial situations in which somehow the pieces mysteriously fell together to save us in one case or support us in another. In addition, a very careful analysis indicates that we had very little or no control over some of the most crucial pieces, and yet without them, success in some aspect of our life would have been impossible. The success-oriented individual is naturally led to question this fascinating phenomenon. For example, is there some way for us to increase the probability that whenever necessary the pieces will always line up in the manner required? By now we must know that we can accomplish this only through the Divine Presence and Power of Almighty God. Nothing, absolutely nothing, is beyond his control. I know there have been many cases in my own life when he has extended his hand to protect me in situations which otherwise seemed to me to be completely intractable. I signed a contract to buy an expensive piece of property. Prior to closing I learned that this property had some environmental issues that would have a detrimental effect on my ability to use it or develop it. Based upon this new data, I wanted to get out of the contract. However, the sellers wanted to get rid of it, and they refused to let me out, even threatening to sue for performance. I was stuck with no visible means of escaping. However, a new investor appeared on the scene—out of nowhere, and was willing to buy the property for what I had agreed to pay. So, the sellers let me out of the contract, and sold the property to him. Hallelujah! I knew that God had his fingerprints all over this deal, and I was so thankful that he had extricated me from it.

---

4. Burns, "Broken Dreams."

I am totally confident that if anyone who endeavors to live in the shadow of Jesus Christ will very thoughtfully review their past, they will be able to recall events in their lives in which impediments to their progress were somehow removed. Furthermore, since our Lord has saved us in so many cases, he will continue to do so. Simple logic dictates that he would not extract us from one catastrophic situation only to destroy us in another.

God asks us to carry only a single day's load. During that day we must forget the past, since it is gone and cannot be repeated. Have no fear of the future, because it is not here yet, and the things we anticipate could change before it arrives. Concentrate only on the tasks at hand. The failures of the past, together with the problems of the future, coupled with the load of the day is too heavy for any of us. In addition, in our upward climb, if we stop to cry each time we stump our toe or scratch our leg, we will never reach the pinnacle we strive to achieve. At the end of the day, when we have done all that we could, Almighty God readily accepts from us our unfinished work. He will then either complete it himself or he will make any adjustments necessary for us before he returns it. Victor Hugo, the French poet, says it well:

> Have courage for the great sorrow of life and patience for the smaller ones; and when you have laboriously accomplished your daily task, go to sleep in peace.[5]

The capability to see only one day at a time provides the impetus for developing and sustaining a strong faith. In Matthew 8:13 we find the passage,

> As you have believed, let it be done for you.

For a moment, think of the awesome importance of this statement. Do we really believe or not? Our answer may have some rather significant consequences. Jesus said, "Except ye become as little children, ye cannot enter the kingdom of heaven" (Matt 18:3). When a small child is told by their mother that something will be done, there is absolute faith that it will indeed be accomplished. Not even the slightest hint of question arises. Although it may be very difficult for us to adhere to this philosophy in every aspect of our lives, we must learn to do so because it is a fundamental component of our winning strategy.

---

5. Hugo, "Victor Hugo Quotes."

Almighty God calls upon us to be faithful to him on a daily basis in the small and sometimes insignificant things of life. Day in and day out we are asked to follow his guidance in a routine fashion. However, if we are truly faithful to him, even during the dark days of our lives, then when we really need him, we can very confidently call upon him with the absolute conviction that he will reward our faithfulness with the best possible answer to our prayers. The answer may not be what we expect, or precisely what we desire, but it will be the best solution for us in the long run.

Each one of us is unique. Therefore, our role in this life cannot be filled by anyone but us. We have special talents and capabilities that are necessary and important for our present position in this world. The knowledge of this truth provides us with a positive, healthy, and productive self-image. As stated in Psalm 82:6, "You are gods, all of you sons of the most high." Therefore, if we are good and faithful servants, success for us is essentially a birthright. In order to achieve that success, however, we must discipline ourselves so that we become an efficient instrument for executing *his* wishes; he will take care of *our* wishes.

As sons and daughters of our Heavenly Father, great things are expected of us. However, he is always with us to aid us in achieving them. He is the same yesterday, today, tomorrow, and forever. Although he is always present at the very core of our being, rarely do we go there to talk to him. We are too busy with the temporal things of this world, and yet the time spent in communion with him is like a shot of high test fuel for our internal engines. Isaiah 40:31 states it well:

> They that hope in the Lord shall renew their strength, they will soar as with eagles' wings; they will run and not grow weary, walk and not grow faint.

How many of us would like to be close personal friends of the President of the United States? So, close, in fact, that we could talk with him whenever we wish and count on him to help us achieve our goals. If we were actually in this position, wouldn't we be winners? The potential we would possess from our close association with him would be incredible. We would undoubtedly feel that we were in a position to accomplish many things that we would like to do that are in the realm of possibility. Now compare for a moment the President with Almighty God. This statement itself is, of course, absolutely ridiculous. How could we possibly compare *any* human being with the creator and master of the entire universe? And yet we can be as close to God as we want to be. Think about it—the potential is utterly astounding! In such a position, how could we be anything but successful? In fact, we must be very careful to pursue only good through a positive and helpful attitude, since we have such awesome power at our disposal. Even within this framework all of our desires may not be fulfilled, and we may never understand the reasons why. However, we can be thankful for what we have. At the very least we are free and we live in the greatest country in the world—even people who hate it live here and they, of course, are free to leave. Whenever I am unable to achieve some particular desire, I am reminded of a sign I saw on the wall in a restaurant in Gulf Shores, Alabama. The sign read "Instead of complaining because you don't get what you want, be thankful you don't get what you deserve."

The Christian Lifestyle

The following advice from Phillips Brooks, an American clergyman, is important as we seek to establish and maintain a Christian lifestyle.

> Do not pray for easy lives! Pray to be stronger men. Do not pray for tasks equal to your powers. Pray for power equal to your tasks. Then the doing of your work shall be no miracle. But you shall be a miracle.[6]

We have to expect to live in a chaotic world where things are in a constant state of change. These changes, which routinely occur in our lives, may at times place us in positions which shift or disturb our normal progress. When this happens, it is not the circumstances that surround us that need to be altered, but rather our perception of them. We must first examine our own mind and make the necessary corrections there; and if we do, the external conditions will naturally follow suit. To begin we have to remember two things: God is in charge, and his plan for us is always our highest good. In addition, it is in dealing with adverse circumstances that we learn and grow. For example, if we lose a job, it may be because there is a better opportunity waiting in the wings if we will only look for it. Through a positive mental attitude, we can turn the lemon into a lemonade by finding that we are capable of much more than we are currently doing. We have to just keep plugging, moving forward with

---

6. Brooks, "Do Not Pray for Easy Lives..."

perseverance, and knowing that Almighty God is managing all of the traffic lights which control the flow of our lives.

We are going to have problems, and we are going to make mistakes; however, we can work more effectively with others if we too have had similar experiences. The Bible recounts a number of occasions in which Saint Peter essentially walked on his own tongue, and yet Jesus selected him to be the first leader of the Catholic Church. Like a tree, we must have a strong root system, firmly based in Christian principles in order to withstand all the trials and tribulations of life. In an analogous manner, a skyscraper must have a very firm and well-constructed foundation. And so it is with us as we strive to reach higher and higher.

Just as the flow of traffic within a city is controlled by traffic signals, the sequence of events in our lives is under God's control. In order to move efficiently through a city, we must obey and cooperate with these traffic signals. If we speed or run a red light, we may be stopped and fined, and if we take detours in our haste to move more quickly, we may end up on dead-end streets. Our lives are much the same. God works at his own pace. He has planned it all, and our best strategy is one of complete cooperation. If we try to speed things up or take a different route, we will more than likely have even more problems. As stated in Deuteronomy 6:16,

> You shall not put the Lord, your God, to the test.

By tempting him, we not only disobey him, but we demonstrate our ignorance, for how could we possibly devise a plan that is better than his?

God defines the way and the pace, and he asks us to conform to it. Although the peer pressure is often enormous, the "I gotta be me" philosophy unfortunately will not work. We cannot simply decide to obey only a subset of the traffic signals, and do whatever we wish with the others.

In order to know God well we must set aside time for communion with Him. He supplies our guidance, the food for our souls, and our inner strength. John 6:35 states the case well:

> I am the Bread of Life; whoever comes to me will not hunger,
> and whoever believes in me will never thirst.

When we center ourselves in Almighty God, we are perfectly balanced. In this sense, we are somewhat like rotating machinery. As anyone who is familiar with this equipment knows, a machine that is a little out of balance causes vibration, and a machine that is way out of balance will completely destroy itself.

All too often we think that we know best, but *obedience* is the real watchword. Recall, for example, Peter's encounter with Jesus in which Peter and his associates in the fishing business had fished throughout the entire night and caught nothing. At this point, Jesus asked them to take their boats out into deep water and lower their nets. Although this was a simple request, it must have appeared to be without merit and a total waste of time. After all, if they could not catch any fish throughout the entire night, why would there be any fish there now. Furthermore, Jesus was a carpenter by trade, and Peter and his associates fished for a living. It would not have been unreasonable for Peter to politely refuse to do it, or at least ask for some data to support what at this point would appear to be a very unusual request. Instead, however, Peter told Jesus that if he wanted them to go out and lower the nets, they would. As we know, Peter's obedience was rewarded, since within a few minutes the boat was completely loaded with fish.

God is always with us, but we must have faith that he knows best. When Peter, fearing for his life, stepped out upon the water, he found that he could indeed walk on it. Not until Peter began to doubt Jesus, did he begin to sink. However, even then Jesus in his infinite mercy gives Peter a hand. We too can do more than we would ever believe is humanly possible if we couple our faith with obedience to God's plan. We have to understand that our needs are God's opportunity to confirm our faith. Our faith is the spark that ignites the awesome power of God to save us. Throughout our lives miracles are sometimes necessary, and therefore they should be an integral part of our game plan. However, remember that miracles are not necessarily the work of a single instant in time; God works at his own pace, everything is under his control and he will not test us beyond our capacity.

On a daily basis our job is very simply that of following the guidance of God. In the absence of some specific turn signal, we are called upon to follow our usual routine. At times we may even wonder whether we are on the right track. However, God made us, and therefore he knows a priori how we will react to any given set of inputs and conditions. For example, if we are faced with alternatives on some issue under some set of circumstances, he knows what our preference will be.

Decades ago, I was offered a position with a company. The deal included a lot of company perks. I thought about the offer long and hard. More importantly, I prayed about it long and hard. However, I never felt that my question was answered. In spite of my efforts, it appeared that

God was not going to tell me what to do. In the final analysis, I stayed put. In retrospect, I think, even though I cannot be sure, that I did the right thing. However, I am convinced that God knew the choice I would make, and therefore it must have been the right one.

When a signal to change direction comes, however, we must promptly move in the right direction. There are times when God casts us in a part in which our function is to help to bring lost souls back home to him. He leads and we must very methodically follow. In some cases, we may not even realize the identity of the target of our efforts, and therefore we must be extremely careful to adhere to his directions or we could spoil the entire plan.

We need not know the future. In a kind and merciful manner God reveals it to us only one day at a time. He is always with us, and our faith takes care of the rest. Taken together, faith and obedience are an awesome force for removing any evil that may lie in our path.

The Christian Chamber of Commerce (CCC) reports that there are, and have been, a host of corporations that are run by very religious individuals, and the number is growing rapidly. Some of the most notable names are Truett Cathy, founder of Chick-fil-A; Sanford McDonnel, Chairman and CEO of McDonnel Douglas Corporation; Kenneth Olsen, founder of Digital Equipment Corporation; Thomas Phillips, CEO of Raytheon Corporation; Richard DeVos, President of Amway; and David Green, the founder of Hobby Lobby. Today, the international headquarters, i.e., ICCC is in Orebro, Sweden, with locations throughout the entire world. Although devout Christians who operate in a Christian manner, they clearly separate religion and business at the office. While they freely give of their time, talents and wealth to help others, they are also extremely competent and efficient businessmen.

The tremendous success enjoyed by many Christian individuals appears to stem, in part, from their basic philosophy that God is first, family is second, and the company is third. An adherence to the relationships within this hierarchy helps to not only retain employees, but keep them happy. Within this structural framework, God is, in essence, a silent managing partner.

We often think of strong leaders as tough, hardnosed individuals, and indeed they usually are; however, behind that no-nonsense appearance is, in many cases, a heart of gold. Christians, regardless of their positions, learn never to judge by appearances. In particular, when it comes to people, what you think you see is not necessarily what you actually get.

We live in eternity, and within that framework our time on this earth is nothing more than a fine line on a time diagram. Within this perspective, we need to constantly remember the words in 2 Corinthians 4:18:

> As we look not to what is seen but to what is unseen; for what is seen is transitory, but what is unseen is eternal.

It is unfortunate that, at times, people who you truly believe to be your friends will stab you in the back. In some cases, their attitude changes to envy because of something you have achieved; others are naïve or easily led. Our natural reaction is to not only get mad, but get even. However, we must resist any thought of revenge. Grudges and resentments can be a very heavy burden, and are at times, too much to carry. Our lesson for handling these types of situations is given in John 21:22. When one of the disciples questioned Jesus concerning the actions of another, Jesus replied, "What is that to you? Follow me." In plain English, Jesus tells us that our job is to follow his guidance. We should not waste time criticizing others or questioning their actions. We should forgive and forget. Almighty God is in control, and he does not need our help or advice. If corrections are required in the lives of others, he will administer them.

We should forgive as often as necessary. When we do this we sweep our minds clear of any ill will. It is an emotional release, and we ourselves are better for it.

Jesus provides the following advice on this topic in Matthew 18:21–22 in the response: "'Lord, if my brother sins against me, how often must I forgive him? As many as seven times?' Jesus answered, 'I say to you not seven times, but seventy-seven times.'" In addition, in Luke 23:34, we recall that when they crucified Jesus, he said, "Father, forgive them, they know not what they do." Therefore, in one of his last acts on earth, Jesus teaches us a lesson in forgiveness.

In the Lord's prayer, we say, "Forgive us our trespasses as we forgive those who trespass against us." Do we *really* realize what we are saying? We are calling upon the all-knowing, all-powerful master of the entire universe to treat us in the exact manner that we treat our fellow man. Do we really want that? We do, of course, if we ourselves forgive and forget. Otherwise, it would appear that we might be on shaky ground.

Life is too short to spend it in hate or revenge. I'm afraid that there are many people who will one day realize that they have spent a significant portion of their lives in these modes. We cannot help but feel sorry for them. These periods of their lives are gone forever. In fact, do you realize that the time you spent reading the previous sentence is gone forever? We can only pray that they change their attitude as quickly as possible.

If we are truly repentant, God forgives us over and over, and as such, he holds no grudges or resentments. On the contrary, he gives to us in so many ways, and it is our faith that activates the process. Imagine for a moment the scenario in which a child asks his father for something easily within his grasp, and then proceeds in a manner which indicates his complete confidence that his father will supply it. Will the father supply the request? Is the Pope a Catholic? Almighty God supplies each of us in a different way, but according to our needs. For example, he gives comfort to those in distress, health to those who are sick and strength to the weak. We are also given talents and gifts, and we are asked to pass them on. Quoting Mother Teresa, "I alone cannot change the world, but I can cast a stone across the water to create many ripples."[7]

As Almighty God gives to us, we should in turn give to others, i.e., as we empty our storage facilities, God fills them up and the cycle repeats. Therefore, we must endeavor to be a clear and clean channel through which Almighty God can help us, as well as others. If we will simply cooperate by following his guidance, he will maneuver us into positions where we can not only improve ourselves, but help others as well. King George VI of the United Kingdom supports this philosophy with the comment, "The highest of distinction is the service of others."[8]

Each of us has much to offer. For example, even more important than material possessions, we can give respect, appreciation, love, time, sympathy, and understanding. At the right time and in the right place, which will of course be selected by Almighty God, these things can have a profound effect on the lives of others. It is interesting that this philosophy is presented in what is considered to be one of the greatest novels of the nineteenth century, *Les Misérables* by Victor Hugo. The novel outlines, in part, the struggles of an ex-convict, Jean Valjean, and his experience of redemption through life-altering changes, because someone (in this case, the Bishop Myriel) showed him great kindness. In a similar manner, the annals of history are replete with examples of people whose entire lives were altered because someone gave of themselves to help them. People have turned away from alcohol, crime, and drugs, while others

---

7. Mother Teresa, "I Alone Cannot Change the World…"
8. King George VI, "Highest of Distinctions…"

have turned unhappy existences into happy and productive lifestyles, or failures in some aspect of their lives into lasting successes.

In some cases it is easy for us to give to others. Family and friends are generally two groups with whom it is relatively easy for us to share. Unfortunately, and this is where it can get really sticky, some of the people that God sends into our lives can tax our system almost to the breaking point. In such situations, maintaining a Christian perspective can be a very difficult challenge. However, just as Almighty God makes the life-sustaining rain and sun to fall on both the good and the bad, we are called upon to give what we can to those that enter our lives regardless of their relationship to us. As Arnold H. Glasgow, an American businessman, has said,

> The true measure of a man is not the number of servants he has, but the number of people he serves.[9]

We can best give to others what we truly are ourselves. Therefore, we not only optimize our own performance, and hence our chances for personal success by matching our interests and capabilities to our career paths, but from this vantage point we are also better prepared to give what we can to others in an effective manner. When we sign up as one of God's foot soldiers, the contract guarantees us that he will constantly resupply us as indicated in Luke 6:38:

> Give and gifts will be given to you; a good measure, packed together, shaken down, and overflowing, will be poured into your lap. For the measure with which you measure will in turn be measured out to you.

When we give such things as our love, time, understanding, and wealth, God resupplies us so that we are always in a position to help those whom he sends our way. As stated in Matthew 22:39, "You should love your neighbor as yourself." If we continuously maintain an attitude of service, we are always in the proper position to give and it comes naturally. Perhaps the finest quality that anyone of us can possess is that of service to others. It is not necessary that we search for opportunities to serve; we must simply always be prepared. God is the architect, and he designs the opportunities. Our task is to implement his design. If our tools are always sharp, we will be ready to act on a moment's notice. As an analogy, cutting down a tree with a dull-bladed chainsaw is an almost impossible task, but when the sawblade is very sharp, the process is easily accomplished.

9. Glasgow, "Arnold Henry Glasgow."

If we are prepared, the seeds that God plants in our brain will bear tremendous fruit. However, if we are unreceptive, there will be no harvest and God's plan to work through us will be blocked. In John 14:12, Jesus says to us,

> Whoever believes in me will do the works that I do, and will do greater ones than these, because I am going to my Father."

Whoa! We should back up and read that quote again. When Jesus was on this earth, He cured the blind and the lame, and even brought Lazurus back to life. In clear view of all these stupendous feats, he tells us that we can even top them! If we are a clear, receptive, well-prepared channel, God will exercise his unlimited power through us, and then we will indeed be able to accomplish great works.

Jesus has set the pace and given us numerous examples to follow. We must learn from these examples so that in our daily lives we will exhibit the qualities he possessed such as love, humility, forgiveness, patience, peace, and understanding. There have been many times in my own life when I have tried to serve others simply by being there for them, and listening as they poured out their troubles upon me. I know that I have also been blessed to have someone there for me when the roles were reversed. Although those and other supportive activities may not appear to be of great significance, they can at times have a tremendous impact, not only on our lives but the lives of others.

As Francis of Assisi has so eloquently said,

> Lord, make me an instrument of your peace.
> Where there is hatred, let me sow love;
> Where there is injury, pardon;
> Where there is doubt, faith;
> Where there is despair, hope;
> Where there is darkness, light;
> Where there is sadness, joy;
> Lord, grant that I may seek to comfort, rather than to be comforted
> To understand rather than to be understood,
> To love rather than to be loved.
> For it is in giving that we receive,
> By forgiving that we are forgiven,
> And by dying that we awaken to eternal life.[10]

---

10. Francis of Assisi, "Peace Prayer of Saint Francis."

I recall that some time ago I was contacted by a man whom I had never met. He had been referred to me by a mutual friend. The man had encountered some problems in a particular organization because of some snafu in the paperwork. Initially, it appeared that it would take an act of Congress to get it straightened out. I knew some people who were in high positions in this organization that could be of help. But instead, I decided to call the individual who was actually handling the man's paperwork. He was very busy, but if something was not done soon, the situation would get worse quickly.

I contacted the individual and explained why I had called, and asked for his advice as to how I should proceed. I told him that I knew some very influential people, and I told him who they were. My friends were high above him in the chain of command, and I stated that I hated to bother them with this issue. I really wanted to secure, if at all possible, *his* help. I explained that if he could fix this situation, then I would be in a position to write to my friends, tell them that he had solved this complicated issue, and that they were so fortunate to have someone of his capability and knowledge on board. Guess what? He fixed the problem, and in addition I followed through and wrote my friends a glowing letter in which I praised this guy up one side and down the other.

Now, I could have taken a more negative approach, started at the top, and let the orders ripple down. Of course, I may have burned a bridge in the process. Unfortunately, when we are dealing with people who are uncooperative, unsympathetic and un-everything else, we may be forced into using what should always be the last approach. However, if he was essentially being attacked, the man handling the paperwork may have been able to find a legitimate reason to block my request. By taking the positive approach, it was in the man's best interest to ignore one if it existed. This was a win-win situation, with no losers in the whole game.

Fundamental to our nature is an inherent feeling of tremendous satisfaction and internal peace when we are able to be of service to someone else. If the people we help are not in a position to return the favor, so much the better. There are literally a myriad of ways in which we can be of service to others. In fact, it is absolutely fascinating that as we work to help others, we find that we cannot give anything away—because it comes right back to us. Smile at someone, and they will smile back. Love someone, and they will love us in return. Just think of the tremendous contributions that each of us can make if we will take the initiative and do something nice for someone else every day. As Aesop, the Greek storyteller, puts it,

> No act of kindness, no matter how small, is ever wasted.[11]

If we have a genuine interest in others, we share with them our time, talents and resources. In so doing, we have an opportunity to significantly impact not only the lives of others, but our own as well, since service to others is generally its own reward.

Through service to others, especially the needy, we give back to God some of the many blessings he has bestowed upon us. After all, we can't take it with us. I have never attended a funeral in which one of the vehicles was a U-Haul trailer, carrying the possessions owned by the deceased.

A simple word of encouragement or a pat on the back can mean a great deal to someone. Correctly timed, it may even change the course of their lives. I believe I can truthfully say that some of the most important events in my own life have been the times that I could provide someone with critical help and know beyond any doubt that I have touched their lives in a special way. Of course, anything that I do cannot be done without the help of God, and thus as stated in Matthew 5:16,

> Your light must shine before others, that they may see your good deeds and glorify your heavenly Father.

Our light, which comes from God, may represent love, kindness, patience, or help of some kind; and like a candle, which loses no light when lighting another, our light is in no way diminished when we give it to others.

An orientation toward service to others is also a fundamental concept in business. Countless individuals with a positive mental attitude have become extremely successful by finding a special way to meet people's needs and thereby be of service to them. Think for a moment about the stores where we shop. Do we shop at stores in which it appears that everything possible is being done to help us in any way that they can? Is the quality good, the price reasonable, are the salespeople friendly, and may they even know us by name? Does the attitude that permeates the store indicate that we are important to them, and they want to ensure that we are satisfied, if not delighted, with every purchase? Of course. On the other hand, do we shop at a store with the same type of merchandise, in which the sales force act like mindless, disinterested robots with little

11. Aesop, "No Act of Kindness…"

or no interest in our business? No need to answer; I know the answer is "No!"

Unfortunately, some salespeople have the attitude that they are doing us an enormous favor just to help us. Whenever this happens to me, I have to bite my tongue as I leave to keep from explaining to them the basic economics of the situation, i.e., people don't buy, store does not make money, store goes out of business, and they go out the door. Or management, who definitely understands the importance of service, observes their attitude and suggests they find employment elsewhere.

There are others who operate under the philosophy that if we will only pay them more, they will work more. These people have the cart before the horse, and any organization that is loaded with them is also probably headed right down the tubes.

While each of us, regardless of our position, can in some small way be of service to others, by virtue of their talents and accomplishments, the winners of this world are typically able to do much more. In situations where they can have a positive, and at times profound, impact on the lives of others, they will hopefully feel compelled to do so, for as stated in Luke 12:48,

> Much will be required of the person entrusted with much, and
> still more will be demanded of the person entrusted with more.

However, service has some unusual benefits for those who provide it. There is, of course, tremendous personal satisfaction in helping someone in any aspect of their life, but if we are really effective at helping others, God will often move us into successive positions of greater authority so we can, in turn, serve even more people. Therefore, an attitude of service to others is an effective strategy for winning. This message is clear in Matthew 25:21 where we read the passage

> Well done, my good and faithful servant. Since you were faithful
> in small matters, I will give you great responsibilities.

Almighty God wants us to be successful. For example, who is in a better position to help the most people: a group supervisor or the president of the company; a wealthy individual or someone living on the edge of poverty; a leader of government or one of the troops; a positive, forward-looking individual with a can-do attitude or the prophet of doom and gloom? Think about it. Life is like a chess game. The more capable players we have in strategic positions, the better. I can only guess that God would view it the same way. Therefore, let's make a giant step toward our own personal success by serving as best we can the needs of others. However, context is very important here. When examining the issue of service to others, the group that stands out among all others is the Saints. Most, if not all, of these individuals embraced poverty, and yet their success in serving others was monumental.

The Achievement of Happiness

You will find as you look back on your life that the moments that stand out above everything else are the moments when you have done things in a spirit of love.

—HENRY DRUMMOND, SCOTTISH WRITER[12]

Although it is extremely unfortunate, I know people who I do not believe will ever achieve happiness. They are simply weighted down with too much excess baggage. This baggage may take any one of a number of different forms such as anger, envy, or resentment. These types of people burn up their energy in heat. They are envious of their brother, sister, or neighbor, because they think that these individuals have more personality, brain power, or wealth. They carry a grudge instead of burying it, and take the attitude that at the very least, they will not get mad, but get even. People who take pride in seeing someone else hurt are sick and should seek medical help. Almighty God is the supreme equalizer, and he is more than capable of handling what he feels are inequities.

What we feel are inequities can often lead to jealously. Recall for example, the lesson we are given in Matthew 20:1–16 concerning the parable of the man with the vineyard. Although the normal rate of pay was a penny for a whole day's work, those laborers who worked only one hour were paid the same as those who worked the entire day. To say that those who had borne the burden of the day's heat were angry is undoubtedly an understatement. Unfortunately, many of us have yet to learn the lesson of this parable, and if a similar situation occurred today, it would perhaps provide the impetus for a Congressional investigation into unfair labor practices.

---

12. Drummond, "Henry Drummond Quotes," para. 11.

The problem with jealously is that it is self-centered and self-destructive. It destroys love, and therefore those that exhibit this characteristic are to be pitied. Our talents and possessions are gifts from Almighty God, and if to the best of our ability we fine-tune our talents and appreciate what we have, we will be happy. Edie and I have always tried to teach our children to be happy for others when something nice happens to them. I believe this positive approach serves them well in every aspect of their lives.

As long as we are on terra firma, we are going to encounter people and situations that tend to rattle our cage in one way or another. An individual may try to harm us in some fashion, or circumstances may develop, through no fault of our own, that cause us grief. When these things happen, we have a choice: we can dwell on them, even to the point that they consume our time and make us miserable, or we can spend those irreplaceable hours in happy and worthwhile pursuits. The manner in which we deal with these things is, to a large extent, a mark of our education. As the Greek philosopher, Epictetus put it,

> To accuse others for one's misfortunes is a sign of want of education; to accuse oneself shows that one's education has begun; to accuse neither one's self nor others shows that one's education is complete.[13]

We only have a finite amount of time on this earth, and none of us really knows exactly when the clock will run out. Wouldn't it be a terrible tragedy to realize, after it is too late, that we have completely wasted a significant portion of our lives?

We cannot change the realities of life. However, we are in complete control of our attitude, and therefore we can decide how we will view them and what their resultant impact on us will be. We can project through a positive mental attitude, faith, and hope, and thereby maintain our health and an exuberance for living, or we can assume a negative attitude and worry, which may result in despair and ill health. Regardless of what we have been doing in the past, last year, last month, last week, or even yesterday, we should realize that right now, whomever we are and whatever we are doing, we can change our attitude because it costs us nothing to do so. If we want to be happy, we can be happy; and if it is our desire, we should take steps to ensure that we are. Abraham Lincoln's advice on this subject is contained in the quote,

---

13. Epictetus, "Epictetus Quotes."

Most folks are just about as happy as they make up their minds to be.[14]

Our attitude is simply the catalytic ingredient. A positive and cheerful attitude, which is based upon faith and an optimistic approach to life, has miracle-working potential. From this frame of mind, we can turn lemons into lemonade and add joy and zest to every waking moment of our day. As the comedian George Carlin has stated,

> Life is not measured by the number of breaths we take, but by the moments that take our breath away.[15]

Happiness is so easy to achieve and yet so elusive. In general, it has nothing to do with material things, but rather is totally dependent upon attitude. Our attitude determines how we react to all the events of our lives, and how we enjoy what we have. Our life is exactly what we think it is. Happiness is right where we are today; therefore, we must seize the opportunity, and do it now. The Persian mathematician, Omar Khayyam, provides some very sound advice on this subject in the following:

> Living Life Tomorrow's fate, though thou be wise
> Thou canst not tell nor yet surmise;
> Pass, therefore, not today in vain,
> For it will never come again.[16]

We can maximize our chances for happiness if we will simply devote whatever time and energy is necessary in order to achieve as good a match between our talents and interests and our total lifestyle, which includes both work and leisure. If we do this one thing very well, we will not only be happy, we will be a real winner and feel good about ourselves and the things we are doing. Regardless of our position in life, if we are happy and are making, in some way, a contribution to this old world, then we are a success. Happiness is not necessarily synonymous with wealth, power, or fame. In fact, splashed before us on the TV screen in living color are many TV personalities that possess a large degree of wealth, power, and fame, and yet a peek into their personal lives indicates that happiness has somehow escaped them. As someone has said, "The best things in life aren't things." As an example, Og Mandino, the American author, states the following: "Treasure the love you receive above all. It will survive long

14. Lincoln, "Abraham Lincoln Quotes."
15. Carlin, "Just Cause You Got the Monkey Off…"
16. Khayyam, "Living Life Tomorrow's Fate…"

after your gold and good health have vanished."[17] In addition, Ziad K. Abdelnour addresses this issue from another perspective with the comment, "A truly rich man is one whose children run into his arms when his hands are empty."[18]

If we have matched ourselves to our environment, then the proper operational characteristics will guarantee both happiness and success. We must therefore resolve to maintain our health, for happiness is almost impossible without it. Faithfully, cheerfully, and calmly execute the daily tasks that Almighty God has set before us. Maximize our potential by continuing to develop through a positive mental attitude our talents and interests, even after retirement. People I have known who retired and went home to sit and watch TV all day didn't live one year. Be loving, compassionate, sympathetic, and tolerant of others, since we will want everyone to treat us in the same manner. Be of service to others in any way that we can, even if our help is known only to God. Just remember on Judgement Day, God's vote is the only one that counts.

Erma Bombeck, an American humorist, offers the following advice in this context: "When I stand before God at the end of my life, I would hope that I would not have a single bit of talent left and could say, I used everything you gave me."[19]

We have many reasons to be completely happy. If we remain close to God, the affairs of our lives are in divine order. Just as he has ordered the Heavens, our lives are also in his care and keeping. For as it is stated in Proverbs 16:9, "In his mind a man plans his course, but the Lord directs his steps."

Although there are times when we become completely disoriented by the chaos that surrounds us, we can stabilize our own mental platform when we remember that divine order and timing always govern the affairs of our lives. Within this environment, we can pursue our goals in a step-by-step fashion, knowing full well that we are doing so in God's perfect plan, i.e., as stated in Ecclesiastics 3:1: "There is an appointed time for everything, and a time for every affair under the heavens."

God carefully and methodically guides us through the maze of life. In fact, God guides our steps not only by opening doors before us, but closing them as well. God wants only the best for each of us. We are his

17. Mandino, "Treasure the Love You Receive…"
18. Abdelnour, "Ziad K. Abdelnour Quotes."
19. Bombeck, "When I Stand before God…"

children. As our Heavenly Father, He sends us signals for directing our activities. We, however, must listen very attentively in order to receive the messages. We are, of course, free to ignore them, but if we do, we must accept the consequences.

I heard a story long ago, which has been repeated many times since then, that addresses this issue. A farmer who lived near a river was caught unaware by rising flood waters. He was a very religious individual, and so believed that in spite of the impending danger, Almighty God would protect him. Soon, the flood waters forced him to the roof of his house. While he was there, a man came by in a boat and offered to take him to safety. The farmer thanked the man in the boat, but refused to go saying that God would take care of him. Later the flood waters forced the farmer to the top of his chimney. The rescue squad came in a helicopter, and they too tried to save the farmer. The farmer refused to go, saying that God would take care of him. Finally, the flood waters rose over the chimney, and the farmer was swept away and drowned. When the farmer reached the pearly gates, Almighty God was there. The farmer asked God why he had not saved him. The Good Lord replied, "I sent you a boat and a helicopter; what in the world did you want?"

As William E. Gladstone, Former Prime Minister of the UK, has said, "There is but one question, and that is the will of God. That settles all other questions."[20] Furthermore, never forget that God's will for us is always our highest good. If we continue to remind ourselves of this fact, these words of encouragement act like very powerful magnets that draw our good to us. In addition, if we truly believe that God is guiding and protecting us, we are as steady as a slate of granite as the storms of life engulf us. Living close to God does not mean we will have a life that is free of problems. It means that we can live a happy life in spite of the problems. A life of faith is unfortunately not a security blanket with which we can protect ourselves from suffering and pain. It is, however, the glue that holds us together whenever circumstances in our lives seem to tear us apart.

We can be absolutely fearless and secure in the execution of our daily tasks for, just as God led the children of Israel through the Red Sea, he leads us today along the proper path to the success he has planned for us. Psalm 121:8 states the case very succinctly: "The Lord will guard your coming and your going, both now and forevermore."

---

20. Gladstone, "Lord Willing!"

In her article, "Living without Calculating Costs," the Venerable Madeliene Delbrel, a French laywoman and writer states

> We can't believe simultaneously in Chance and Providence. We do in fact believe in Providence, but we live as if we believed in Chance. It is from this that the inconsistencies in our lives stem; both the situations in which we get over-active and the situations in which we are unduly passive...
>
> And yet we receive each morning and each day in its entirety from the hands of God. God gives us a day which has been prepared for us by Him... If we could research the history of the world and watch this day as it was being developed and formed from the beginning of time, we would grasp the unique value of one single human day...
>
> Each minute of our day, wherever we're supposed to be and whatever we're supposed to be doing, allows Christ to live through us in the midst of human beings. So there is no more question of calculating the effectiveness of our time... We make our humble measurement of the will of God.[21]

We should delight in every encounter for there are, of course, no chance meetings; each has been planned and blessed in advance by Almighty God.

One of my close friends, Harry, who had lost his wife some time ago, while traveling home left his credit card at the airline counter when purchasing a ticket. The lady at the ticket counter, realizing he had left his card there, made an announcement over the airport's loudspeaker system asking Harry to return to the ticket counter. When the lady at the counter made the announcement and mentioned Harry's name, Harry's childhood sweetheart was in the airport at the same time and heard the announcement. So, she went to the ticket counter too to meet him. As they talked, Harry learned that she too had lost her spouse some time ago. Harry was a very religious person, and was fascinated by the coincidence. As Harry related the incident to me, I told him that it was no coincidence, this meeting was planned by God. About six months later, Harry called me to tell me that they had gotten married. I reminded him of my comment, and he had to agree that the meeting in the airport was indeed planned by God.

Our route to happiness and success is a life in which the guidance, control, and communication functions are centered in Almighty God.

---

21. Delbrêl, "Living Without Calculating Costs," 119.

Therefore, in order to ensure that our directional vectors keep pointing us along our appointed path, we must first surrender our wills to him, knowing that his will for us is always our highest good; second, be completely confident that he, and he alone, is infinitely powerful and therefore capable of doing whatever is necessary; and third, know beyond any doubt that everything will work out right, because it is in the hands of the master controller. Along a guided life we not only find happiness and success, but protection as well, for not even the balance of the whole human race can alter God's will for us.

We must trust God with complete confidence knowing that he will always prevail. He is with us to meet every challenge and show us the way. As long as we trust to the absolute limit, somehow and in some way he will deliver us. If we believe beyond any doubt, then a miracle may be the vehicle for our deliverance, and not because we deserve it—we don't. If we are granted a miracle, it is only because of God's infinite love and mercy.

We must learn that there is an established hierarchy in the control space, and that it is the spiritual that controls the material. Within this context, miracles are simply manifestations in the material plane that are activated by forces in the spiritual plane. Recall the statement from Matthew 6:33 which states, "But seek first the kingdom [of God] and his righteousness, and all these things will be given you besides." Therefore, the most direct path to material success in our lives is via Almighty God.

The material and spiritual planes are tightly coupled. For example, the spiritual may support the material in order to achieve some particular success; then the material will support the spiritual in order to satisfy some portion of God's plan. The mathematics which accompanies this interaction is often very strange in that one plus one is always greater than two. The operational characteristics of the two planes are quite different. In the material plane strength lies in action; however in the spiritual plane Isaiah 30:15 clearly indicates that "In quiet and in trust your strength lies."

In other words, it is in quiet communion with Almighty God that we make the progress which assures our success. I believe that I have read somewhere that Martin Luther, in commenting on the very heavy schedule that lay before him, said that he would have to spend even more time in prayer in order to accomplish all the tasks at hand.

We need quiet time alone with God. It is during these periods that he resets our systems and recharges our batteries so that we are prepared to do the work he has planned for us. What is perhaps even more important is the fact that God is our resting place, and only in him can we be truly happy. Regardless of whatever else we have achieved, there is a fundamental need within us that can never be satisfied until we rest in him. For example, fullness does not produce happiness, as anyone who has eaten too much can plainly attest. The same can be said for any other thing in the material plane.

Our lives, when lived in concert with Almighty God, are free from worry and doubt. They are not, however, free from work. We have to do our part by working as diligently as we can. God blesses our efforts by preparing the way, and his blessing and our work are the optimum mix. Our work must be performed to the very best of our ability in an orderly and calm fashion, and we should periodically rest and talk to God along the way. It is during these rest periods that he can perhaps best communicate to us any midcourse corrections. If, however, our work is performed in a state of frenzy, we will not even hear his directions.

If we have done our very best, then what remains for us is to trust that Almighty God, in his infinite wisdom and mercy, will do the rest. As John Jay, the first Chief Justice of the United States Supreme Court, has said,

> *God is great*, and therefore He will be sought; He is good, and therefore He will be found. If in the day of sorrow we own *God's presence* in the cloud, we shall find Him also in the pillar of fire, brightening and cheering our way as the night comes on.
>
> In all His dispensations *God* is at work for our good. In prosperity He tries our gratitude; in mediocrity, our contentment, in misfortune our submission; in darkness, our faith; under temptation, our steadfastness; and at all times, our obedience and trust in Him.
>
> *God governs the world*, and we have only to do *our duty wisely and leave the issue to Him*.[22]

If we simply practice Monday through Saturday what we learn in church on Sundays, we will be a tremendous success. If we treat everyone the way we would like to be treated, we will not only be successful, but happy. Where we do this in our business, we will achieve our goals and get out of life everything we want from it. The trick, however, is not simply to get it, but to enjoy it, and only the wisest among us do the latter.

God is with us every moment of the day. Therefore, we don't have to make an appointment to talk to him. However, when he speaks to us, we must strain our systems to hear everything he has to say. Since his

22. Federer, "American Minute," paras. 96–98.

directions always point to our highest good, the surrender of every moment to his wishes is the basis for a happy and successful life.

In prayer we talk to him, and we should do so as often as possible. It is so easy to be distracted by the constant pressure or our day-to-day activities, that without a regular reminder, we tend to forget the lessons we have learned. He, and he alone, is our strength, and in prayer we do not simply acknowledge that he can produce some desired effect, but rather we strongly affirm that we *know* he *will* do it.

In God we have, at our constant disposal, the most awesome force in the universe. Our faith and efforts and God's power comprise the winning combination. Therefore, we must believe beyond any doubt that if we are opposed by another individual, and in the final analysis that person is triumphant, it is only because our omnipotent Lord and Savior knows that this result is in our best interest.

In this life we must remember that we are on a journey, and our destination is heaven. Therefore, our final goal is not something or somewhere in this world. However, what we do and what we have in this world should be an aid to us as we strive to reach the next.

Today we stand at the threshold of the rest of our lives. Behind us is the past which we cannot change or impact in any way. Directly ahead lies the excitement of the future, which is only revealed to us one day at a time. As we approach the balance of our lives in search of happiness and success, we should be guided by the words written by Minnie Louise Haskins and spoken by King George VI of England in his 1939 Christmas message to the British Empire,

> I said to the man who stood at the gate of the year:
> "Give me a light that I may tread safely into the unknown."
> And he replied:
> "Go out into the darkness and put your hand into the hand of God.
> That shall be to you better than light and safer than a known way."[23]

As I complete my time here on terra firma, I keep reminding myself that God is in charge, and that the trials I encounter are here to speed up my spiritual progress, not arrest it. I am here to serve him as best I can, and in the final analysis, which of course is his analysis, I hope and pray that he will believe I have done that well.

---

23. Haskins, "God Knows," ll. 1–5.

Appendix

Book Club Discussion Questions

Introduction

Are the items in this chapter in sync with the title of the book?

Chapter 1

Is the basic inventory identified in this chapter complete, or are there other items that are important, but not mentioned?

Is planning really important in achieving a goal, or is it sufficient to simply have the goal fixed in your mind?

Chapter 2

Are there critical items in personal development that have been omitted from this chapter? If so, what are they?

Do you believe that continuing education, in whatever form, is a key component in personal development?

Are there areas of personal development in which social graces can essentially be ignored?

Chapter 3

Can you identify areas of development in which time is not a factor?

Can time be traded for information, and vice versa?

Is information always valuable, or are there times when information can be detrimental?

Have the various facets of power been clearly identified, or is there some facet of power that is not discussed?

Chapter 4

What role does teamwork play in trying to ensure that everyone in an organization is a contributor?

What are the consequences of having employees who do not contribute to the goals of the organization?

Is it necessary to approach every goal with a positive attitude?

Do you believe that mutual support is a necessary ingredient in the success of any endeavor?

What are the consequences of poor communication in small/large organizations?

Chapter 5

Does the author do an adequate job of identifying the critical aspects of leadership, or are there others not mentioned?

Will a failsafe environment always produce good performance?

What is the biggest problem associated with hiring the wrong people?

Are there any items associated with the development of personnel that have been omitted in the presentation?

Are there environments in which careful listening is really not an issue?

What is the most effective way in which to reward someone when financial compensation is not a possibility?

Chapter 6

Is stress always a result of poor time management? If so, why? If not, why not?

What role does attitude play in dealing with stress?

Are there actions that can be taken to reduce the consequences of unplanned change?

Are there effective techniques for dealing with adversity not mentioned in the book?

Are there areas in which power has to be applied in a somewhat dictatorial fashion?

What are the top three personal benefits obtained from a strong faith?

How does faith protect us in times of trials and disappointments?

Chapter 7

Is there a connection between a positive attitude and perseverance?

Is belief in oneself a prerequisite for success?

Is there a downside to thinking big?

Is an individual operating at their best a winner, regardless of the circumstances?

Can hard work be traded for information? If so, under what conditions?

Are there advantages in encountering lemons in life?

Are there effective methods for turning a lemon into a lemonade not identified in the book?

Chapter 8

What role does discipline play in achieving a balanced lifestyle?

Does tunnel vision in pursuit of a goal preclude the establishment of a balanced lifestyle?

Book Club Discussion Questions

What role does God play in a balanced lifestyle?

Does faith play any role in our approach to a happy life?

How is a happy lifestyle achieved when it appears that everything is going wrong?

Are Christians better prepared to deal with life's difficulties? If so, why? If not, why not?

How is success defined in a Christian lifestyle?

Is it possible that God's definition of success for each individual is different than the individual's?

Are success and happiness interlocked?

Are happiness and achievement interlocked?

Is there one trait that is common to all winners?

Is service in some form related to winning?

Can happiness be achieved without God's help?

What role does love play in the achievement of happiness?

Does God guarantee happiness? If so, under what conditions?

If the communication lines to God are broken, how are they repaired?

Why does God's guidance always point to our highest good?

Bibliography

"26 Positivity Quotes on Thoughts, Attitude, and Mindset (2021)." *Kites and Roses* (blog), April 13, 2021. https://kitesandroses.com/positive-thinking-quotes/.
Abdelnour, Ziad K. "Ziad K. Abdelnour Quotes." https://www.goodreads.com/quotes/1138959-a-truly-rich-man-is-one-whose-children-run-into.
Aesop. "No Act of Kindness..." https://www.brainyquote.com/quotes/aesop_109734.
Aquinas, Thomas. "To One Who Has Faith..." https://www.brainyquote.com/quotes/thomas_aquinas_186900.
Balkenhol, Klaus. "Quoteable Quote." https://www.goodreads.com/quotes/23879-there-is-a-difference-between-being-a-leader-and-being.
Beecher, Henry Ward. "It Is Defeat that Turns Bone to Flint..." https://www.forbes.com/quotes/4216/.
Bombeck, Erma. "When I Stand before God..." https://www.forbes.com/quotes/2760/.
Brengle, Samuel. "One of the Outstanding Ironies..." https://www.goodreads.com/quotes/6871472-one-of-the-outstanding-ironies-of-history-is-the-utter.
Brooks, Phillips. "Do Not Pray for Easy Lives..." https://www.goodreads.com/quotes/180411-do-not-pray-for-easy-lives-pray-to-be-stronger.
Brown, Ken, and Gail Brown. "In Deepest Sleep..." https://www.kenbrown.com/product-page/god-s-footprints.
Burns, Loretta P. "Broken Dreams." https://www.scrapbook.com/poems/doc/27113.html.
Carlin, George. "Just Cause You Got the Monkey Off..." https://www.brainyquote.com/quotes/george_carlin_385217.
———. "Life Is Not Measured..." https://quoteinvestigator.com/2013/12/17/breaths/.
Carlyle, Thomas. "Today Is Not Yesterday..." https://quotefancy.com/quote/916851/Thomas-Carlyle-Today-is-not-yesterday-we-ourselves-change-how-can-our-works-and-thoughts.
Carnegie, Andrew. "47 Empowering Andrew Carnegie Quotes." https://wealthygorilla.com/47-empowering-andrew-carnegie-quotes/.
Caretto, Carlo. *Letters from the Desert*. Translated by Rose Mary Hancock. Maryknoll, NY: Orbis, 2002.
Churchill, Winston. "Quotes." https://draganprimorac.org/quotes/.
———. "Success Is Going from Failure..." https://quoteinvestigator.com/2014/06/28/success/.
Collier, Robert. "We Can Do Only What We Think..." https://www.azquotes.com/quote/850137.

Delbrêl, Madeleine. "Living without Calculating Costs." *Magnificat* 22.5 (July 2020) 119.

"Developing a Positive Conflict Culture." https://www.conflictdynamics.org/developing-a-positive-conflict-culture/?gclid=EAIaIQobChMIk__S9p_55AIVicDACh35Zwiy EAAYASAAEgIf4PD_BwE.

Devos, Richard M. "The Only Thing That Stands . . ." https://www.goodreads.com/author/quotes/1414622.Richard_M_Devos.

Disraeli, Benjamin. "Benjamin Disraeli Quotes." https://www.successories.com/iquote/author/594/benjamin-disraeli-quotes/1?gclid=EAIaIQobChMI9fLgpej47gIV9ebj Bx30QAJKEAAYASAAEgIPFvD_BwE.

Don'tgiveupworld. "Introspective Poem What's Your Wage by Jessie Belle Rittenhouse." https://medium.com/@Dontgiveup/introspective-poem-whats-your-wage-by-jessie-belle-rittenhouse-cfaf3747e9fe.

Drucker, Peter. "Peter Drucker Quotes." https://www.successories.com/iquote/author/451/peter-drucker-quotes/2.

Drummond, Henry. "Henry Drummond Quotes about Living a Beautiful Life." https://everydaypower.com/henry-drummond-quotes/.

Edison, Thomas A. "Genius Is One Percent Inspiration . . ." https://www.brainyquote.com/quotes/thomas_a_edison_109928.

———. "Quotation Details." http://www.quotationspage.com/quote/39629.html.

Einstein, Albert. "Albert Einstein Quotes." https://www.successories.com/iquote/author/99/albert-einstein-quotes/19.

Eliot, George. "Quotable Quotes." https://www.goodreads.com/quotes/38095-blessed-is-the-man-who-having-nothing-to-say-abstains.

Emerson, Ralph Waldo. "Do Not Be Too Timid . . ." https://www.quotes.net/quote/546.

Epictetus. "Epictetus Quotes." https://www.goodreads.com/author/quotes/13852.Epictetus.

Federer, Bill. "American Minute with Bill Federer." https://myemail.constantcontact.com/First-Chief-Justice-John-Jay-was-also-President-of-American-Bible-Society-.html?soid=1108762609255&aid=k4Q-vvuxLUc.

Ford, Henry. "Failure Is Simply the Opportunity . . ." https://www.brainyquote.com/quotes/henry_ford_121339.

Francis of Assisi, Saint. "Peace Prayer of Saint Francis." https://www.loyolapress.com/catholic-resources/prayer/traditional-catholic-prayers/saints-prayers/peace-prayer-of-saint-francis/.

Franklin, Benjamin. "Quotable Quotes." https://www.goodreads.com/quotes/670282-after-crosses-and-losses-men-grow-humbler-and-wiser.

Frost, Robert. "Robert Frost Quotes." https://www.successories.com/iquote/author/3/robert-frost-quotes/.

Gladstone, William E. "Lord Willing!" https://www.cbckinston.com/morning-memos/2017/10/26/lord-willing.

Glasgow, Arnold H. "Arnold Henry Glasgow." http://www.greatthoughtstreasury.com/author/arnold-henry-glasgow.

Goldhill, Olivia. "A Philosopher's 350-year-old Trick to Get People to Change Their Minds Is Now Backed Up by Psychologists." *Quartz* (blog), September 11, 2016. https://qz.com/778767/to-tell-someone-theyre-wrong-first-tell-them-how-theyre-right/.

Grizzard, Lewis. "Life Is Like a Dogsled . . ." https://www.brainyquote.com/quotes/lewis_grizzard_471566.

Bibliography

Harrison, Elizabeth. "Quotable Quote." https://www.goodreads.com/quotes/58565-those-who-are-lifting-the-world-upward-and-onward-are.

Haskins, Minnie Louise. "God Knows." https://ctntp.files.wordpress.com/2018/12/God-Knows.pdf.

Hazlitt, William. "A Strong Passion for Any Object . . ." https://www.greatest-quotations.com/search/william_hazlitt/23027/quote-a-strong-passion-for-any-object-will-ensure-success-for-the.html.

Henry, Patrick. "Founding Father Quote #687." https://www.foundingfatherquotes.com/quote/687.

Hill, Napoleon. "The 35 Most Notorious Napoleon Hill Quotes." https://wealthygorilla.com/the-35-most-notorious-napoleon-hill-quotes/.

———. "Through Some Strange and Powerful Principle . . ." https://quotefancy.com/quote/871194/Napoleon-Hill-Through-some-strange-and-powerful-prin.

———. "Whatever the Mind of Man . . ." https://www.brainyquote.com/quotes/napoleon_hill_392258.

Holmes, Oliver Wendell. "Oliver Wendell Holmes Quotes." https://www.successories.com/iquote/author/61/oliver-wendell-holmes-quotes/3.

Hoover, Herbert. "Herbert Hoover Quotes." https://www.successories.com/iquote/author/441/herbert-hoover-quotes/1?gclid=EAIaIQobChMI467tyIP57gIVuubjBx26gA-kEAAYASAAEgLok_D_BwE.

Hugo, Victor. "Victor Hugo Quotes." https://www.successories.com/iquote/author/27/victor-hugo-quotes/3.

Keller, Helen. "Famous Quote From: Helen Keller." http://famousquotefrom.com/helen-keller/.

Kettering, Charles F. "Have Faith in Yourself and in Your Ideas." https://www.knowol.com/wisdom/have-faith-in-yourself-and-ideas/.

Khayyam, Omar. "Living Life Tomorrow's Fate . . ." https://www.brainyquote.com/quotes/omar_khayyam_165612.

King George VI. "The Highest of Distinctions . . ." https://www.nimibriggs.org/in-pursuit-of-justice-and-equity-rooting-for-the-health-of-t.

Kipling, Rudyard. "We Have Forty Million Reasons . . ." https://www.forbes.com/quotes/8250/.

Korda, Michael. "Michael Korda Quotes." https://www.successories.com/iquote/author/505/michael-korda-quotes/1.

Landers, Ann. "If I Were Asked . . ." https://www.goodreads.com/quotes/46809-if-i-were-asked-to-give-what-i-consid.

———. "Quotable Quote." https://www.goodreads.com/quotes/281866-it-is-not-what-you-do-for-your-children-but.

Law, Vernon. "Experience Is a Hard Teacher . . ." https://www.brainyquote.com/quotes/vernon_law_115255.

Lincoln, Abraham. "Abraham Lincoln Quotes." https://www.successories.com/iquote/author/291/abraham-lincoln-quotes/2.

———. "Quotable Quotes." https://www.goodreads.com/quotes/155759-if-i-were-to-try-to-read-much-less-answer.

Lombardi, Vincent T. "The Quality of a Person's Life . . ." https://www.brainyquote.com/quotes/vince_lombardi_121318.

Longfellow, Henry Wadsworth. "Perseverance Is a Great Element . . ." https://www.brainyquote.com/quotes/henry_wadsworth_longfello_124652.

Mandino, Og. "Treasure the Love You Receive . . ." http://www.famousquotesabout.com/quote/Treasure-the-love-you/21381

Marshall, Peter. "Give To Us Clear Vision . . ." https://www.brainyquote.com/authors/peter-marshall-quotes.

Maugham, W. Somerset. "At a Dinner Party . . ." https://www.brainyquote.com/quotes/w_somerset_maugham_397144.

Maxwell, John C. *The 21 Indispensable Qualities of a Leader: Becoming the Person Others Will Want to Follow*. Nashville: Nelson, 1999.

McGeady, Mary Rose. "Quotable Quote." https://www.goodreads.com/quotes/900530-there-is-no-greater-joy-nor-greater-reward-than-to.

Medina, Jennifer, et al. "Actresses, Business Leaders and Other Wealthy Parents Charged in U.S. College Entry Fraud." *The New York Times*, March 12, 2019. https://www.nytimes.com/2019/03/12/us/college-admissions-cheating-scandal.html.

Mill, John Stuart. "So What Is Coaching." http://coaching-4-everyone.com/.

Milton, John. *Paradise Lost*. Edited by Merritt Y. Hughes. New York: Odyssey, 1935.

Mother Teresa. "I Alone Cannot Change the World . . ." https://wordsofwisdom.app/i-alone-cannot-change-the-world-but-i-can-cast-a-stone-across.

———. "In This Life . . ." https://www.quotesaga.com/quote/742.

"Motivational Quote: What Did Confucius Mean By 'Our Greatest Glory Is Not in Never Failing, But in Rising Every Time We Fall.'" https://www.quora.com/Motivational-Quote-What-did-Confucius-mean-by-Our-greatest-glory-is-not-in-never-failing-but-in-rising-every-time-we-fall.

Niebuhr, Reinhold. "God Grant Me the Serenity . . ." https://www.brainyquote.com/quotes/reinhold_niebuhr_100884.

Pais, Abraham. *Niels Bohr's Times, in Physics, Philosophy, and Polity*. Oxford: Clarendon, 1991.

"Power Perception Matrix," http://changingminds.org/explanations/power/power_perception.htm.

Pythagoras. "Rest Satisfied with Doing Well . . ." https://www.forbes.com/quotes/7651/.

Rankin, Ormond. "It's Worth Quoting: 50 Quotes for the Business Minded." *BCG Consulting* (blog), March 8, 2012. https://ormondrankin.wordpress.com/2012/03/08/its-worth-quoting-50-quotes-for-the-business-minded/.

Reagan, Ronald. "Live Simply, Love Generously." https://www.goodreads.com/quotes/128645-live-simply-love-generously-care-deeply-s.

Rogers, Will. "Will Rogers Quotes." https://www.successories.com/iquote/author/444/will-rogers-quotes/1?gclid=EAIaIQobChMIx4Sf9fH77gIV2zizAB3GNwWrEAAYASAAEgJ3CPD_BwE.

Roosevelt, Theodore. "Theodore Roosevelt Quotes." https://www.successories.com/iquote/author/63/theodore-roosevelt-quotes/.

Schwab, Charles. "A Man Can Succeed . . ." https://www.brainyquote.com/quotes/charles_schwab_125728.

Scott, Elizabeth. "What It Means to Have 'Type A' Personality Traits." https://www.verywellmind.com/type-a-personality-traits-3145240.

Shaw, George Bernard. "The Man Who Listens to Reason . . ." https://www.quotes.net/quote/377.

———. "People Are Always Blaming Their Circumstances . . ." https://www.forbes.com/quotes/3370/.

———. "The Secret of Being Miserable . . ." https://www.quotes.net/quote/400.

Bibliography

Stevenson, Robert Louis. "48 Inspiring Quotes By Robert Louis Stevenson, the Renowned Scottish Novelist." https://quotes.thefamouspeople.com/robert-louis-stevenson-2707.php.

Stillman, Jessica. "Employee Leadership Is Dead. Good Riddance." *CBS News*, May 20, 2010. https://www.cbsnews.com/news/employee-loyalty-is-dead-good-riddance/.

Sweet, Laurel J. "Hollywood Stars among Those Arrested in College Admissions Scam." *Boston Herald*, March 12, 2019. https://www.bostonherald.com/2019/03/12/hollywood-actresses-among-those-arrested-in-college-admissions-scam/.

Swisher, Matt. "A Resolution Succeed." *Matt Swisher* (blog), October 30, 2019. https://pastorswish.medium.com/a-resolution-to-succeed-f01965e9837d.

Washington, George. "We Ought Not to Look Back . . ." https://www.azquotes.com/quote/701688.

"We Have Done So Much . . ." https://quoteinvestigator.com/2017/05/13/anything/.

Wells, H. G. "H. G. Well Quotes." https://www.successories.com/iquote/author/323/h-g-wells-quotes/1.

Will, George Frederick. "Don't Just Do Something; Stand There." https://quoteinvestigator.com/2014/03/22/stand-there/.

Wintle, Walter D. "Quotable Quotes." https://www.goodreads.com/quotes/1033193-if-you-think-you-are-beaten-you-are-.

ylenfest. "Psychoneuroimmunology and the Mind's Impact on Health." *Bill of Health* (blog), March 5, 2018. https://blog.petrieflom.law.harvard.edu/2018/03/05/psychoneuroimmunology-and-the-minds-impact-on-health/.

www.ingramcontent.com/pod-product-compliance
Lightning Source LLC
Chambersburg PA
CBHW071439150426
43191CB00008B/1177